Yours,
Helen

TRADING GRENADES *for* CANDY

A KURDISH REFUGEE'S AMERICAN JOURNEY

TRADING GRENADES *for* CANDY

A KURDISH REFUGEE'S AMERICAN JOURNEY

DR. HELEN SAIRANY

atmosphere press

Published by Atmosphere Press

Cover design by Kevin Stone

atmospherepress.com

THE GUEST HOUSE

This being human is a guest house.
Every morning a new arrival.

A joy, a depression, a meanness,
some momentary awareness comes
as an unexpected visitor.

Welcome and entertain them all!
Even if they're a crowd of sorrows,
who violently sweep your house
empty of its furniture,
still, treat each guest honorably.
He may be clearing you out
for some new delight.

The dark thought, the shame, the malice,
meet them at the door laughing,
and invite them in.

Be grateful for whoever comes,
because each has been sent
as a guide from beyond.

– *Jalal ad-Din Mohammad Rumi*

To the unnamed U.S. Marine who, many years ago,
saved the life of a curious little Kurdish girl

&

My loving mother, Fatima, who selflessly raised
my ten siblings and me without being literate.
Although she cannot read this book herself,
every word is written with my full heart for her.

CONTENTS

KURDISH INHABITATED AREAS (KURDISTAN)

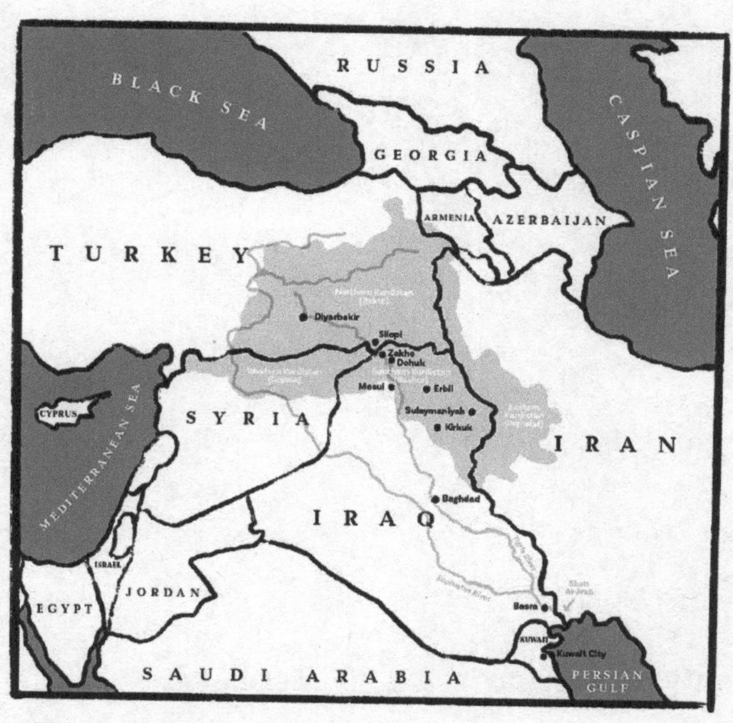

KURDISTAN INHABITED AREA

AUTHOR'S NOTE

The historical details and stories shared throughout this book reflect my vivid childhood memories and those whom I was in close contact. While everything I have shared stands true to the best of my knowledge, the stories I share are not meant to be a treatise on any religion or political ideology, but rather a reflection of how religious and political conflicts have shaped the trajectory of my life as a first-generation immigrant woman of Kurdish descent.

My focus over the pages that follow was to share my story through my own voice, but this was only possible by walking you through a precise account of historical events. I have tried my best to provide accurate dates, times, and narratives reconstructed throughout my story.

Of note, since security remains a concern and out of respect for their safety and privacy, I have changed the names and omitted identifying life details of almost all the individuals mentioned in my story.

INTRODUCTION

They say home belongs to those who never have left it. While a body cannot be in two places at the same time, a mind and a soul certainly can. As a Kurdish refugee living in the United States, I often find myself inextricably caught between two worlds. When I landed in America at the age of fifteen, I had no doubt in my mind that I was a Kurdish refugee from Iraqi Kurdistan. However, after living in the U.S. for over 25 years, I no longer feel entirely at home in Kurdistan, and I'm never entirely at home in America, either. It can be a challenge to split myself in half, looking at America through my Kurdish eyes and at Kurdistan through my American ones.

I was born during the tumultuous Iraq-Iran war (1980-1988). As a result, my early life was shaped by violence, tension, economic sanctions, and conflict. On any day, I could have been deformed or killed by one of the 25 million landmines scattered across our landscape.

The pages that follow track the story of my refugee family as we immigrated to the United States from Iraqi Kurdistan through Asia, over the Pacific to the United States, back to Kurdistan, and then returned to the United States. It's the story of an eager and precocious teenager who was hungry to succeed and live the American dream. It is also the story of my yearning to return to my motherland to serve the countless number of displaced refugees, only to find a maze of roadblocks designed to prevent me from serving those mirror images of my younger self, simply because I was a young female native in a region battling nepotism and the traditions of patriarchy.

When you finish this memoir with a better understanding of what it is like to be a Kurd, a Kurdish woman, a refugee, a Muslim in the West, a woman who wore and then took off her hijab, a pharmacist, and a village girl raised in a mud house who adventures the world in search of home and a sense of belonging—then my objective in sharing my story and opening up my life to you will be achieved.

Sairany Family Tree

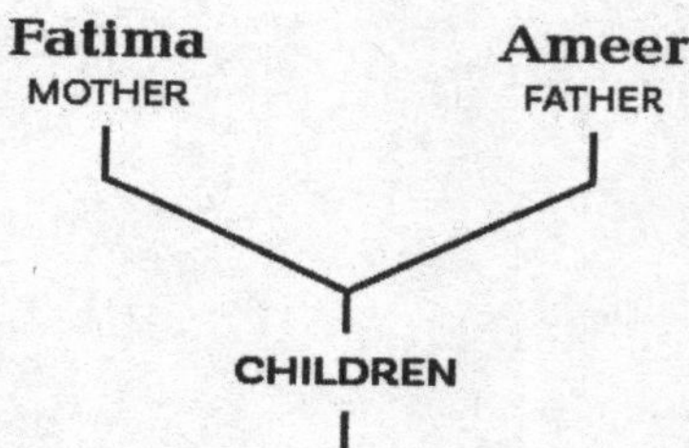

BROTHER **Omed,**
which means hope.

BROTHER **Hoger,**
which means friend.

SISTER **Jowan**
which means beauty.

SISTER **Zyan,**
which means life.

SISTER **Jehan,**
which means world.

BROTHER **Zerak,**
which means clever.

ME **Helen (Heleen)**
which means nest of love birds.

BROTHER **Dlovan,**
which means mercy.

SISTER **Dilven,**
which means heartily needed.

BROTHER **Blend,**
which means tall.

BROTHER **Reveng (Pambo)**
which means nomad.

CHAPTER I:
EVEN THE MOUNTAINS ARE UNFRIENDLY

"Why did I have to witness all this in a single lifetime? A war in my childhood, sanctions as a teenager, and a new war with advanced smart bombs when I have not yet reached twenty. How can a normal person tell their personal life story when they move from one war to another as they grow older?"
– *The Baghdad Clock*

Mass Exodus of 1991 where Kurds fled their homes seeking refuge in the mountains. Photo courtesy of bbc.co.uk/news.

I am a Kurd. This sentence may seem simple, but it contains within it a wide range of implications: cultural pride, historical baggage, collective grief, and communal obligations—both positive and negative. Such a declaration, depending on where you say it, can endanger your life or end in arrest from the states who occupy the Kurds while denying us our rights; it's also the first most definable trait one needs to know about me to fully comprehend who I am.

To start, there are many words and phrases used to describe us Kurds: "The race with no home," "The nation with no country," and the people who have "no friends but the mountains." Divided among the four countries of southeastern Turkey ("Northern Kurdistan"), northwestern Iran ("Eastern Kurdistan"), northern Iraq ("Southern Kurdistan"), and northern Syria ("Western Kurdistan"), Greater Kurdistan is a melting pot of dialects, religious beliefs, and numerous political factions. Kurds also widely vary in ethnic appearance (thanks to centuries of outside invasion), which can confuse outsiders as to who is and is not a Kurd.

Kurdistan, once found on historical maps, no longer exists on the modern maps of internationally recognized nations due to division by the visitors of World War I. As such, the forty-plus million Kurds remain the largest ethnic group in the world without their own country.

The first hope of an independent Kurdistan came immediately after the collapse of the Ottoman Empire at the end of WWI in 1918, when Western powers redrew the map of the Middle East. The 1920 Treaty of Sevres granted Kurds a separate country in accordance with U.S. President Woodrow Wilson's position that non-Turkish minorities—which primarily meant Kurds—should be granted the opportunity to become independent.

The Kemalist movement of Turkey, a political revolution that changed the Ottoman Empire to the establishment of the nation-state of Turkey and development of the national identity of modern Turkey, however, provoked a change in British foreign policy, and the 1923 Treaty of Lausanne superseded the Treaty of Sevres, dividing the Ottoman Kurds among what would become the countries of Turkey, Iraq, and Syria, while the Kurds of the Persian Empire remained within Iran. One area where the Kurds have semi-autonomy presently is in northern Iraq, or Iraqi Kurdistan, where Kurds now have their own Kurdish Regional Government—that is the site where my story begins.

I was born to a middle-class, Kurdish Sunni family in Erbil (referred to as Hewler by Kurds), which today is the capital of the Kurdistan Region of Iraq. I was the seventh of eleven children born to Fatima Jaff and Ameer Sairany. Since my parents came from opposite ends of the Kurdistan Region, Kurds sometimes ask how my parents met.

My father was from Zakho, a city close to Iraq's border with Turkey to the northwest. He was the only educated member of his family, with a Bachelor of Science degree in accounting from the University of Baghdad. As one of the few college graduates in Erbil, my father had a high-ranking position directing the largest hospital. In contrast, my mother came from a humble family in Hawraman, far to the east along the border with Iran. When my maternal grandfather moved from Hawraman to Erbil for work, he met my maternal grandmother and settled in Erbil permanently.

My mother was the youngest girl in the family and was known for her beauty. People were often misled by my mother's age, since she was taller and appeared older than she was. My father noticed my mother while she was with her sister seeking healthcare at the hospital where my father worked. Inspired by her beauty and unaware of her age, my father asked the provider who cared for my mother about her and started to follow my mother and her sister to their house. My mother noticed a stranger following her in pursuit, so once she was home, she purposefully told my grandfather that a stranger was instead following her older sister. My grandfather questioned my aunt and blamed her for my father's wanting to know where they lived, and she was warned to be careful when they went out again.

Soon, my father took the initiative and visited my grandfather's house to propose marriage to my mother. However, remembering my father as the stranger who followed my mother and her sister not long before, my grandfather thought that my father was proposing to my aunt who was several years older than my mother. When my father clarified that he was interested in my mother rather than her sister, my grandfather objected because my mother was only thirteen years old. My father, who was then twenty-seven, was not willing to give up and used his connections to convince my grandfather to agree to the marriage.

The civil court, however, refused to proceed with the marriage because of my mother's young age. Undeterred, my grandfather, with assistance from my father, arranged to change my mother's birth year by two years, making her fifteen years of age, which was permissible for marriage according to the law. My mother, too respectful and young to deny her father, indeed married a stranger. Someone fourteen years older, whom she at first disliked because he smoked, drank, and did not practice his faith.

My parents lived a nomadic life and would move among three cities of Iraqi Kurdistan, Erbil, Zakho, and Duhok. Soon after their marriage, my father was transferred to Duhok and my mother became the caretaker of the new house that my father built. Alone and without family support, my mother passed through puberty while married to my father, became a full-time housewife, and began having and raising children at an incredibly young age. The people of Duhok taught my mother to clean the house and cook Kurdish dishes. My father, who was overly protective and controlling of my mother, was always determined that she stay home, fearing she would encounter strange men if she went outside.

My mother dutifully honored my father's wishes, never questioned his strict dictates, or complained about his extreme jealousy. When my father was cruel to her, she would lower her head, hide her tears, and go about her day. She had her first child at the age of fifteen, and without any formal education, not knowing how to read or write a single word, miraculously raised eleven children, giving birth to a child naturally every other year for the next two decades. She grew up with her children and we became the center of her world. She was the most selfless woman I knew, always the last to eat after ensuring her family was fed. My father was the sole breadwinner of the family, and the Iraqi government had a system where my father would receive a salary increase for every child born to him and my mother.

My parents took pride in their heritage and were not shy to say that they were from Kurdistan (i.e. "the land of Kurds"). It is no surprise, then, that my parents defiantly gave all eleven children Kurdish names, each with a special meaning. Their oldest child was a boy named Omed, which means "hope" in the Kurdish language. Hoger, also a boy, was next. His name means "friend." After their first two boys, my parents gave birth to three of my older sisters, Jowan ("beauty"), Zhyan ("life"), and Jehan ("world"), which all sound so similar that it confuses not only Americans but native Kurds as well. Next came my brother Zerak ("clever"), and then me, Heleen ("nest of love birds"). According to my parents, I was supposed to be their last child, and they had no plans for the additional children born after me: my brother Dlovan ("Mercy"), sister Dilven ("heartily needed"), brother Blend ("tall") and brother Reveng ("nomad").

My parents insisted we learn the names of our great grandparents because in Kurdish culture you are secondary to the name of the family to whom you belong. Therefore, it was critical for us to know the names of our ancestors because they defined who we were. Whenever we met a stranger, they would always ask for the name of our family and then would often trace our ancestry back as far as they could until we found a common forefather. As a result, we joked how all Kurds in Iraq were cousins or distant blood relatives.

Before I was born, my father was offered a senior official position in Erbil, where the former Iraqi government provided him with a spacious house in one of Erbil's finer neighborhoods. The new house had a large garden where my father would team us up to play soccer in spring and summer afternoons. This is the home in which my mother gave birth to me.

My mother would prepare afternoon tea, often with a homemade vanilla cake that she baked. She would sit on the patio and wait until we were done playing so we could join her for tea and cake. With so many of us still young, my mother would serve us tea in large cups while she and my father enjoyed theirs in little hourglass-like teacups. At night, we would lie on our mats and my parents would tell us stories. We loved listening to them ritually repeat the same three or four stories almost every other night. However, the stories were not told upon our request, as my parents would only tell them when we were well behaved. My favorite story was about the porter and the fava bean, which went as follows:

After a long day of carrying goods for people, the porter would spend his daily earnings on fava beans that he liked to eat while sitting on the side of a stream. He would throw the beans up to the sky and try to catch them in his mouth. One night, the last fava bean he threw to the sky fell into the stream and the porter started weeping. He returned to the same spot every day and continued to weep for the fava bean. After days of weeping, a mermaid came out of the stream asking the porter why he was crying. He told her that he had dropped his fava bean into the stream. The mermaid then gave him several things that were much better than the bean he had been weeping for: a donkey that produced gold when placed on a dirty carpet, a cupboard that would fill up with food as soon as he shouted "food," and an angel that would brighten the room at all times. However, the porter was naïve, and people took advantage of him and stole the valuables he had received from the mermaid. He then returned to the stream to weep for the fava bean. The mermaid came out of the water to again ask why he was weeping. He told her that his next-door neighbor had stolen the things she had given him. The mermaid recommended he sue the neighbor. This time, she gave him a smart lawyer to win his case in court so he could get his valuables back and return them to the mermaid in exchange for his lost fava bean.

As soon as the story ended, my parents would always ask what lessons we learned from it. We would be excited to share the lessons, but we were only allowed to speak one at a time. "The porter was not smart; he should have been more careful sharing the valuables he got from the mermaid and he should not have been so trusting," we theorized. We also added, "How valuable something is can only be determined by each person." Our parents would always agree with our conclusions. My parents would tell stories from their childhood that were told to them by their grandparents. They shared stories about their lives as children and the things they enjoyed doing when they were our age.

As we grew older, the stories evolved to indirectly bring our awareness to the struggle of the Kurdish people. One of my favorites was a tragic love story entitled Mem and Zin (Mem û Zîn in Kurdish) by the poet Ahmad Khani. The story is sort of like a Kurdish Romeo and Juliet, which features a man, Mem Alan—heir to a city, and Zin—daughter of the Governor of Botan (an area of Northern Kurdistan). They meet and fall in love at a New Year's celebration. However, their relationship is opposed by

Mem's rival, a man named Bakr. Bakr conspires to poison Mem and kills him, and when Zin learns of the news, she dies of grief and the two of them are buried next to each other. A friend of Mem's named Tacdîn then takes revenge and kills Bakr, and buries him next to the two lovers, as it was Mem's last dying wish to make Bakr witness for eternity the love that he opposed. However, Bakr's blood nourishes a thorn bush, which grows between Mem and Zin and divides them even in death. The story is used as a metaphor, with Mem being the Kurdish people, and Zin as Kurdistan, which is always just out of our reach.

I was born during the Iraq-Iran war (1980-1988), which became a catalyst for changing the trajectory of both political and regional dynamics. The war affected many aspects of my daily life, perhaps some unconsciously, but mostly, it defined the person I became. The exact cause of this war is entirely contingent on who narrates this history, but the root lies in the political-religious dispute between both countries, combined with a geographical dispute over the Shatt al-Arab, a navigable waterway where the Tigris and Euphrates Rivers merge and flow toward the strategically important Persian Gulf. In 1980, soon after the overthrow of the Shah of Iran, Iraq's Saddam Hussein took advantage of Iran's isolation from the world and the support he received from the United States.

Saddam Hussein, a Sunni Muslim Arab, actively opposed Iran's Shia Islamic Revolution that led to the fall of the Shah, partly because of the turmoil it could foster among Iraq's Shia majority. These Muslim sects, Sunnis and Shia, originated from opposing views following the death of the Prophet Muhammad. The Sunnis believe that Muhammed has no heir and his successor should be elected by the Muslim community, while the Shia believe that only God (Allah) can select religious leaders, and therefore Muhammed's successors must be direct descendants of his family.

The Republic of Iraq is one of the most ethnically diverse countries in the Middle East. Before World War I, Iraq was part of the Ottoman Empire, which included parts of ancient Mesopotamia, "the land between two rivers." Ethnically, Iraq is 70% Arab and 30% other minorities, primarily Kurdish, but also Turkmen, Assyrian, Armenian, Persian, and others. By religion, Iraqis are 60% Shia and the rest are Sunni, Christian (Church of the East, Chaldean, Syriac, Armenian), Kakai, Yazidi, and others. Kurds were the largest non-Arab ethnic group in Iraq at around 20% of the total population.

As the Iraq-Iran War continued, my mother gave birth to my two younger siblings, Dlovan and Dilven, who became known in the family as the children of war. Both grew up with sirens, bombs, and instability. Growing up in Erbil during the war, the blaring sirens sounded regularly. My parents would gather all the children and hurry to the tunnel they had dug by hand in the garden behind our house. We would often hear intense bombardment and the noise of explosions, while my mother would recite verses from the Quran and prayers to protect us. We would stay in the tunnel for hours until we could no longer hear any bombs falling.

On one occasion as the siren went off, we all rushed out of the living room and forgot baby Dilven, who was only three at the time. My mother thought that one of my older siblings had grabbed her as we all rushed to the tunnel. Dilven, noticing she was being left behind, froze in place, and began screaming. Eventually, my mother rushed back to retrieve her and bring her to the tunnel, but by that time she was already traumatized. For the next thirty minutes, she yelled in terror, and every other time the sirens went off from that point on she flashed back to that moment and began screaming in fear. My siblings and I would try our best to dance or make jokes to calm her down, but it usually did not help.

During this time, I was six years old and registered to attend the first grade. My mother would dress me and braid my hair, and my father would then hold my hand and walk me to school every morning and then return and drive everyone else to school. My sisters Jowan and Zhyan, fourteen and twelve then, were in middle school and would often dress in navy uniforms and help my mother get Jehan and Zerak, ten and eight, ready for school and prepare breakfast for everyone else. As soon as my father returned home each morning, to his surprise, he would find me back at home playing with baby Dilven and Dlovan. I vastly preferred playing with my younger siblings to going to school. "You need to be attending class and you can wait to play with them until after school," he would explain.

As the war continued, my teacher told my father that she was worried about me running away from school every morning. After multiple failed attempts that year at first grade, my parents decided it was best that I miss the school year and they would try registering me the following year. Around the same time, I not only ran away from school but also from home. If anyone upset me, I would repeatedly sneak into my bedroom, pack my clothes, and leave the house. I would be found later by other children in the neighborhood, who would return me to my family. One of the neighboring children who assisted in my return was Brwa, a sweet little boy with long straight hair and bangs. We often played outside, where I would pour sand on his head and he would return the favor by pouring a bowl full of sand on my curly hair. Brwa and I went our separate ways over the years during the war, but we managed to reconnect many years later through Facebook, as I will discuss in a later chapter.

Iraqi Kurdistan became an area of general unrest during the early stages of the Iraq-Iran War. The two prominent Kurdish political groups, the Kurdistan Democratic Party (KDP) and the Patriotic Union of Kurdistan (PUK), combined their forces known as Peshmerga ("those who face death") with support from Iran to fight against Saddam's Baathist regime, the government of Iraq. The word "Baathist" is used to refer to those who follow the Baath political movement. In Arabic, Baath means "renaissance" or "resurrection." Sadly, it never felt that way to us, as every Kurdish family, including my own, hated the constant fear we experienced under the Baathists.

Saddam's regime decided to annihilate both the KDP and PUK by striking at the Peshmerga, using all the means at their disposal. This included the large-scale punishment of civilians and the use of chemical weapons. The two most severe atrocities committed against the Kurds were the scorched earth Al-Anfal Campaign and the chemical weapon attack on the Kurdish city of Halabja. Unfortunately for us, these massacres were not officially recognized by the international community until the 1991 Gulf War following Iraq's invasion of Kuwait in 1990.

Ali Hassan al-Majid, also known as "Chemical Ali," the cousin of Iraq's President Saddam Hussein, was tasked with leading the Al-Anfal operation. The operation captured and transported thousands of Kurdish civilians to detention centers. Kurdish males of military age were treated as insurgents and executed, while women and children were forced to starve or trafficked as far away as Egypt.

On March 16, 1988, during the final days of the Iran-Iraq War, Chemical Ali ordered the bombing of the Kurdish city of Halabja with mustard gas and the deadly nerve agent Sarin. Halabja was where most of my mother's distant cousins lived. Many survivors still suffer from the aftermath of the chemicals to this day.

Perhaps one of the most notable victims of the Halabja massacre was Mam Omar ("Uncle Omar") who now symbolizes the genocide in Halabja. Omar had one infant son, who was his youngest child after eight daughters. When the Iraqi regime started gassing Halabja, Omar, with his infant son, ran to a neighbor for shelter. Tragically, he never made it there and neither Omar nor the rest of the family survived. He died on the neighbor's doorstep, holding his precious little boy in his arms. When I visited the Halabja National Memorial years later, I saw the heartbreaking image and memorial statue of Mam Omar with his infant son.

After eight years of mass killing, including the use of

weapons of mass destruction by both Iraq and Iran, the lack of international sympathy for civilians, and the failure to reach a diplomatic agreement, the United Nations negotiated a ceasefire in August of 1988. By then, the Iraq-Iran War had cost both countries over a million lives. The end of the war brought neither compensation for the victims nor border changes, just mass graves on both sides of the shared border and enough tears to fill up an ocean. It split so many families of their loved ones far too soon and ripped the security from the lives of so many children. For my childhood self, it was a dream for the day to go by without sirens, bombs, or the need to run for our lives.

Predictably, because of their alliance with Iran against Saddam, following the war, the Baathist regime became extremely suspicious of Kurds and their movement for autonomy or an independent Kurdish state. Kurds in Iraq were all now potential "traitors" to Iraq. To prevent us from being killed, my parents made sure that we refrained from any public declarations that indicated our support and love for Kurdistan. They also made sure that we knew all the songs and anthems that were praising the Baathist government and we would sing them to deter any suspicion of our loyalty. Our fear became extreme, to the point where we were afraid that any action could be misinterpreted by the Baathist regime and would cost us our lives.

To survive we did whatever it took to show our loyalty and support to the Baathist regime. We even hung a white flag outside our door to indicate our symbolic "surrender" to peace. Moreover, as children we each had a small white flag we would wave as soon as we heard military helicopters fly over the city to bomb houses whose inhabitants were suspected of supporting the Kurdish resistance.

Throughout the summer of 1988, my aunts and uncles traveled from Zakho to spend a few weeks with us in Erbil. My oldest aunt, Mati Soad, was a divorcee in her thirties. Mati was the oldest of my father's two sisters and had also gone to the University of Baghdad for her bachelor's degree. She often showed us pictures from her college days where she would dress in short dresses with puffy hair, the style of less-conservative 1970's Baghdad. She was also well-traveled for a woman her age. She showed us photos of her recent trips to Europe which left all of us in awe.

During her college days, Mati had fallen in love with a college classmate of hers who was a Shia Arab and the breadwinner to a group of younger siblings. The family never approved of him because of his background and the fact that he was obligated to provide for his younger siblings. My grandmother felt that he should not be responsible for supporting his younger siblings now that he was married to Mati, and he was eventually given an ultimatum by her to choose between the two. In response, he broke off the relationship with my Mati and chose his family responsibilities. Although I was too young to understand the magnitude of what Mati was telling us about her breakup, I could read the sadness on her face for ending her marriage and it was disappointing when I later learned how my grandmother interfered and played a role in it.

On the plus side, I was happy to have Mati spend the summer with us, but also regretted seeing her so sad and heartbroken. Mati never considered marriage after her divorce. Instead, she chose to look after my grandmother, and both would often visit us in Erbil.

As for my grandmother, she and my grandfather had gone their separate ways years before. I never understood the relationship between my grandmother and grandfather. She never talked nicely about him and when we visited my grandfather, he often told us how harsh our grandmother was. Curiously, my grandparents did not ever legally divorce. With so much shame associated with divorce, couples in Kurdistan in the 1980s often chose to simply separate instead of filing for divorce and never went public about their split to avoid being criticized by society and family members. We lost my grandmother when I was only seven years old and looking back I am bothered by the fact that I cannot remember her ever being pleasant to me or my sisters. My grandfather was right; she was very harsh and bitter and preferred my brothers. She saw girls as a societal and social burden, while boys were assets as the breadwinners of the house.

My grandmother was also often disturbed by my loud voice. Since I was my father's favorite child, my grandmother and father would quarrel over me. During one of their visits when I was six, I was being my usual self, a goof who tried to get my grandmother's attention. In doing so, I put my hands behind my back and started walking on my knees to impress her. In the middle of the walk, I fell on my face, breaking my front jaw, and my face was covered with blood. With my father out of town, my mother and oldest brother, Omed, rushed me to the emergency room. The oral surgeon was called to check on my jaw. The surgeon informed them that I had damaged all my front teeth and he did not think they would ever grow in properly. My mother was devastated.

On our way home that night, my mother and Omed were presented with twin infants who had been abandoned and left outside the hospital. The emergency room officer told my mother that the infants needed a home and asked if she was willing to adopt them. My mother, who was already overwhelmed by my condition, did not know how to respond. She looked at Omed hoping he would say something that would comfort her. "Mom, we have Heleen to worry about and you already have nine children at home," Omed reminded her. Omed grew up to be not only my mother's oldest child, but her best friend, and she relied on him for all family-related matters.

When my father returned home, he froze on the spot at the sight of my damaged face. When my mother and Omed told him the story, he was tearful and held me tight. "Heleen is so young! Her front teeth will grow," he asserted. "Plus, who said science is always right?"

Indeed, my father was right. Six months after the accident, my front teeth started growing again, but I ended up with an overbite. Ever the problem solver, my father assured me that the overbite was an easy fix. He took me to the best orthodontist in the country for braces and would later take me to my monthly appointments in Mosul to tighten the braces.

I was one of my father's favorites for many reasons. I resemble my mother—tall, curly-haired, with dark brown eyes, and a thick unibrow. Likewise, as a child, my father was my whole world. When he would leave for work in the morning, I would sit in his chair and refuse to move until he returned from the hospital. He took me with him to the hospital almost every week to keep him company in the office. When I finally started the first grade, I spent long hours studying so I could earn A+ grades and trophies to make my father proud.

This tight-knit relationship between my father and me was not limited to grades but extended to many areas of my life. I would go out of my way to please him, and he was always willing to listen to me brag about my accomplishments. This special bond between us continued until my father was detained by the Baathist regime and kept in prison for forty-five days. I remember it was around the holiday season when my mother dressed us all to go visit my father in prison. After his release, I noticed a drastic change in his temperament, as well as his passions. Following the torture he endured in prison, many things affected my father's mental state. He no longer enjoyed the little things he used to do for pleasure, such as taking care of the cattle, planting the garden, or cooking. He no longer wanted to dress in business clothes and was not passionate about the work he did for the hospital.

You might be wondering about the reasons for my father's imprisonment. My father was an educated Kurd from Zakho, with twenty-eight years of service and no affiliation or connection to the Baath regime. Because of this, his credentials and loyalty were constantly questioned by Iraqi government officials in Erbil. The Baath officials used the fursan (a Kurdish military unit that cooperated with the Iraqi government), whom we derogatorily referred to as Jash (offspring of donkeys), to detect any suspicious activity by Kurds in Iraqi Kurdistan. The fursan finally managed to come up with some accusations against my father, questioning his integrity and fitness to manage the hospital system in Erbil. After a thorough investigation, they failed to find anything substantive against my father and eventually released him.

After his release, my father was given the option of joining the Baath movement to keep his current post and benefits, or to retire immediately. He chose the latter. I later learned that this was not the first time my father was targeted because of his Kurdish identity. Immediately after graduating from high school, my father went to Baghdad to join the aviation school with the hope of becoming the first-ever Kurdish pilot in Iraq. However, the admissions committee used his Kurdish identity as an excuse to deny him acceptance into the program. Disappointed, my father opted for a degree in accounting.

After his incarceration in Erbil, my father informed my mother and the older children of his decision to leave his post at the Erbil hospital. My parents thought that his resignation was the safest decision for our family. Having nine children then, my parents packed our belongings and hired a van to travel the long road to my father's hometown of Zakho near the Iraq-Turkey border where we would live. Over the years, my parents got used to this constant drumbeat of injustice and it became an inseparable part of our lives and who we were as Kurds.

The main Kurdish cities of Iraq include Erbil, Sulaymaniyah, Duhok, Kirkuk, Halabja, and Zakho. The Kurdish dialect spoken in Erbil, Halabja, Sulaymaniyah, and Kirkuk is Sorani, spoken by my mother, while the Kurdish dialect spoken in Duhok and Zakho and surrounding areas is Bahdini, spoken by my father. When we lived in Erbil, they always referred to us as the "Bahdini people," and when we moved to Zakho, they referred to us as the "Sorani people." With my parents from opposite ends of Southern Kurdistan, and each speaking a different dialect of Kurdish, we grew up speaking both dialects with a slight accent and were thus treated as foreigners by both groups for not speaking like natives. My father—worried about our ability to find work in Iraq later in life—insisted that we go to a school that taught in Arabic. So, while we spoke Kurdish at home, Arabic was the main language we learned in school. Once we got to Zakho, the first thing my father did was register us in decent schools. Being around seven then, I started first grade in Zeen Primary School. The only challenge I had in school in Zakho was mastering the Bahdini dialect.

To make a living and provide for the family, my father went into the hospitality business by opening a restaurant, which he named Abu Omed ("the father of Omed"). From formerly being a white-collar professional, my father turned out to become a skilled kabob maker. He did not seem to care about giving up the profession he had worked so hard for because the restaurant business meant providing a comfortable life for his family. He prepared meals himself for the customers and obtained flatbread from a neighboring bakery. My father's restaurant became known regionally for his signature tashreeb dish (tomato stew made with dried limes from Basra, in the far south of Iraq). Once the soup was ready, the limey residue of the soup would be poured on a plate of chopped fresh bread.

In addition to my father's business, to help make ends meet my mother would buy five to ten kilograms of sunflower seeds from the bazaar in Zakho. She would wash them with salt water and spread them on big trays to dry on the roof during sunny days. Once dry, she would then roast the big pile of sunflower seeds while we made cone containers for my mother from our used journal books that we no longer needed for school. Each cone was filled with an hourglass full of seeds, our attempt in making sure to have an equal amount in each one. My mother would then line all the cones up for Zerak in a large basket that he carried to the soccer field in our neighborhood whenever there was a match. Zerak would shout, "wara verie tufkit garm u narm!" ("Come here for warm and soft sunflower seeds"). My mother's roasted sunflower seeds became so popular that we had to open a little stand for the neighborhood kids to buy them on a daily basis. Zerak would return home after he sold all the cones and hand the earnings to my father. However, one Friday, instead of making sales, Zerak returned with all the cones opened in his basket and his shirt ripped open. It seemed he had gotten into a fight with a guy who insultingly asked if Zerak had "soft and warm sisters" instead of seeds.

My brother, Zerak, and my sister, Jehan, who were nine and eleven at the time, were my proverbial "partners in crime." We were often caught getting into minor trouble together. We would make noise during my father's afternoon nap and he would wake up in a rage for interrupting his sleep.

Once when we split a piece of chocolate among us, Zerak took the bigger portion. I then complained that he was being greedy. "Well," he said, "If it was up to you, what portion would you take?"

I told him, "I would be fairer than you and take the smaller piece."

"What's the big deal, then?" he said, "I left you the small piece."

I began screaming in protest, waking my father who came storming in. Usually, when we were in trouble, my father would angrily chase all three of us through the house. Zerak and I would usually manage to escape, but Jehan would get caught all the time because of the lengthy gown she had to wear for "modesty," a consequence of her starting to show signs of puberty. On days when our father took his afternoon naps, we were all expected to either take naps as well or keep silent. For if our father was awakened from any noise made by us, he would launch into a rage and beat all of us, regardless of who was the actual offender.

To make up for our mischief and contribute to the family's meals, my siblings and I would collect free beans. During the garbanzo bean harvest season, farmers would bring piles of garbanzo bushes and spread them in the nearby soccer field to deseed. Jehan, Zerak, and I would make our way to the field to collect any garbanzo beans the farmers had left behind. We each often collected up to a bowl full of beans for our mother to cook.

However, no trip was free of adventure with Jehan and Zerak. One night, as we were searching for beans, Jehan's male teacher who was into wrestling walked by us wearing a tight pair of shorts. Zerak, spotting his fat behind in those shorts, started clapping and chanting a rhythm that aligned with the bouncing of his butt cheeks. Hearing the mocking, the teacher turned around and told Zerak to essentially "shut the fuck up!" Jehan and I quickly hid in the bushes, so the teacher did not notice we were there as well.

Of all my siblings, I was always closest to Jehan, even

though she was very nosy. From a young age, she constantly got Zerak and me in trouble as she was snooping into our business to investigate what we were up to. By the time I began middle school, Jehan was entering the tenth grade, and we were in the same school. She was someone I looked up to and would often find opportunities to hang out with during school picnics. Humorously, for one of those picnics, Jehan and I fixed a pot full of dolma and I kept referring to it as "manjal" which was a Sorani term for a decent size pot, but in Bahdini, a manjal meant a big pot of dolma that would feed the entire village. So, our friends thought we had cooked for the whole class, only to be disappointed once we arrived and they discovered how small it was.

My family and I soon found ourselves in the midst of another war, Iraq's invasion of Kuwait (the "Gulf War" to Americans), with many tough years ahead of us due to UN sanctions imposed on the whole country, sanctions which would eventually cost my father his business. I was about nine years old at the time and we were living in Zakho.

Displaying the perpetual nature of war, the origins of the latest conflict were rooted in the previous one. Not long after Iraq's ceasefire with Iran, we learned the Baathist regime had financial obligations towards Kuwait from the previous eight years of war. Kuwait, located south of Iraq, took a neutral stance in the Iraq-Iran War, until it began to fear that the Iranian Revolution would spread to its own land. This forced Kuwait to side with the Iraqi government.

During the Iraq-Iran War, Kuwait provided substantial financial support to Iraq, and played an instrumental role by providing access to all its ports when the major Iraqi southern port near Basra was destroyed by Iranian forces. When the war was finally over, Iraq was not able to repay Kuwait the money it had borrowed and asked for loan forgiveness, claiming that the war had also benefited Kuwait.

To offset the cost of the war, Kuwait decided to increase oil production. With the abundance of oil in the market, the price of oil from Iraq could not be increased, which caused its economy to falter. Later, we learned that there were allegations by the Iraqi government that Kuwait was illegally drilling for oil from the Rumaila field in Iraq. Iraq insisted that Kuwait, with its advanced technology, was slant-drilling, which cost Iraq billions of dollars in oil revenue.

In 1989, the Iraqi government demanded immediate repayment for the oil taken from Rumaila. After a year of failed diplomatic talks between the two countries, Iraqi forces invaded Kuwait in August 1990. Within a few days of the invasion, the United Nations Security Council (UNSC) formally opposed the invasion and demanded Iraq withdraw its forces from Kuwait. The Iraqi government, however, ignored the demand. The UNSC then enacted an international trade ban on Iraq.

The Iraqi government led by Saddam Hussein remained unfazed and five days later, on August 9th, President George H. W. Bush ordered the deployment of U.S. troops to the Persian Gulf. The Iraqi regime responded by increasing its troops in Kuwait. The UNSC established a deadline for the Iraqi government to withdraw from Kuwait, no later than November 29th, and stated that force would be used if it did not remove its troops by January 15th.

On January 17th, an international coalition of thirty-two countries led by the U.S. began airstrikes against Iraq. The ground invasion (referred to in America as "Operation Desert Storm") began on February 24th, and in only four days Iraq withdrew from Kuwait and President Bush declared a ceasefire.

Economic sanctions were imposed on Iraq by the United Nations four days after the Baathist regime's invasion of Kuwait. The sanctions involved a near-total economic and trade embargo, except for medicine and "in humanitarian circumstances," food imports. The sanctions remained in effect until the Baathists were forced from power years later during the second Gulf War in May 2003.

Before the sanctions were imposed on Iraq, my family had access to healthcare. In addition, Iraq had a social welfare policy in place to assist handicapped citizens and orphans, as well as poor families. The sanctions imposed on the country (which were supposedly enacted to help us) created a dramatic decline in our living standards and sanitary conditions. The hospital conditions were deplorable due to a lack of basic medical supplies, equipment, and maintenance. Healthcare and higher education standards dropped dramatically due to a lack of training and research. Schools and public offices were closed for weeks, and sometimes months. The death toll from 1991 to 1998 was estimated to be close to one million (half of whom were children), while Saddam Hussein remained unaffected in his palaces. The United Nations was criticized for targeting the Iraqi people with sanctions and not the Baathist regime. The disruption in the economy led to heightened levels of crime, corruption, and violence. Also, many public offices and houses were burned and looted.

One loss I experienced during this time in Zakho—and one that remains with me to this day—was the death of our pet sheep named Gundoor ("melon" in Kurdish). He was an adorable little lamb that my father got for us. Gundoor was stricken by a terrible skin disease for which we had no treatment, and no veterinary services were available. We watched poor Gundoor suffer terribly and die during those tough days under economic sanctions.

Our lives were soon turned upside down and any daily joy was stolen from us. Women and men in the neighborhood no longer paid attention to their physical appearances, as all mental energy turned to survival and making it through the day. My family and I lived through difficult years during the sanctions. From three healthy meals pre-sanctions, my parents now struggled to provide us with one meal. We knocked on countless doors begging for food. As food became scarce, the neighbors started sharing whatever they had in their possession with each other, mostly sugar, rice, and tea. My father, Omed, and Hoger would wake up early and begin searching for food and come back with whatever they could get their hands on.

There was no electricity or clean drinking water, so my siblings and I would walk for miles in search of tire rubber that we could use to make a fire to sterilize the water, which we would carry in buckets from the Khabur River. At night, my father and other men in the neighborhood would gather to listen to the news on the radio to see what would befall Iraq next. Within the dark neighborhood, my father would take the oil lamp to find his way to his friend's house through the narrow alleys. One night, I heard my father proclaim, "That son of a gun Gorbachev needs to do more to get rid of Saddam," to his two older friends as he lit a cigarette.

Of course, I did not know who Soviet leader Mikhail Gorbachev was at the time, other than that he was the guy with the stain on his forehead and somehow powerful enough to stop our misery under Saddam, according to my father.

Despite the difficulties, we were able to claw out some moments of fleeting happiness. For instance, my favorite thing about the sanctions was how close everyone had gotten in the community. I loved the neighbors and the kids that I used to play with. We would use chalk that we had taken from school to scribble cartoon images on the narrow alleys and walls of the neighborhoods. That was one of the few sources of entertainment we had as kids amidst the constant power outages. I also loved hanging out with Hajji Shukor and Aunt Aziza, an old couple who had no children but treated us as their own. Every night the children from the neighborhood would gather at Aunt Aziza's house for storytelling time, where she made yummy sugar cookies that she gladly shared with all of us.

Due to the unsanitary conditions, infectious diseases were easily contracted and spread. At eight years of age, I remember being infected with chickenpox. I had to endure the symptoms of the disease in the heat of summer with no proper treatment, electricity, or drinking water. I sobbed for hours, my whole body itching and in agony, yet I was not allowed to scratch. Being one of ten children then, my mother kept me in isolation, fearing I would transmit the infection to my younger siblings.

After my father lost his restaurant during the sanctions, times were difficult, even though we lived in a supposedly "high-end" neighborhood. In the 1990s, this was simply a cement house with running water, electricity, and a yard. To stay afloat financially, my parents decided to open a teahouse serving tea and naani saaj (flatbread fried in corn oil). My mother would fix the dough at night and let the yeast grow until morning. She woke up at sunrise to fix 200 to 300 pieces of flatbread and fry them in the oil to be ready by 8 am. Once the first few batches were ready, one of us would hand-deliver the bread to the teahouse, about a twenty-minute walk from where we lived. Civilians and Iraqi soldiers would stop by the tea house to buy a flatbread and tea to go. The business model was not ideal because making the bread left my mother physically exhausted, but my parents knew this was the only way of providing for the family amid the crippling sanctions. Luckily, my mother was worth fifty Kurdish men (as our saying goes) when it came to having strength and devotion to her children. But not only to us; she would cook and bake extra to feed any hungry neighborhood kids as well.

In the wake of the devastating defeat of the Iraqi forces in Kuwait, the Iraqi regime started to lose the power it previously held. Consequently, revolutionary Arab Shia forces launched a rebellion against the Baathist regime in southern Iraq, which soon also spread to the Kurdish region in the north. Kurdish forces slowly but deliberately began taking control of the Kurdish cities of northern Iraq, in the famous Kurdish uprisings of 1991. Baathist forces soon tried to regain control of the Kurdish towns and cities, resulting in one of the largest mass exoduses in recent history.

Hundreds of thousands of Kurdish families, including my own, began fleeing our homes, fearing another gas attack like Halabja. The United Nations estimates that over one million Kurds fled their homes to escape bombardment by Saddam's Baathist military, seeking refuge in Turkey and Iran during extreme winter conditions. Most refugee families, like my own, left their homes with nothing and walked towards the mountains along the borders. None of us knew how many days we would be walking and how far we needed to go. We walked as quickly as possible for what seemed like hundreds of miles. The paths from "Kurdish Iraq" to "Kurdish Iran" and "Kurdish Turkey" consisted of twists and turns through the mountains. For the thousands of people suddenly embarking on a journey towards survival, the potential gas attack could not have been more real.

Our shoes wore out or got stuck in the mud, and some of us continued barefoot. We felt completely abandoned by the rest of the world and in danger of starvation while stranded in the freezing mountains. The children were in the most danger from lack of food, water, unsanitary conditions, and extreme cold. Parents became scavengers, looking for water, and forced us to suck on snow to stay alive. We would squeeze against each other for the heat and rub our hands against each other to prevent our fingers from freezing. I would also go under my mother's arm to keep me warm. On our way to the mountains, my brother Omed spotted a blanket. He got excited about using it to warm up. But when he pulled the blanket towards himself, he found the dead body of an infant hidden inside the blanket, leaving me terrified.

Every day, there was more illness and disease because we were living in appallingly filthy conditions. At night we slept under plastic tarps. Every morning, the dead bodies that did not make it through the cold, wet, sleepless nights, were carried away. Families slept just a few feet away from the corpses of their loved ones. No one was able to provide their loved ones with a proper funeral. They had to leave the bodies behind and continue walking to the next safe destination in tears. Their desire to live ended up outweighing their human need to grieve.

Witnessing all the human suffering at such a young age, I couldn't think about anything but disappearing from the world. I walked to my mother in freezing cold weather in the uncertain world we were living in. "Ouda?"

"Yes, Dai Guri."

"Why is this happening to us?"

"Why do you ask?"

"I am hungry. I am cold. I am homeless. I lost all my friends. I don't want to be in this world."

With desperation, my mother held me tight, "There is no looking back, Heleen. We must fight through this. We have no choice but to look ahead and see what the future holds for us."

Once we made it to the first "safe" destination, thousands of refugees would wait every morning for medical workers, food, and aid to arrive from the Turkish military, who themselves were not happy to see Kurds, as they did not treat Kurds any better in their country than Iraq did in ours. The supplies would usually not meet the demand. Blankets, rice, bread, and tents were dropped from helicopters and military planes and thousands of us would run as fast as we could to catch them. On one occasion the packages were dropped in a minefield and when the refugees ran to get them, men died from being blown up. There was no medical care, just a few medications that could not meet the demand of thousands of refugees.

A political commentator traced the uprising and chaos in Iraq to a statement made by President H.W. Bush at the height of the war, "...there's another way for the bloodshed to stop, and that is for the Iraqi military and the Iraqi people to take matters into their own hands to force Saddam Hussein, the dictator, to step aside and to comply with the United Nations and then rejoin the family of peace-loving nations." To incite this, the U.S. military dropped planeloads of pamphlets telling Kurds and Shiites to revolt against Saddam. However, when the people did so, no U.S. assistance arrived alongside them.

The media began airing pictures of the hundreds of thousands of Kurds seeking refuge in the mountains, dying of starvation, dehydration, and suffering under extreme winter conditions. In some locations, Turkey, claiming it did not have the resources to accommodate thousands of Kurdish refugees, refused to open its borders and forced the Kurdish refugees back into Iraq. Any refugee who attempted to get past the Turkish soldiers was hunted down. The images were extremely uncomfortable for the coalition forces, especially the United

States. To the international community, it appeared the gains of the Kuwait war were being erased along the mountainous borders of Iraq.

Once again, the Kurds were abandoned by Western powers and had their dream of becoming an independent state crushed. In several Western nations, including the U.S. and Great Britain, there was a growing public demand for action to end the suffering of the Kurdish people along the Iraqi northern borders. After intense public pressure, the United Nations Security Council (UNSC) passed a resolution condemning the Baathist regime's oppression of the Kurds. The U.S. military began dropping food and medical supplies to Kurdish refugees in Turkey. However, the limited supplies provided still did not meet the demand. In addition, the U.S., Great Britain, and France implemented a no-fly zone that prevented Iraqi military aircraft from flying into Iraqi Kurdistan. Generously supported by the international community, The United Nations responded with a major relief effort, setting up camps with semi-permanent structures to care for the Kurdish refugees until they could return to their homes. The coalition forces had also deployed military forces to secure a safe haven in northern Iraq, called Operation Provide Comfort.

Despite the aid, my family decided to take their chances and return home. To my father, it was better for us to die in our homes than out of starvation in the mountains. While other families chose to stay because the UN built refugee camps and airdropped food and supplies, my siblings and I took enough food from the camp and made our way back. We slept in the mountains and eventually returned to Zakho and our rental house.

We found our house's walls intact but were disappointed to see all our valuables stolen. On a macro level, everywhere we looked we saw public offices and government buildings turned into rubble, burned cars, and damaged windows. Statues and large public posters of the former Iraqi regime that previously were everywhere in Zakho, were now all shot with bullets and burned. The once lively city felt like a cross between a ghost town and a war movie set. Peshmergas and coalition forces peered down at us from machine gun nests on the rooftops. Even though the Kurdish region was no longer under Baathist control, everyone and his cousin seemed to be carrying a weapon and young kids would even be seen driving vehicles as a state of lawlessness reigned.

Upon our return home, we heard intense bombardments that followed the long sirens, which proceeded the violent explosions close to where we lived. One of those nights, we heard a bomb explode in the Khabur in front of our house. My parents rushed us all to the closest air-raid shelter to seek refuge in the middle of the night until the bombing eventually stopped. A few families who chose to stay behind or return from the mountains would soon join us in the air-raid shelter. As for me, I was with other girls my age, and would narrate stories to distract us from the terror we lived in. While the darkness surrounded my family and I from every angle as war tore the country apart, the deep connection to those girls at the air raid shelter is what kept me sane.

As more families returned from the mountains, they would join us in the shelter and share their stories of suffering. After so many stories, the child in me could not help but wonder why the common denominator to all our stories involved suffering and the struggle to stay alive. One of those nights, we were all rejoiced to have Hajji Shawkat and Aunt Aziz reunite with us. Aunt Aziza's hands were blistered from the unforgiving living conditions in the mountains. As sad as I was to see how frail she looked, I was ecstatic to learn she was alive and back to Zakho all safe and sound.

There was little comfort, though, when we returned home to Zakho from the mountains. Three decades of conflict had left millions of landmines and other unexploded ordnance scattered across the region. In Zakho, grenades, bullets, guns, and other weapons were left behind. The concentration of landmines was especially dense. From 1980 to 1988, the Baathist regime planted thousands of mines in and around Kurdish cities bordering Iran to prevent Iranian forces from moving into those cities. Additionally, during the first Gulf War, mines were laid by the Baathist regime along the border with Turkey to keep the Kurds confined. As a result, the Kurdish region of Iraq became one of the most densely landmine-contaminated areas in the world.

A pile of stones, if not marked appropriately with skull and crossbones, might look harmless to children, but in the Kurdistan Region of Iraq it was indicative of danger. To this day, I feel blessed that I am not missing a limb or have other permanent injuries from the high number of explosives we were exposed to. Access to mines was easy; we would play with them and even exchange them for money. In one of those instances, two of my little brothers chose to light one of the explosives they were holding. It exploded immediately and burned my brother Dlovan's entire face. With scarce medical aid available due to sanctions, we were extremely worried. My mother rushed Dlovan to the hospital and we learned that the burn thankfully did not impact his eyesight. Dlovan was brought home where we cared for him until his face healed.

Around three months later, things were finally calming down in northern Iraq, meaning no sounds of shooting and bombing, or fighting for our lives in the mountains. We started to feel safe. By then, most refugee Kurds had descended from the mountains and returned to their homes only to find them looted.

To keep the peace, U.S.-led coalition forces were deployed to the Kurdish region of Iraq to ensure our safety from Saddam's regime. As kids, my siblings and I loved interacting with the U.S.-led coalition forces. From teaching us a few English words to giving us candy, we always left the encounter feeling happy to have Americans talk to us. The next day, we would be back on the streets of Zakho to wave at the military Humvees and yell, "Mister, Mister, chocolate? Please, Mister, chocolate." We would then add "Mister baba (father) no", to show how hungry and desperate we were for food. The friendly soldiers would stop their cars to share their snacks with us and even have us pose for photos. Unlike the Iraqi army soldiers that were deployed to Zakho, the American soldiers were extremely friendly. To ingratiate ourselves we would tell them, "Mister yes yes Bush, no no Saddam," to show our displeasure of having the Baathists still in power in Baghdad.

For more security, we moved into an abandoned house that previously had been occupied by a Baathist official, and was in a mostly deserted neighborhood near where the U.S. forces were stationed. I was nine at the time. Our new place faced a government high-rise building that was occupied by coalition forces, which my family felt would provide some degree of safety.

Humorously, one hot summer day we noticed the U.S. soldiers out on the balconies sunbathing naked, which came as a funny shock to me and my sisters. We would cover our eyes and giggle in embarrassment at how comfortable these men were being outside with no clothes on. Not knowing any English, my father and uncles flagged down the U.S. soldiers and struggled to explain to them that exposing themselves in public was against our cultural and religious practices. At one point my uncle started pointing to his own penis and then covering his face, while saying "no!" (one of the only words he knew) to the soldiers. After multiple attempts, my uncle was convinced they understood his message, and the following day the soldiers were wearing towels around their waists when sunbathing.

Not long after my brother Dlovan had been burned by an exploding munition, I had my own close call that could have altered the course of my life.

My brother and sister and I were exploring an abandoned house that previously had been occupied by a

Baathist official in Zakho. I spied this shiny, mysterious-looking thing in army green, not realizing that it was a grenade. I picked it up quickly, before anyone else could, and made my way with my prize out to the interstate. I didn't think it was dangerous; I thought it was an exciting new find.

There were several U.S. Humvees out on the highway driving by. I was startled when one Humvee screeched to a stop and honked at me. A marine jumped out. He was looking at me and my prize and he was walking toward me slowly...cautiously.

I clutched the grenade tighter.

He smiled at me and pointed to the grenade.

I clutched it tighter still.

He held up a bag of candy.

A bag of candy! It had been a long time since I'd had a bag of candy. I smiled back at him. Slowly, I made my way toward him, holding out the grenade, never taking my eyes off the sweets.

He handed me the bag of candy, and I handed him the grenade, certain I got the better part of the deal. Totally unaware at the time that this marine might have saved my life, I ran off to share my newly earned candy with my siblings.

A few months into living in the deserted area of Zakho, we were asked to evacuate the area for the families of the Kurdish martyrs (Kurds who died fighting to remove the Baathists). As much as we loved living in those houses, it was time for us to leave the area.

We next found a two-floor spacious house for rent in the Abasiki area of Zakho and were relieved. However, not too long after we moved into the house, the landlord's relatives were also returning from the mountains and asked us to vacate. We begged to stay and after countless attempts, the landlord allowed us to, under one condition: that the second floor be left for their returning relatives. We agreed, considering it was becoming impossible to find a good place to rent with everyone returning from the mountains.

We now had two big households sharing one house with one bathroom. One positive was that all the kids from both families could play with each other. I often found myself playing with their little girls on the balcony of the second floor where the family kept their onions and potatoes. And since hunger will make a thief of anyone, I would often take onions when no one was around, and throw them down to where my sister Jehan would collect them for our mother. After multiple attempts, Jehan and I were caught stealing onions and their mother complained to our mother.

Their family also had a single son of marriageable age who took a liking to two of my sisters, asking my mother if one of them was available. My mother refused, as she believed their family was merely exploiting our poverty. Turning them down on such an offer, however, meant that we had to also find a new place to live, as we were no longer welcome in the home.

My father often felt hopeless for not being able to provide for the family. To cope with the stress, he would pull out his tobacco pouch and paper from his pocket, roll a cigarette, and smoke one after another. Soon after, my father decided to move the family back to Erbil. He felt there were more job opportunities now that the city was no longer under Baathist control. He was certain he would find a job in Erbil to provide for our family. Since they spoke some English, my two older brothers chose to stay in Zakho, working as translators for coalition forces and non-profit organizations.

We managed to find a decent two-bedroom house on Chadai Surchian Street in Erbil. This was 1992. I was ten years old. Surchian Street was a decent neighborhood consisting of mostly middle-class families. Over time, Jehan had come up with a nickname for every one of our neighbors. One neighbor, whose son was taken hostage by the Baathist regime, would often tell my mother that her son Aziz would detu (meaning "eventually return"), so she became "detu detu." Another, a midwife who delivered all the babies in the neighborhood named Ayesha, became Guara Gawra ("big earrings") for her large golden earrings. Then there was mala Badala ("telephone house"), since he possessed the only working phone that we could call our aunts and uncles in Zakho on. Next was the mala Sufi ("religious house"), because they were devout followers of Sufiism and generous enough to let us use their water pump to fill the tanks that Jehan and I would have to continuously carry.

Perhaps the most memorable experience from my childhood in Surchian was witnessing the nomadic Darwish (Sufi holy man) passing through our neighborhood. It was fascinating for us as kids to watch him and learn about his beliefs. He only had one eye, very long hair, a traditional Kurdish outfit, and a daf drum. He would rhythmically chant "Ya Allah" (Hey God) as he bent down and struck himself to perform dhikr (remembering God). He spoke perfect Sorani and told Jehan that Satan had stolen one of his eyes, which instead of weakening him, only strengthened his resolve. "My focus, and my love allow me to repel all self-desires of the ego," he would explain. "Remembering God feeds the soul just as food nourishes the body," was another of his repetitive statements. Unlike the profoundly serious religious men we were used to seeing, Darwishes like him were free spirits who often quoted the poet Rumi and took ascetic vows of poverty where they did not own any possessions. Instead, they relied on charity for their survival.

While some holy men sustained themselves on devotion, the rest of us required food, and that was becoming scarcer. Making matters worse, as the whole country struggled under the sanctions, the northern region of Iraq suffered from a double embargo. After the U.S. declared it a "safe zone" in October 1991, the Iraqi government began withdrawing funding and services from the northern provinces of Duhok, Erbil, and Sulaymaniyah, imposing its own economic blockade on the Kurdish region. This led to the creation of the de facto Kurdistan Region of Iraq. The United Nations, however; did not alter the scope of the international sanctions since Kurdistan was still technically part of Iraq. This double embargo, one by the United Nations and the other by Iraq's Baathist regime, led to the development of a non-productive economy, based almost solely on revenues derived from smuggling goods from Turkey, Iran, and government-controlled areas of Iraq.

The double embargo on the Kurdistan Region of Iraq directly impacted my father's pension. Because he was employed and retired when Erbil was under Baathist control, his pension came from the Baghdad government. However, with the regime now withdrawn from the Kurdistan region, those like my father were forced to commute to an Iraqi city under Baathist control outside the region to receive their pensions. In his case, that city was Mosul, which was a two-hour drive from where we lived.

The road to Mosul was often shut down for weeks and sometimes months at a time, preventing my father from making the trip to receive his pension. When the road finally opened, he was able to commute to Mosul by bus to obtain his pay. He was owed back pay for all the months he missed his salary, leaving him with a relatively large amount. Once he received his pension, he hopped on the bus back to Erbil, but at one of the checkpoints on the way out of Mosul he was stopped for inspection. When they found the large sum of money he was now carrying, the Baathist officers took it, handcuffed my father, and took him to a local prison in Mosul before transferring him to Abu Ghraib prison in Baghdad.

With the complete separation of the Kurdistan Region from the rest of the country, the lack of electricity, and no reliable telephone system, there was no way we could learn about my father's status and we were deliberately kept in limbo. Our case was not unique. In fact, many young Kurdish students studying at the University of Mosul went missing like my father on their way to the city. Their primary "crime" usually was possessing Kurdish music (such as cassette tapes of Şivan Perwer) or anything that indicated pride or loyalty to the Kurdish resistance movement. My brother Hoger, eighteen years old then, was studying agricultural science at the University of Mosul. He was often humiliated at the checkpoints because he was a Kurd. My mother would cook and pack him food when he visited to take back with him. However, the Arab Baathist officers at the checkpoints would dig into his box of goods and ridicule him over the food that my mother had packed for him, while also seizing whatever they wanted for themselves. Such humiliation was done intentionally to cause a reaction for which the person could be arrested and disappear.

There was no sense of closure when Kurdish family members vanished, as you would constantly worry about where your loved ones had gone. Were they alive, dead, or being tortured? We were not able to prepare for their return, or their funeral, as we had no idea of their fate. This psychological trauma also had the effect of keeping people docile about resisting, as people did not know if their loved ones were alive, and feared that if they caused any problems, revenge would be taken on their loved ones for their actions. The regime wanted all Kurds in a constant state of fear, worry, unfinished grief, and anxiety, which allowed them to rule more easily. In our own personal case we waited for weeks, then months, and still there was no news about my father. It felt like an intentional move to threaten our sanity and force us to anguish in despair.

We were renting our home at the time, and the first of the month was approaching with no information about my father's whereabouts. We had to borrow money to pay the month's rent while he was gone. As time went by, and to keep up with our school needs, my mother started selling her jewelry and our furniture. A month after my father's disappearance, my mother had managed to save some money from the jewelry and furniture she sold. Then, pregnant with her 11th child, my mother took it upon herself to make the trip to Mosul to search for my father. With Hoger already in Mosul, she met up with him and they went looking for my father. After begging the Baathist officials countless times at checkpoints and telling them that my father had ten children in desperate need of his financial support, my mother was given empty promises and sent from one office to the next without getting anywhere. She had nothing to offer those officials and recalled how it gave them a sadistic pleasure to look at my mother's desperate face trying to find her husband's whereabouts.

She was a beautiful, modest Kurdish lady in her early forties with her college-age son. She had no makeup on, and no flirtatious smiles to grant these corrupt officers to ease the process for her. With the limited cash she had, she bribed a few of them until they finally told my mother about my father's whereabouts in Mosul. My father had been sent to Salamiya prison. My mother and Hoger hopped into the next taxi, determined to find him. After arriving and further bribing, my mother was crushed to learn that my dad had been transferred to Abu Ghraib in Baghdad. My mother was devastated as she would be forced to return home without my father.

Once my mother returned, with all the stress she was under, her water broke. After ten prior pregnancies, she recognized well the pattern of contractions, knew she was about to deliver a baby, and needed to be taken to the hospital immediately. We did not have a car, so my brothers, Jowan and Zhyan, started knocking on neighbors' doors, asking whether one of them was willing to drive our mother to the hospital. Our next-door neighbor, who had a truck, kindly agreed. Before we knew the gender of the 11th child, my sisters and I wanted the baby to be a girl so we would outnumber the boys. Of course, my brothers wanted the baby to be a boy to outnumber the girls! Once my mother delivered the baby, she was discharged from the hospital immediately. The same neighbor drove my mother, Jowan, and the baby home. Once they arrived, we were informed the baby was a boy. They named him Reveng, ("someone with no home") as had been my father's wish, reflecting the time when we had fled to the mountains. We all called him Pambo (cotton ball in Kurdish), because of his fat baby cheeks and cute curly hair.

Baby Reveng was put into a special kind of cradle, which is still seen all over Kurdistan. The cradle consisted of a flat wooden bottom on two rockers. The bottom had two holes, which were used for waste passage. At each end of the flat wood, there was a large transverse loop of wood connected by a thick twisted bar. My mother had hand made a colored cotton mattress with a hole that aligned with the hole on the flat wood bottom of the cradle. My mother would fold a soft towel and place it under Reveng's neck, and he was arranged to be fastened to the cradle by colored cords that were the width of my hand. A handmade wooden pipe was put through the hole in the mattress and the bottom of the cradle into a bowl. My mother had it raised above the mattress and covered with a soft cloth to prevent any discomfort to the baby. While Reveng was fastened in the cradle, my mother would breastfeed him by sitting on the floor and holding the cradle towards her. Once she was done, she would cover the cradle with a colored blanket and rock the cradle until Reveng went to sleep.

A few days after Reveng was born, my mother, who should have been resting, started looking for a source of income to provide for her children. I remember her being worried about getting cursed by "the evil eye," because a woman was obviously unfit to be seeking work when she had just delivered a baby. However, with our living conditions and finances depleted, she had no choice. She would leave the house early in the morning or when no one was outside to see her. On days where she could not find a job or a source of income, she would come home with a dealer to sell one of the items from our home. When our hunger got extreme, we would be in search of anything edible, including random chickens wandering on the streets of our neighborhood. Once we spotted one, we would rush to grab the chicken and bring it home alive for my mother to kill it and prepare dinner. My mother warned us not to tell the other children in the neighborhood that we had chicken for dinner. Considering how expensive chicken was, we would likely be caught for taking the missing chickens.

There were days when Reveng would cry all night. Complaints started to come in from the neighbors about Reveng's cries and how it kept them up. With that, my siblings and I started taking turns rocking Reveng's cradle at night to keep him quiet. When Reveng was born, Blend was only two years old. When classes were out, I oversaw caring for both Reveng and Blend. Not being able to afford diapers, Blend would just soil himself when he needed to go.

On cold winter days, I would boil water in a big teapot on the stove, mix the boiled water with cold tap water to bring it to room temperature, and wash Blend's butt. One day, I forgot to cool the boiled water, and instead poured the boiling water on Blend's butt and he started screaming. My mother was not home, and my sisters frantically rushed in to see what had happened. I told them that I had forgotten to cool the water and burned Blend's butt. They took the two-year-old Blend to a neighbor we knew who was a nurse. She examined Blend and told us he was suffering from second-degree burns and needed to be taken to the emergency care unit. I felt extremely guilty for causing my little brother so much pain and adding to my mother's burden when she was already under so much stress. I asked my sister to let me accompany Blend to the hospital, but I was told to stay behind. I waited for hours until my sisters finally came back from the hospital with Blend's butt covered with ointment and bandages. He would eventually recover, but he had to endure a lot of pain that night.

For my mother, so many things remind me of how brave she was. She was a fighter and never accepted no for an answer. She often went by "Jinka Drij" (tall lady) in the Bazaar for her height and beautiful posture. Very stoic with a silent dignity about her, my mother always covered her hair with a beautiful white scarf made from silk.

Modest in certain matters, she covered her face with her left hand when she laughed to conceal her teeth. She was beautiful with a perfectly fit body despite giving birth to eleven children. She also breastfed all her kids, which meant the front top of her dress would constantly be open with milk dripping from her breasts. Growing up, my sisters and I longed for the day when our mother's dress would finally be buttoned up, as it would signify that she was finally finished bearing children. My mother had learned over the years to grind down any of her own dreams and prioritize her children.

Photo of mother, Fatima Jaff, at 59 years of age.

With my father still away, our mother was the center of our life. She was obsessively attached to each one of us. Each morning, she would wake up at sunrise regardless of how she felt to start a fire in the tandoor oven that she had made by hand in the courtyard. My mother's tandoor oven was made of clay that was cylindrical and curved inward towards the top to concentrate the heat. The tandoor oven was covered with mud, which served as the insulating material. She would make countless numbers of dough balls, flatten them, and then slap them against the sides of the tandoor wall until they were puffy and blistered. She would then call on us to have the fresh warm naan (bread) to dip into a bowl of homemade yogurt, accompanied by a cup of chai (tea) with cardamom.

I would wake up every morning to the rhythmic slap of the flattened dough against the tandoor wall. At times, I offered to help in making the balls of dough for her. Mine varied greatly in size and shape. Seeing the lack of consistency and focus as metaphorical, she would remind me how I would never be able to discern my friend from my enemy because the balls I made were so variable. I would then stand by the tandoor to warm my hands during cold winter days, while sharing stories from school with her and what my friends were up to.

Despite not being able to read or write herself, she insisted that all her kids go to school and finish college. This showed the extent of how being deprived of education by her parents and my father had bothered her. Growing up, my mother was adamant about two things for her kids: that eventually we own our own home, and that we acquire a college degree. "Not having a house is like leaving home without underwear," she would explain. Over the years we would all share with our mother what we learned in school. I would show my mother the notes and lessons we discussed in class. I would also tell her how the teacher was so pleased with my performance because I showed up prepared, meaning my nails were clipped, my uniform was clean, and my books were wrapped with paper covers.

I knew those types of updates made my mother happy that her hard work raising all of us was paying off. Of all the classes I took, I remember telling my mother how much I hated English at first. She would often joke using the few English words she knew to tease me and show how easy the English language supposedly was. I needed a dictionary for my English class, but I could never ask her for money. I used to share the tandoor naan with my classmates. They loved the naan so much that they asked me to bring more and they were willing to pay for it. I was initially hesitant to accept payment because sharing your food was part of our culture and something that my parents had encouraged us to do. But because they had asked for whole pieces of my mother's tandoor naan, I was convinced to accept payment, especially when I needed to get my dictionary. So I started bringing more naan and sold each piece for a dinar, money that allowed me to purchase school supplies for my siblings and the dictionary that I desperately needed to help me with my English class.

I should add that despite our hardships, I do not recall my mother ever complaining about why we were so poor. Instead, she would manage with whatever she had access to in order to provide for my siblings and me. She often got frustrated with us, but instantly regretted her anger and thanked God by praying for ease to come her way after a rough day with my father still away. Despite all the struggles she had gone through to make a living for us, she called each one of us "Dai Guri," a Bahdini term that meant, "May your mother sacrifice her soul for you." My mother spoke Sorani to us all except when it came to the term Dai Guri, because, without us, she found no point in living. My cousins often asked my mother why she used the term Dai Guri. "My whole life is about my children," she would respond.

If one genuinely wants to understand the struggle and perseverance of the Kurdish people, they must first focus on the mothers like mine, the silent pillars that quietly held up our society and culture. To my mother, we were her whole world, and to us, my mother will always be "Gula Ganim," the beautiful wheat flower that grows all around the valleys in Kurdistan, nourishing countless Kurdish souls over the centuries.

CHAPTER II:
HOLDING ON TO HOPE IN A BROKEN PLACE

"no one leaves home unless
home is the mouth of a shark
you only run for the border
when you see the whole city running as well
your neighbors running faster than you
breath bloody in their throats
the boy you went to school with
who kissed you dizzy behind the old tin factory
is holding a gun bigger than his body
you only leave home
when home won't let you stay."
– "Home," poem by Warsan Shire

Pira Delal (the beautiful bridge) at sunset, Zakho, Kurdistan.
Photo courtesy of Salam Abdullah.

One cold winter morning, I was walking to Shayma, the primary school where my parents had registered me in the third grade when we settled in Erbil. Shayma was in the high-end neighborhood of Shorsh, home to many of Erbil's Turkmen. My mother had braided my hair as she usually did for school days, and I was dressed in my required navy-blue uniform with a matching bag. We did not have a school bus system, nor proper public transportation, so I would walk for forty-five minutes each day to reach the only school in the area that taught an Arabic language curriculum. I hand-wrote the poetry we were required to memorize that day for my Arabic literature class, and I repeated the lines as I walked from one neighborhood to the next, paying attention to the busy morning traffic.

One day, as I was getting close to the school, I saw hundreds of my schoolmates and their parents standing outside the building. I also noticed police officers on top of the building inspecting the roof and the corners of the school. I asked what was going on. Apparently, neighbors had spotted some terrorists the previous night setting up bombs that were timed to explode when classes were in session.

Not long after I arrived, the school principal was instructed to send the students home for the day, and he asked everyone to leave the area. We could return to school when we were informed it was safe. I was terrified, yet also disappointed that I would miss classes and my classmates for who knew how long. My only source of entertainment was going to school and seeing my classmates.

I was finally told to return to school, but it would not be for long, because the situation in the city became unstable and violent due to the economic sanctions. After the Kurdish region of Iraq was granted de facto autonomy, the region was self-ruled by the two opposing Kurdish political parties, the KDP and PUK. In parliamentary elections in 1992, the KDP gained an absolute majority of votes in the Kurdish cities of Zakho, Duhok, and Erbil, under the leadership of Masoud Barzani, while the PUK gained the Sulaymaniyah governorate, as well as the Kurdish portions of the Diyala, Kifri, and Khanaqin districts, under the leadership of Jalal Talabani. With little experience at governing, the two parties now had to manage the refugee crisis and respond to the demands of the international humanitarian agencies.

A year after the election, tensions grew between the two ruling parties over land rights. Ultimately, this resulted in the Kurdish Civil War in 1994, a bitter conflict which lasted four long years. Each party sided with a larger state neighbor to defeat its adversary. The PUK sided with Iran and Kurdish guerrillas of the PKK fighting Turkey, while the KDP sided with Turkey and Iraq. The KDP then undertook negotiations with the Baathist regime in Baghdad to expel the PUK from Erbil. If you ask Kurds about this civil war, they will say, "You mean the Bira Kuji (Brothers War)?" Indeed, it was a "Fratricide War" when brothers killed brothers, choosing to ally with the enemies of Kurds to defeat each other. The Fratricide War destroyed what little was left intact from the earlier wars waged by the Baathist regime, killing over 5,000 Peshmerga and civilians, and leaving thousands more displaced. Schools were used for Peshmerga stations, and hospitals were shut down for months. Due to the constant gunfire, the city of Erbil, once known for its nightlife, became a ghost town.

One of the victims of the Fratricide War was my first cousin, Jalil, who was in his early twenties in 1994, and a supporter of Barzani under the KDP. Jalil was living in Erbil, and at that time, the city was under the control of the PUK. One night during the tensions, Jalil was kidnapped by PUK forces and tortured to death. Just before he took his last breath, Jalil was returned to his parents. To this day, my aunt and uncle grieve over Jalil's death and the torture he endured at the hands of his own Kurdish brothers.

The Fratricide War is a complicated black spot on every Kurdish politician's history. The mothers and spouses of the lost Peshmerga, including my aunt, criticize even their own KDP politicians for siding with the Baathist regime. Did they forget what the Baathist regime had done to the Kurds? The regime that had gassed and massacred the Kurds for years and was now the KDP's ally against their own blood brothers.

The living conditions were difficult during the Fratricide War. My paternal grandfather, who went by Babu Ali, passed away while my father was still in Abu Ghraib prison in Baghdad. My oldest sister Jowan (20 years old then) joined my oldest uncle, Yousif, alongside his wife, for the long road trip to Zakho to attend Babu Ali's funeral. Babu Ali owned a mud hut in the poorest neighborhood of Zakho, the historic Mahala Reeta ("the naked neighborhood"). The neighborhood was called Reeta because of its proximity to the Khabur River and Mahala for the young boys from the neighborhood who would jump from a cliff into the Khabur and swim naked. Babu Ali lived in the mud hut all by himself after he was separated from my grandmother. Together, they gave birth to five boys and two girls. My father was the third child in line.

A formal mourning period for Babu Ali was held at my Uncle Anwar's house. Anwar was the oldest uncle after Uncle Yousif. When Jowan arrived there, she met up with both of my oldest brothers, Omed and Hoger, 26 and 22 years old then. On the second day of mourning, everyone stopped by the mud hut to sort through Babu Ali's belongings. When we were kids, I remember we were fascinated by the pocket watch that Babu Ali carried with him everywhere and his cane that was made from a walnut tree. Both the pocket watch and the cane were retrieved by Jowan, which she brought with her to Erbil to us.

Knowing how difficult our financial situation was after my father's imprisonment in 1993, my three uncles suggested that my oldest brother move the family from Erbil to Zakho, where we could stay at my grandfather's house to avoid rental costs. This sounded like a great idea; however, there was one major problem. For us to make the trip from Erbil to Zakho, we had to travel through Mosul. The city of Mosul was still under the control of the Baathist regime, and if we went through the checkpoints of Mosul, my older brothers, Omed and Hoger, would be taken and forced to join the Iraqi military. Our only other option was to take the unpaved mountainous path in the middle of winter, which would have been extremely dangerous.

My mother, a very tough and wise lady, decided to seek assistance from one of the local United Nations (UN) offices. The UN office agreed to send security officers to guard us until we crossed through the Mosul checkpoint. When the Baathist officers at the first checkpoint approached my older brothers, the UN officers intervened immediately, emphasizing that we were refugees under the protection of the UN. Only then were we able to continue through the remaining checkpoints without any further interrogations or problems. Six hours later, at dark, we reached Zakho. When we arrived at Babu Ali's house, there was no power or running water. In the dark, we walked to the nearby Khabur River to get water to boil for drinking.

Mahala Reeta used to be a cemetery, and most houses were built on old, historic gravesites, though the graves of religious figures were kept intact out of respect. The houses in the Mahala Reeta were made from crude mud. Pipes poking from the mud walls would spew wastewater into the alleys, washing rotten food and other waste items into the Khabur River, where neighborhood children swam. Thousands of laundry lines and satellite dishes were bolstered to rusted bed frames assembled on the roofs of the mud huts. During the hot summer days without power, the locals would wait until dark to go up to the roof to sleep, waking at sunrise to gather their mats and blankets and head down.

When it came to television entertainment in Mahala Reeta in 1993, our options consisted of only a few Arabic channels broadcasting news and programs on Islamic practices for ten hours a day. There was one Spanish soap opera that was subtitled in Arabic. The story revolved around a gypsy maiden named Casandra marrying into a rich family. However, Casandra did not realize that she was the granddaughter of the man in the house. On her wedding day, Casandra's husband got killed and she was blamed for his murder. I remember we were instructed to close our eyes every time a kissing scene would pop up. All Mahala Reeta residents watched the same show and would talk about their predictions of what would happen in the next episode. Friday afternoons were the highlights of our week, when they broadcast Egyptian movies showing starlets in smoky eye makeup and big hair styles. I would watch with my mother. On windy days, the channels would go blurry on us and one of my brothers would go on top of the roof and try to tinker with the antenna until the quality of the broadcast was satisfactory.

During summer days in Mahala Reeta, my younger siblings and I would climb the ladder to the roof at night where we counted the stars while my mother cut open a melon to help us cool off. After a good night's sleep, my mother would wake to the sunrise call to prayer. Quietly, my mother went down first to start baking bread and wait for us to awaken later in the summer heat.

Babu Ali's mud hut had only one bedroom and one bathroom, which was a cesspool. My mother and all eleven children slept crowded next to each other in one room, with mattresses pushed together. During a power outage, we used an oil lamp to light the room that we shared. When we needed to study or complete our homework assignments, we would sit around that one oil lamp for hours. At times, we would all get distracted by the noise the mice and rats made as they cruised within the wood-mud ceiling of the hut. Rats were everywhere and at times, they would even pop out of the cesspool. Terrified of rats, I would get as close to Zerak as I could to feel safe.

There were times Zerak (eleven then) was annoyed by the noise I unconsciously made as I studied. Because the education system in Iraq was memory-based, I would often repeat the same sentence over and over until I felt I had it memorized. With so many loud repetitions, you can only imagine how disturbing that would have been to my siblings, and Zerak was the most impatient of all. He would try to pull my ear to get me to stop.

Frustrated, I would hit him in the head with my book. My mother would try to jump in to calm things down. She suggested that instead of repeating the same sentence over and over, I write it down, which I did.

Jehan, on the other hand, (thirteen at the time) would complain about the noise Zerak made when he breathed, and she would try to push him away. Recalling these childhood memories brings back so much laughter and joy. Despite poverty and countless struggles, we were happy.

The mud huts were challenging to maintain during winter, especially when it rained. When rain was in the forecast, my mother asked one of us to go up on the ban (roof) to spray salt and start rolling the bagurdan. The bagurdan, a Kurdish invention, was a large cement cylinder with a hole running through the center and a thick piece of rope threaded through the hole. We would tie both ends of the rope, pulling the cylinder back and forth behind us on the ban. This ancient method of keeping the mud roof intact and preventing leaks is still practiced in the city of Zakho. Many times, despite our efforts, the rain leaked through the roof and we would feel the drops fall on us as we were studying. When that happened, my mother put bowls under the leaks to collect the water, leaving them until it stopped. She would simply move the oil lamp and ask us to study in the dry corner of the room. If the leaking was too bad, my mother would take the oil lamp, rush to the roof to smooth it, and then return with her feet soaked in mud.

Babu Ali's mud hut was located on top of a hill, where the Khabur River split between two neighborhoods. As picturesque as this might sound, we had to deal with cold winds during the winter season. There was one window, and a doorway to the balcony overlooking the scenic view. The window's broken glass was covered with a thin layer of plastic that did not stop the cold wind from coming in when we were sleeping. After the first night of this, we woke up to the sound of knocking. One of my uncles had come with homemade baked goods for breakfast. After a yummy warm breakfast, my brothers went with my uncle to shop for more plastic and tape for the broken window. We also had to create a little fireplace to light a fire and warm the house.

There was a shortage of oil during the sanctions even though Iraq was one of the richest countries in the world when it came to oil reserves. My siblings and I would stand in long lines for hours with our oil canisters. Sometimes we would get oil, while other times after a long wait, we would give up and burn truck tires that we collected from trash zones in the neighborhoods. To do so, my mother heated water in a big pot on the burning tires and we would use the water for baths. With our limited resources, we only had a bath once or twice a month.

After a few months of living in Mahala Reeta, it was

clear that the neighborhood came with a lot of scandalous stories and gossip. This was possibly due to the poverty, economic sanctions, and lack of employment that afforded everyone the free time to focus on everyone else's business. The notorious Jehan, with her nicknaming skills, was at it again. But this time the names were in line with all the stories in the neighborhood. There was this cute looking guy "Drawin" (liar), who lived next door to us and would flirt with all the neighborhood young women. Since the young women were naïve and sex deprived, Drawin was their only source of self-esteem. His tactic to get their attention was to flirt with winks, while blowing a kiss and making hand gestures, which made the young women swoon.

There was also "Zig Dahul" (woman with the drum belly) because she was always popping out babies and possessed a big goiter. Persistent rumors circulated that her husband was not into her, and instead had a crush on the single lady whose husband had gone missing during the Anfal genocide. Another curious neighbor was "Dayka Peni Rashki" (mother of the guy with big black mole), who constantly cursed all the Sorani speakers (my mother included) because my brother Dlovan had once beaten up her son. My mother had tried to convince her not to blame all Sorani speakers for our family's offense, but she did not care, and would proclaim "hama, hama," meaning all Sorani people were screwed up for hurting her son. Finally, three houses down from us, lived a nice, simple lady named Azar, who became "Azara ben kandala" (the Azar living under the valley). Azar was a mother of seven daughters with a handicapped husband, whose family experienced extreme poverty to the point where she had to sell off two of her daughters in marriage to rich Turkish merchants in order to financially provide for her remaining children.

Even though everyone carried unspeakable burdens from their past, there were still traditions to uphold. One day a month, women in Mahala Reeta gathered for a communal waxing session. With no men allowed, the women and marriage-aged girls dressed in lingerie and openly flouted all the flesh that was usually hidden under layers of fabric. They sat there with arms showing, legs spread apart, and mouths full of obscene language regarding their sexual desires. The smell of the bubbled wax mixture made of water, lemon, and sugar would arrive from the kitchen. When the wax was ready, they would spread it on a piece of cloth and press it against their hairy skin, before wincing in pain with each pull. Amidst the agony was a flood of social gossip and rumors, which left ten-year-old me mostly flabbergasted that these loud women in skimpy outfits were the same modest and pious women I would see every day walking on the streets.

Cognizant of such poverty and our past, my mother always wanted to make sure that we had enough dried vegetables, meat, and wheat in storage in case we had to seek refuge in the mountains again. One of the common traditions for Kurds in Zakho was boiling 100 to 200 kilograms of wheat for winter. During the wheat harvest season, my family would buy wheat from local farmers. Then at the very beginning of the fall season, families in Mahala Reeta took turns boiling the wheat. My mother would place a large bucket over a big fire, fill it with water and wheat and let it boil until the wheat softened. The little children would line up with their empty bowls, hoping they would each get a small share of boiled wheat to eat. Once the water cooked off, she would lay big sheets of fabric on the ground where we spread the wheat until it was completely dry. Once it was dry, she bagged the dried wheat and took it to the local factory for grinding into bulgur wheat for cooking and powdered wheat for bread.

Additionally, my mother would buy a large side of sheep meat and fat from a local butcher and chop the meat and fat into small pieces, cooking it with an excessive amount of salt until the fat turned to oil. Meat prepared with this method (known as qali) did not need refrigeration. On cold winter days, my mother would take several scoops of qali and cook it with the bulgur wheat that she had prepared for the winter season.

Another task my mother undertook to prepare for winter was to buy a bulk amount of small globular aubergines (eggplants). The small aubergines would be cut in half, have the inside carved out, be rubbed with salt, and hung on ropes to dry. Aubergines prepared in this traditional way did not require refrigeration and would be used for the signature Kurdish dish, "dolma."

Kurds say that you are not Kurdish if you do not love eating dolma, a delicacy of stuffed grape leaves and vegetables. To make dolma, the vegetables are prepared first. The squash is halved and hollowed. Onions are beaten to loosen their skins and separate the inner layers, and the dried aubergines are softened by soaking them in water. Once the vegetables are ready, they are stuffed with a mixture of uncooked rice or bulgur wheat, diced onion, Kurdish herbs and spices, tomato paste, chopped meat, salt, and hot oil. The onion and grape leaves are filled with the mixture, rolled, and skillfully placed in the cooking pot with the other vegetables. The dish is cooked with sumac (a Kurdish spice, sour in taste) until the bulgur wheat or rice softens.

With the water shortage and power outages, living in a house on the Khabur River was ideal. One drawback, however, was that since the city of Zakho was so small and many people had a lot of free time, almost everyone in the city knew the daily business and whereabouts of everyone else. Especially my brother Hoger, who now owned a small bookstore stand that he would assemble in front of Hajji Ibrahim mosque, the biggest mosque on Khabur River in downtown Zakho. The spot Hoger secured for his small business granted him a lot of book sales because of the busy traffic in and out of the mosque, which also kept him up to date on everything going on in the area. Knowing about such gossip, my family was cautious about what others thought or said about us, so they did not let my older sisters leave the house except for work or school.

Luckily, my sister, Jowan, had worked as a teacher when we moved to Zakho. The government hiring policy was that new graduates had to serve a year in the villages outside Zakho. So, my sister would take the bus with other new hires to a nearby village every day to teach for four hours. She was soon hired to become my teacher at the elementary school, and I could not have been happier. When Jowan walked into class, I felt the whole world belonged to me. However, she was often harsh towards my siblings and me, as she viewed herself as a second mother when my real one was busy with other siblings. Since my mother was illiterate, it was often Jowan who guided us through school. She did not believe in favoritism when she was teaching class; to achieve this, she would pretend we were strangers by asking for my name in front of my classmates, confusing everyone.

I was ten years old at the time and since the older girls were confined indoors, I was the one assigned to take the dishes and wash them on the Khabur. When we were done eating, we gathered all the dishes, silverware, cooking pots and pans and placed them in a big tasht (round tray) with dishwashing detergent. Two of my sisters placed the tasht on my head while I was standing. With a thirteen-member household, the tasht was often heavy and Jowan would fold a big towel and put it on my head before placing the tasht there to prevent it from hurting my skull. I walked for fifteen minutes from our house to the Khabur River. Once on the Khabur, I would ask whoever I encountered first to help me put down the tasht and find a spot with good flowing water to rinse the dishes. At times, I had to cross the first part of the Khabur to the other side where the water ran cleaner and was faster flowing. I would find a big rock on which to place the tasht and start separating the dishes from larger pieces, wash every piece by hand, and place them back in the tasht before heading home. At times, girls I met for the first time would wonder aloud if we recently had a wedding because of the volume of dishes they saw me washing.

I often walked to the Khabur barefoot. One time, as I was crossing the first part of the Khabur with the tasht on my head, I felt something sharp go deep into the sole of my foot. It paralyzed me on the spot and soon I started seeing blood flowing down the river. I started screaming for help. The girls and boys took the tasht off my head and I looked down to see a big glass bottle deep into the bottom of my foot. The girls rushed to the house to bring my mother and siblings to the rescue. I eventually got the broken bottle out of my foot and wrapped the injury with the towel that Jowan placed on my head. I knew I had to fight the injury with everything I had. I did not surrender to the pain and suffering until I spotted my mother from far with my siblings running to help and that was when I felt lightheaded and fainted.

During one of those adventurous trips to the Khabur, while I was crossing to the other side, I lost my balance and the tasht fell off my head into the river and all the big plates and pans started washing away. Helpless and fearing the consequences, I screamed for help. Luckily, some of the older neighborhood boys who were swimming there heard me and ran to catch the plates and pans for me.

In the summer, after hours of washing dishes, my family would let me swim in the Khabur with the other girls from Mahala Reeta. When I was done with the dishes, I covered the tasht with the towel from my head and jumped into the Khabur with my clothes on! Since Zakho was patriarchal, girls were not allowed to swim in bathing suits. Once I got bored with swimming, I would wait in the sun for my clothes to dry and then head home with my tasht. Being out in the 104-degree Fahrenheit heat (40 Celsius) for hours, my face, hands, and skin would crack from the sunburn and my hair turned to a bleached yellow.

In the early 1990s, Zakho did not have any source of entertainment like movie theatres, parks, or a shopping mall for young people in the city. Other than visiting my uncles and aunts once a week, we would go to Pira Delal (the beautiful bridge) occasionally or rent a bus to go to the countryside for a picnic. Pira Delal, made of stones on the Khabur river, was an iconic tourist site for many Kurdish families in the region including my own. The bridge was roughly 36 feet (11 meters) long and 52 feet (16 meters) high. As a child, I was intrigued by the story of the architect who built Pira Delal, a story that was first told to us by my paternal grandmother, Miryam, who was a Zakho native. She would tell the story in such a captivating way that Pira Delal and its builder reside in the recesses of my mind to this day. Here is how Ouda Miryam (Grandma Miryam) recounted the story for us:

A skilled architect was asked to build a bridge on the Tigris River in Bohtan (essentially Northern Kurdistan, which is in what is now southeastern Turkey). Once the bridge was completed, the architect's hands were chopped off to prevent him from doing similar work elsewhere. When the architect arrived in Zakho, the mayor of the city asked if he could build a bridge that connected both sides of the Khabur River. The architect agreed to build the bridge; however, the bridge would collapse whenever the architect got to the middle part. Seeking guidance from a fortune teller, the architect was advised to bury whoever set foot on the bridge first as a human sacrifice. The architect's niece was named "Delal," and one day she, along with her dog, brought her uncle lunch. Her uncle was not worried about her coming, thinking that the dog would run in front of her onto the bridge and he would take the dog as a sacrifice. However, the dog stopped and Delal stepped onto the bridge first. The architect told Delal about what the fortune teller had said about the need for a sacrifice. Delal immediately agreed to be sacrificed for the bridge. The architect then buried his niece under the bridge. When Delal's husband found out what had happened to his wife, he rushed to Pira Delal and started digging for her until he heard Delal's muffled voice asking him to stop digging and to accept her wish of wanting to stay under the bridge to keep it together for eternity. Since then, the locals in Zakho grow two lengthy plants in one of the gaps between stones on one side of the bridge, referring to them as Delal's hair braids.

Only twelve miles away from Turkey's border, Zakho was an ideal hub for Turkish trucks bringing food and medicine into the Kurdish region and returning with diesel fuel in exchange. This type of trade was allowed, under the United Nations "Oil-for-Food Program." In Zakho, the KDP leadership collected lucrative tolls from the Turkish truck drivers and kept 100% of the money for their party personnel. This made the PUK angry, considering both parties shared power in the local parliament and administration, based in Erbil, and had an obligation to serve the Kurdish people and Peshmerga who fought to overcome the Baathist regime.

In time, the Kurdish region started to crumble due to corruption and nepotism by the two conflicting parties. You were guaranteed a high-ranking job in the government, for example, if you knew someone from either party. There were even situations where those who were granted high-ranking posts could not read or write and had no expertise or experience suitable for their positions. Jobs were delegated based on presumed loyalty and family ties rather than proven competence or qualifications. The government personnel would simply collect the cash from the Oil-for-Food program and provide minimal services, leaving the Kurdish civilians hopeless after all the years of war. As corruption continued, along with a lack of a defined governing body, many Kurdish people began to pledge their allegiance to their tribes and the religious clerics that led the Friday sermons at local mosques. With this sectarian divide, violence and extremism started to spread.

Like thousands of vulnerable uneducated Kurdish youth, my brother Zerak became susceptible to the religious clerics who would refer the public to the Holy Quran for concerns related to daily living. These same clerics, with financial support from the Muslim Brotherhood in Saudi Arabia, opened madrasas (schools) to spread the teachings of the Quran. This included giving free food and meat to the public inside the mosque to encourage their participation in the Friday sermons. They also filled a social need and opened hospitals to provide free medical care to all.

For Zerak, it started with a friendly encounter in a billiard lounge where he hung out with his friends. As time went by, Zerak started coming home late. When my mother, along with Hoger and Omed, went to the lounge looking for Zerak, he was nowhere to be found. When Zerak finally returned home past midnight, a long session of beating was in store for him. After a couple of hits and slaps, Zerak gave in. He told my mother and brothers that he had met a group of religious guys and they asked him to attend the halaqas (religious circles where they studied Quran and discussed the nature of the Prophet Muhammad's message). They had tempted Zerak with food and given him goods as well as clothes to share with his family. Zerak had been forbidden to be friendly with this group, until one of the halaqa leaders visited my mother to assure her that Zerak was in good hands. My family had not understood the potential danger that came with these halaqas and allowed Zerak to participate as long as he returned home before midnight.

Over the next several weeks, Zerak's attitude started to change. Rather than a brother, he began to view himself as a family savior who had been divinely sent by Allah (God). He started to tell the girls and women in the family that we were being disobedient to Allah for showing our hair in public. He sang the Islamic anashiids (songs) in the shower which made us all wonder how he knew the lyrics. Zerak started to cry during the call to prayer every afternoon from the local masjid (mosque) and spent his Thursday afternoons in the cemetery where ladies would hire him to read a chapter of Quran to the soul of their dead. At sunset, Zerak would return home with a pocket full of cash that he made from these readings.

The formerly sweet, loving Zerak we knew had turned into a fanatic, stubborn twelve-year-old boy who was always displeased with how we performed our daily activities. His extreme outlook started to concern us all. Before things got out of hand, my mother and older siblings sat Zerak down and lectured him on his abnormal and unhealthy choices. From then on, Zerak was not allowed to attend halaqas or interact with any of the religious brothers from there. His experience taught me that fundamentalist religion can fill gaps in social spaces and prey on impressionable people looking for meaning and purpose. I also learned that with conflict and war, comes hunger, corruption, and loss of civilization. As Kurds, we have become the victims of failed foreign policies by the Western powers, leaving us vulnerable to the hands of religious fanatics and extremist ideologies that used the Kurds for their political gains for far too long. Thankfully, Zerak was spared from this fate.

I had always been serious about school and envisioned myself becoming a healthcare provider one day as an adult. To be admitted into medical, dental, or pharmacy school and ultimately serve as a healthcare provider in Iraq, I knew I needed to get high grades. So, I studied extremely hard, sometimes staying up all night, to advance to the next level in school. However, this was only possible until an attack or suicide bomber would strike Zakho, which would invariably cost us weeks of our education. As sad as this may sound, bombing was becoming a routine, almost daily occurrence in our lives. We felt blessed if a day or two went by without an explosion or tragedy of some sort.

When I graduated from elementary school, I got the highest exam grades in both Zakho and Duhok. It was the first time I received recognition for my achievements at a regional level. My mother and siblings were extremely proud of my hard work, but to be honest, none of us ever dreamed that I would excel like that. The highest I had hoped for was to graduate as valedictorian of my class. I was excited, yet sad, because summer was about to begin, which meant that school would be closed for months.

Growing up in Zakho I had two talents—writing in Arabic calligraphy and creating pencil drawings depicting the pain we had endured over the years. A favorite image I created for an art exhibit in Zakho was a revolutionary fist breaking through the ground. The fist represented the powerful Kurds, and the hard ground represented the hardships imposed on us over the years by war. As an eleven-year-old, I remember showing my artwork to the founders of some women's non-governmental organizations and hoping for a job opportunity of some sort to keep me busy over the long summer. Almost everyone was impressed by my artwork, but no one would consider giving me a job because of my young age.

As I grew older, I started to lose confidence in myself and my creativity because I was discouraged from thinking outside the box. I was often warned to be careful because my inventiveness could bring shame to my family. In addition, I was a girl and the culture in Zakho was male dominated. People would judge a woman by the way she dressed, her make-up, and even the number of times she would leave the house to run errands. Every trip outside was seen as something suspicious and potentially salacious, as if merely leaving the home was connected to sexual promiscuity.

The best time of the day during the summer was late afternoon, an hour or two before sunset, when the temperature would cool down. The men would congregate in the chaykhana (teahouse) and sip tea in tiny cups, while the women gathered in front of their doors with a handful of pistachios or roasted sunflower seeds and chat, sharing news about who recently got married, had a baby, and of course, judging those unfortunate women who walked by, while husking the nuts they held in their hands. As part of this late afternoon tradition, the women in the neighborhood would put on a black abaya, a gown that covered their whole body and their face with a kheili, a soft black cloth to prevent anyone from recognizing them. It was unfair that it was even necessary, but the abaya and kheili did give women a little more freedom through anonymity and a bit of protection from society's judgment if they needed to step out of their house multiple times to run errands.

The strict culture and male-dominated society did not bother me until I reached puberty, at about the age of eleven, when I had a growth spurt. Suddenly, the fast growth made me uncomfortable in my new seemingly adult-sized body. I was much taller than the other girls in my age group and therefore looked older. I remember being judged by neighbors for wanting to play with their daughters, who were my own age. I overheard these women wondering why a "marriage-age" woman would want to play with their ten-year-old daughters. They would go so far as to mention my breast size when I was caught doing the mischievous things that all eleven-year-old girls do. I would be reminded that I was now at an age where girls had a menstrual cycle, and I was a disgrace to my family for acting like a child. I felt embarrassed and ashamed every time I heard these kinds of comments from the neighborhood and even my family, including my own mother. Consequently, I started walking and sitting in a hunched-over position to hide my chest. To this day, decades later, I am still working on correcting my posture with little luck.

Things got worse for me when I tried to intervene to stop a physical fight between two young men outside my school. It bothered me to see a big crowd watch these two young men physically hurt each other with whatever it took. At the time, I could not think of anything but the fact that these two would eventually kill one another if the fighting continued. Someone needed to stop them, even if that someone meant me! I did not care what the community was going to think of me then. What mattered was that I was doing the right thing. *After all, was this not what Islam was promoting?* I reminded myself. I walked toward the fight, pushed myself between the two men, extended my arms as hard as I could, and shouted, "Time out!"

When the crowd noticed me, a few men joined me to stop the fight. And that was when I heard one of the men involved in the fight utter, "I will have to stop out of respect for this young lady but do not think I am done with you!"

When I returned home, the news had already reached my mother. She yelled at me and hit me a lot. She reminded me how I was bringing shame to the family and would not let this one pass. Jowan, after getting me out of my mother's hands, asked my mother to let her handle the situation. My sister, Jowan, who was the first female in our family to finish college, was a role model to us all. She sat me down and told me that I was rebelling because of the critical period I was going through as a teenager.

"But I did the right thing," I asserted. "Why is our

mother so unreasonable?"

She reminded me how much pain and suffering our mother had endured. "Her anger is not directed at you but at the cruelty, the abuse, and the poverty we are all under without father around," she explained.

Jowan also took advantage of the situation to tell me about the menstrual cycle, something I was clueless about because my sixth-grade biology class was taught by a young religious male teacher who intentionally skipped every section in the textbook that discussed the female reproductive system. Jowan shared all the details I needed to know. She also handed me a few sanitary napkins and asked me to use them when I needed to.

As a child in a woman's body, I felt a constant sense of shame, which pretty much destroyed my self-esteem. Being a perfectionist by nature, I felt ashamed that I was not following the cultural norms in Zakho, which included modesty, always staying at home, and being obedient to my parents. At the same time, I wanted to excel academically and take advantage of the limited opportunities available to my eleven-year-old self. Instead of playing with kids my age, I chose to hold Quran lessons, where I would gather the little girls in the neighborhood, encourage them to recite Quran with me, and discuss the significance of the Quranic verses to our everyday living. This task meant no judgment and earned my family and me a lot of praise. I worked hard to do things that warranted approval, not only from my family but the neighborhood. It was not about what I wanted, but what was okay according to the cultural standards. Since teaching Quran to the little girls was honorable, it was approved by everyone and gave me some sense of personal agency.

In Kurdistan, my family practiced Islam, but our understanding was relaxed and moderate. We would rush when we heard the call to prayer, washing and covering our bodies and hair so we could line up to pray. However, my parents had always made sure we stayed away from religious extremism. We understood the teachings of Islam through school, a mandatory class that every Muslim student had to take at every grade level. In those courses, Set Amina (how we addressed our teachers) would excuse the Christian students from class to the courtyard while the Muslim students had to stay to discuss verses from Quran: Hadith (the sayings of the Prophet Muhammad), Seerah (the biography of the Prophet's life) and Sharia (Islamic law). Our class discussions often revolved around deeds we should avoid because they were haram (forbidden) in Islam, such as showing your hair, dating, drinking, stealing, and lying. Set Amina instilled fear in us by sharing the consequences that came with these haram deeds on the day of judgment. However, before his imprisonment, my father did his best to rationally explain the Islamic teachings in a non-fundamentalist way. He made sure we understood why certain deeds were looked at as haram.

One of the things we were told in school was that wishing bad for others was haram. However, I never understood why a more conservative religious cleric or imam would chant "Death to America and Israel!" after Friday's sermon. "Was wishing death to others not haram?" I asked.

"Well America and Israel are the sources of our misery here in Iraq," Set Amina once responded. At eleven, with mingled memories of war and loss swirling through my mind, I was in no position to doubt her. I no longer questioned if it was haram or not.

With the unstable living conditions in Zakho, going abroad was extremely desirable. It became something that locals were taking pride in. Almost everyone who had an income, or a property of some sort would invest in finding a smuggler to get him or her out of Kurdistan. I had cousins, aunts, and uncles who had left for Europe this way, and their families including us were simply waiting to hear back from them. Any family who was doing well in Zakho during the early 1990s likely had family in Europe who were sending them money. American dollars and European currencies were worth a lot in Iraqi dinars. At least a half-dozen of my female teachers in middle school were engaged to fiancés who had escaped to Europe; they were simply awaiting paperwork to join them. Often, those same female teachers would assign us meaningless busy work so they could have free time to stare out of the classroom windows and imagine their new lives once abroad. Because of this, the sassier students in class would say that the teacher's heart and mind were no longer with us, accusing her of already abandoning us mentally for Europe where her fiancé was.

Going abroad would come up in every conversation and was constantly on everyone's mind. One afternoon, we had a fortune teller knock on the door. She offered to read the inside of our coffee cup for us (interpreting the cup residue) if we offered her a few dinars. For fun, my mother welcomed her in and asked her to read Jowan's cup. She was hoping that she would tell my mother the reason Jowan was objecting to all the marriage proposals she was getting. Instead, the fortune teller told Jowan that she would be going abroad soon. We all laughed because going abroad was everyone's dream at the time and we honestly thought she just made it up to curry favor with us and perhaps get a cash tip. She then read my mother the cup residues for Zhyan, Jehan, Hoger, Omed, Zerak, Dlovan and finally me—and the result was always the same. She kept saying that we would all be going aboard soon. Eventually, my mother got frustrated with her and gave her a few dinars so she would leave and go about her day, unaware that the fortune teller was correct and that, indeed, we would all soon be immigrating to America.

When I look back at my life as an immigrant, the sadness that comes with emigrating and leaving your loved ones behind feels like taking a one-way path, death in another form. There is no guarantee that we will ever be able to see those individuals again, so in a way, they die and move on to an afterlife that we were not invited to. The goodbyes we hold are more like a funeral. Emigrating is a huge undertaking, and it takes place under very risky conditions in illegal ways by paying large sums of cash to smugglers. While we may never see our loved ones again, they too must fear that we will not survive the journey.

To say the least, war had damaged the Kurdistan region in Iraq beyond repair. To stay and wait for improvement was not patriotism, as much as it was collective suicide and wasting the only life any of us would ever get on earth. The only hope left to us was leaving. There was nothing anyone could do other than adapt to the sad reality that Iraq was no longer the country we could call home because of constant war and economic sanctions. People fail to understand that the comfort of home comes from the comfort of its inhabitants, its people. However, when your loved ones are gone, the country never feels the same again. By this point, I had stopped questioning why I had been cursed to be born amidst war and watch all my loved ones either leave through death or migration (with a similar result either way). I started to feel as if I was abandoned by the universe to a reality of poverty and wondered what I had done to deserve this life. It seemed that being a Kurd from Iraq was our fate and we would never be able to alter our destiny. However, in the back of my mind, I knew that if my family and I could somehow escape our beloved but forsaken homeland, a new life might be possible—even if that meant risking our lives in the harsh conditions of crossing the Mediterranean Sea to Europe through motorboats steered by human traffickers.

I thought of the sirens and how our house would shake from the falling missiles that would destroy the houses nearby. I thought of the fear I grew up with of being crushed from the roof above me collapsing while I slept. I thought of the daily fear that each time I left my house I might not be returning home later that day. Would my school be attacked? Would that next car driving by me suddenly explode? Was any loud voice in public a madman with a gun about to open fire, or simply the usual noise of living in a city? I thought of the countless nights I went to bed hungry, the growl of my stomach ringing in my ears, as if to remind me that for some reason, God had decided I did not need more food to eat. I often wondered, was anything uglier and more damaging to the human mind and soul than war? As humans, we are not wired or made to witness such things. Our psyche was not able to process such devastation and despair while still believing in tomorrow. But in the end, tomorrow was all we had.

"All your life, you are taught not to speak to strangers, and suddenly, you are asked to sleep with one!"

My father was still in prison at this time and Omed worked hard to provide for our family. In addition, the neighboring shepherds would bring the wool that they had sheared from their flock for my mother to wash, sterilize, and turn into pillows for the limited cash she was paid and that got us through the day. The only job available to Omed was housekeeping for two Turkish merchants who were in Zakho for various business dealings. The merchants needed someone trustworthy who could clean the house, do laundry, and cook meals. Omed was recommended to them as someone who would go above and beyond for the job. The payment was not ideal, but it was enough to provide for the family. While working for these two merchants, Omed practiced his English-speaking skills, hoping for an opportunity to work for the Americans in Zakho. A year into his work for the merchants—though his English skills were limited—Omed landed a translating job with the Military Coordination Center (MCC).

The MCC was a military organization representing Turkey, Britain, France, and the U.S. It provided humanitarian assistance to thousands of Iraqi Kurds in the early 1990s. The MCC was also tasked with disarming landmines in Kurdish villages, and thankfully for us, it paid salaries in dollars. With the salary Omed was making at MCC and the dollar value so high in the Iraqi market (70 dinars for 1 U.S. dollar), we were able to purchase my grandfather's house from my uncles. My brother paid each uncle and aunt their share from the sale. Once it was purchased, we decided to rent out the property and move to a better neighborhood in Zakho. Life started to look a little more promising for all of us. My mother could not have been happier, taking pride in the fact that she was a homeowner for the first time in her life.

In the late afternoon on a spring day in 1994, there was a sudden knock at the door. When we opened the door, there he was—my father! After fourteen long months in Abu Ghraib prison, the Baathist regime had finally released him. With no money, my father had managed to find his way to us in Zakho. To celebrate his return, my family bought a sheep from the maydan (a market where shepherds of Zakho would sell goats and sheep to locals) to offer for qurbani, which is the slaughter of an animal for the pleasure of God. Qurbani is a tradition practiced by many Muslims around the world when they buy a house, have a baby, get married, or survive a bad car accident. In our case, we did it to celebrate my father surviving the cruelty of the Baathist regime and his safe return home.

It felt extremely good to have the family together after all those months, and with Omed's income, we lived comfortably in Zakho. Unfortunately, however, it felt a bit strange to have our father back among us. He was almost like a stranger since we had gotten used to his being away.

When he returned, he did many unsanitary things that grossed us out because of the harsh prison conditions he had become accustomed to, such as spitting on the floor, openly picking his nose, and drying his hands on his shirt. We were all surprised at how he now carried himself, without realizing that the harsh conditions he had suffered had made him that way. Another troubling trait he had developed was being cruel to Reveng, his son who was born while he was away. He became very jealous and controlling of my mother when she left his sight and seemed irritated by everything we did. His temper was uncontrollable. It was almost as if the tortures he had endured cut into his body and created a new person. From then on my parents' relationship was never the same and through the years they would gradually drift further and further apart.

Nevertheless, we carried on and soon moved to the high-end neighborhood in Zakho where we could afford renting a decent house. Now that we had enough money, my parents were able to afford buying each one of my siblings and me a new dress or outfit each year. My parents soon decided that it was time for my brother, who was in his early twenties, to get married. During the summer, my parents took Omed to Erbil for two weeks to find him a wife. Even though we lived in Zakho, my family avoided the girls there because of the hefty dowry required, as well as the amount of gold that the girl's family usually requested for their daughters. When they arrived in Erbil, my parents and Omed stayed with my maternal uncles. My uncles' wives had already identified a few girls in the neighborhood who were the right age for my brother. My parents narrowed the search, settling on one of the girls. Shortly after, my parents had Omed visit the girl's family. While there, the girl was asked to serve tea and nuts to the guests. This was Omed's chance to see her, and that was pretty much the extent of their introduction. Omed seemed fine moving forward and asking the family to let him marry their daughter. However, the family asked for a large dowry, which ended the proposal.

The next day, a female neighbor came to my uncle's house to meet my parents. Once she learned that my parents were looking for a wife for Omed, she told them that she had two daughters of an appropriate age (by her standards) and she would like to arrange for Omed and the family to meet them. As strange as it may sound, my parents decided to honor this lady's request. Of the two daughters, my parents decided on the younger sister, Shayma, who was still in high school. Neither Omed nor Shayma had any idea that this marriage proposal would happen so quickly. Omed, who had never had a relationship with a girl or dated, was excited to marry Shayma. My parents arranged for a religious cleric to perform Nikah (a religious marriage contract) between Omed and Shayma the following day. Their marriage contract was not official since their marriage was not documented through the civil court, but this was how many Kurds arranged marriages for their children. Instead of the official documentation, Kurdish Muslims would have two witnesses aged eighteen or older present when the couple was married by the cleric. The families of the newlywed couple also arranged a dinner party, where Omed and Shayma could exchange rings.

Both families had agreed on a dowry of 15,000 Iraqi

dinars, which equaled roughly 200 U.S. dollars. My family also bought Shayma a set of 21 karat gold jewelry and a suitcase full of brand-new clothes and other items, known as nishani. In Kurdish culture, when a girl gets married, the groom's family buys her everything new before the engagement day–things like lingerie, clothing, makeup, hygiene products, and home goods. On the engagement day, when the new couple exchanges rings, the groom's family opens the suitcase to show the party guests what the groom had gotten for his future wife. Two weeks after the engagement, Shayma quit high school and embarked on a new chapter of her life with Omed in Zakho.

Omed's wedding went on for three long days. On the first day, which was called Khene Bendan, we dipped the pinky fingers of Shayma and Omed in henna and wrapped them in paper money. Shayma and Omed's pinkies were each wrapped with a U.S. one dollar bill (worth 70 Iraqi dinars). This ritual was believed to bring the new couple good fortune in their marriage. There were many eyes on the two dollar bills. For my part, I kept myself close to the couple during Khene Bendan to get my hands on a dollar bill before anyone else (I succeeded).

On the second day of the wedding, the groom's family decorated the car for the groom to use to pick up the bride from her family's house. The decorations included colored ribbons, balloons, and soda cans dangling from the car. While the dancing and celebration are going on, the groom and close family members sneak out of the celebration to pick up the bride, the day she officially becomes a member of her husband's family.

Since Shayma was living in Erbil and the wedding was in Zakho, we had Omed pick her up from the salon, where she was dressed and prepared for her big day. When he arrived, all the women on the street and in the salon began their celebratory ululation of "kililili, kililili," which could be heard throughout the entire neighborhood, accompanied by blessings that he "father many sons" (since our society values boys). As soon as Shayma was picked up, a long line of cars driven by close friends and cousins started following the decorated car that carried Omed and Shayma for a quick trip around the city before arriving at the wedding venue with a lot of honking and loud music. My Aunt Bahiya was known to be the first in every wedding she attended to hold her baby high and then place him or her in the bride's lap for the cash that the bride would give to the baby, a tradition that my family had maintained over the years. Also, it was during the second day that the bride and the groom shared a bed for the first time, while the guests celebrated and danced until late in the evening waiting for the spot of blood on the white piece of cloth to show that the bride was virgin.

The most memorable experience I remember from Omed's wedding was meeting the American officers from the MCC, who surprised Omed at his wedding. I remember how honored we felt to have the American personnel in their military uniforms celebrating Omed's big day with him. With the Americans, Omed would have silly conversations in Arabic that had all of us laughing. "You are a big donkey," Omed would jokingly say to his American co-worker in Arabic. "And you are a small donkey," his American co-worker would respond in Arabic. I remember the whole city talking about how Omed had Americans show up to his wedding.

On the third and last day of the wedding, the guests

brought congratulatory gifts for the newlywed couple, and the celebration ended around noon. (Shayma and Omed have been happily married for over twenty-five years, and now live in Colorado, which we jokingly call "Kurdarado" because of its similar mountains to Kurdistan, with their two children, Miriam and Issa.)

Soon after Omed became settled and life seemed to be back to normal, my father and I started hitting the road once again to Mosul to get me braces as a result of the accident where I had broken my jaw. Because of my increasingly prominent overbite, the schoolgirls often made fun of how I use to smile like a mouse with my front teeth sticking out. I talked with my father about my overbite and how it was bothering me. A family friend of ours recommended that we see Dr. Kheiri Qasm in Mosul. Despite the last incident he had at the Mosul checkpoint, my father agreed to risk his life once again and take me back to Mosul to fix my front teeth.

Iraq was and still is a country of endless checkpoints each with their own dark story. If these checkpoints could talk, we would hear tales of abuse, tension, violence, and sadness. Stories of missing Kurdish youth. Stories of Kurdish patriots tortured for opposing Baathist ideologies. Stories of atrocities that would bring even the strongest among us, to their knees. So, as a Kurdish youth, I feared the checkpoints. Would my father and I make it through safely? Would we be stopped, interrogated, humiliated, or tortured simply because our veins carried Kurdish blood?

To get to Mosul from Zakho, we had to go through a countless number of checkpoints by both the KDP and the Baathist regime. On a Friday morning, my father and I walked to the nearby Zakho Garage (taxi gathering spot), which was busy that morning, and waited for a shared taxi to take us to Mosul. Once the taxi driver had four passengers with my father and me included, the driver asked for our IDs and looked at them. We then took off until we reached the first checkpoint outside Zakho that was decorated with the bright colors of the Kurdistan flag: red, yellow, green, and white. No one talked to us at the checkpoint and we were let go. We then drove for about an hour until we reached the first checkpoint that was under Baathist control. Predictably, we were stopped, asked for our Iraqi IDs and the reason we were visiting Mosul. My father told the officer that I needed dental care. Once they were convinced, they let us get out of the taxi, go through the checkpoint to make sure we were not carrying any explosives, and then asked us to get in the back of trucks to take us to the first checkpoint outside Mosul. Once we were cleared at that checkpoint, my father and I got into another private taxi to take us to our destination in Mosul.

When we were finally inside Mosul, we asked our taxi driver to take us to the medical campus at the University of Mosul, where we would be visiting Dr. Kheiri Qasim, an orthodontist and professor at the college of dentistry. Once at the medical campus, we were told Dr. Qasim was gone for the day, but he was practicing at his private clinic in the afternoon. We got into another taxi to the clinic only to be asked to return the following day to see Dr. Qasim. My father and I then stopped by a local shawarma (shaved meat sandwich) shop where we had a late lunch. From there, he asked if I was interested to tag along to go see a few of his friends at the old city of Mosul.

Surprisingly, the solo trip with my father through Mosul ended up being the trip of my life. There was something special about the city that made me fall for it. Described as the "pearl of the north," Mosul was the second largest city in Iraq and known as al-khadrah (the Green) for its beautiful greenery and landscape. From the historic alleyways, neighborhoods, bazaar with skillful goldsmiths, carpenters, artists, and religious or historic sites, Mosul had something for everyone. My dad took me to visit his friends in the gold bazaar in Mosul, where I was mesmerized by the jewelry being made. The songs by two of my favorite childhood Iraqi Arab singers, Kadim Al-Sahir and Haitham Yousif, were played in every other shop in the bazaar. Shy at the time, I consumed the tea and sweets my father's friends offered me while hiding my face behind my father's arm. My father reminded me not to be shy. The uncle who was offering me treats asked my father in Arabic what brought my father to Mosul after all these years. "Heleen needs dental care," my father responded.

The uncle replied, "Heleen looks like a warda (flower) and nothing is wrong with her front teeth." Once again I blushed and hid my face behind my father's arm.

The following day, my father treated me to one of Mosul's delicacies for breakfast called gaymar (heavy cream made with corn starch), which was served with honey, warm bread, and chai flavored with cardamom served in one of my father's favorite teahouses on the Tigers River. Folk songs by Nazim Al Ghazali played in the background. In response, my father leaned back and sang every lyric in a truly beautiful voice.

After breakfast, my father and I continued the tour of the city. He took me to the bazaar to buy me a backpack, school supplies, and anything else at a fraction of what it would have cost us in Zakho. The currency that was used in Mosul at the time was the fake version of the actual Iraqi dinar used in the Kurdistan region of Iraq. These fake dinars were worth much less than the real ones, meaning items were cheaper. My father and I both knew we had to be mindful of what we bought and took with us because we had to go through all the checkpoints, and it could be seized from us. With my sister Jowan being a new hire at her school, she asked me to get her a pair of suede high heels. Yet, I knew if I carried her shoes in my hands the officers at the checkpoints would have taken them from me, so at age eleven (though thankfully tall for my age) I chose to put the heels on and wear them, as I knew this was my only chance to get them for her.

We finally met Dr. Qasim in the afternoon where he examined my upper front teeth and noticed my overbite. My father had told him what had happened to me when I was younger and how the overbite was causing me ridicule. Dr. Qasim told my father that he was glad to see me and would be happy to assist, but I needed to see him every month. He asked my father whether he was able to bring me to Mosul every month so he could tighten my braces. Of course, my father agreed to go through the brutal checkpoints to get me the care I needed. Dr. Qasim got my measurements and asked us to return the following day for the braces. Once the braces were put on, I could hardly stand the pain, but my father was there to comfort me. He reminded me that we had to head back because my mother and siblings would be worried about us since we had no phone or way to call them.

On our way back, I put Jowan's heels on. At the first checkpoint, when we got out of the private taxi to get on the truck, the officer at the checkpoint spotted eleven-year-old me walking awkwardly in pumps. He then stopped me to tease me and asked if my shoes were new? With the pain I was in due to the new braces, I stuttered and said yes! I told him they were new and meant to be for Eid. The officer knew very well I was making up lies so he laughed and let me go in amusement. I soon found myself taking the heels off and running barefoot as fast as I could to the back of the truck to catch up with my father. Once I was in the truck, I looked back and saw the officers were still laughing at me.

Because of the differences in currency value between Mosul and the Kurdistan region, smuggling goods from Mosul became rampant; however, it could land you in jail if caught. My aunt, who was trying to smuggle goods had a humorous situation at the same checkpoint on a different occasion, where she put on ten pairs of pants in order to bring them out of Mosul and was caught by the guards. She claimed it was because she was cold, but her lie was unsuccessful, as the guard made her take off eight of the ten pairs and leave them behind. Although a minor anecdote, the absurdity that we had to wear things to keep from having them taken from us sums up a lot about Iraqi occupied Southern Kurdistan at the time.

In late February of 1995, the whole city of Zakho was getting ready to celebrate Eid ul Fitr, the "Festival of Breaking the Fast." Eid ul Fitr is a religious holiday celebrated by Kurdish Muslims worldwide that marks the end of the holy month. Fasting during Ramadan is one of the obligatory tasks for every Muslim and involves having no food or drink from sunrise to sunset for 30 days. For those who know little about Ramadan, it is during this month that Muslims practice an act of worship to show empathy for the world's less fortunate, for whom hunger is not a choice. We have a chance to reflect, deepen spiritually, and strengthen bonds with our family and friends. Ramadan is divided into three parts, each of which consists of ten days. The first ten days are referred to as the Mercy days, when Muslims seek God's mercy and share it with others, especially in family bonding. The second ten days are Forgiveness days, when Muslims repent, seek forgiveness, and make amends for their mistakes. Finally, the last ten days of Ramadan symbolize Emancipation from Hellfire, and Muslims spend these last ten nights in solid devotion, immersing themselves even more in worship.

My whole family fasted during Ramadan. Right before the sunrise meal, a local person would walk around the alleys of Mahala Reetah banging drums to awaken people for Ramadan. In our family, the first person to awaken would be my mother, who would make bulgur wheat and mix it with homemade yogurt with a cup of cardamom chai (tea). At times, it was tempting to sleep through the drum, but my mother insisted that we get up to eat so we would have enough energy to last us during a long day of fasting. We would then wait for the adhan (call) to the fajr (sunrise) prayer. The calls would go off one after another, like a synchronized chain that we heard five times every day. They would always start with a cry coming out of one masjid followed by the next, and the next until all masjids would be chanting all at once across the city. We then rushed to have the last drink before the start of a long day of fasting.

At sunset, my family celebrated the breaking of the fast with a big feast where we all sat around a sofreh (food spread).

Immediately following Ramadan, Kurdish Muslims celebrate the end of fasting with Eid ul Fitr. During Eid, adults and children dress in new outfits for Eid prayer in the morning, which often takes place in the masjid. Locals then visit the houses of grandparents for Eid breakfast and Eid celebration. It is a tradition in Zakho for children to get cash from their grandparents first and then walk through the neighborhood and knock on doors asking for candy, the same way children trick or treat on Halloween in America.

During the last few days of Ramadan, I was always excited and eager for classes to be over, so I could join the family in holiday preparations. Those last few days were always remembered by prayers. Neighborhood women gathered at each other's houses every night to prepare holiday cookies. The men of the household then carried the trays of cookies to the closest neighborhood bakery to have them professionally baked. The cookies, known as kulicha, were similar to an empanada, shaped and stuffed with various types of nuts: crushed pistachios, walnuts, coconut, and chopped dates with roasted sesame. Preparing and baking kulicha was labor-intensive and time-consuming, usually taking several women at least four or five hours to complete.

On the last day of school, and a few days before the holiday, we were still in class when we heard a loud explosion. It shook the whole building. We rushed to the roof and saw smoke coming from the Dollar Market in Zakho. We were dismissed from school to check on our families. As soon as I got home, I learned that a car bomb had exploded at the busiest market in Zakho while people were shopping for the holidays. The first person I thought of was my father, who would go to that same market to spend time with some of his friends from childhood. I rushed home with my cross-body bag and my schoolbooks to check on my family. On the run back, so many awful thoughts came to me. I wondered whether my father was alive and what life would be like without him. Through tear stained cheeks and swollen eyes, I ran finding all the shortcuts through the narrow alleys of Zakho. As soon as I made it to the entrance of the neighborhood, I saw a crowd and wondered what had happened earlier that morning. My father stood in the middle of the crowd. I immediately fell to my knees and thanked God for his safety.

The bomb killed at least eighty-three civilians, wounding over 100 more. According to a senior KDP official the bomb contained up to 330 pounds of dynamite and was hidden in a red Volkswagen Passat. When I walked through the Dollar Market, I saw parts of human bodies on the ground and blood everywhere. The holiday preparations turned into funeral preparations that day, and the whole city joined in collecting body parts, carrying them to the river to be washed, and placing them in white coffins. The young men found a spot high up on the mountain of Zakho and started digging a mass grave for the victims, while the rest of us carried bodies up the mountain to be buried.

School was shut down for days with everyone in a state of shock over what had happened. The whole city of Zakho had been shaken to its core by the event. Almost every family had lost a loved one in the explosion. Words cannot describe the cloud that had come and stopped over our city. Every heart was aching, every soul destroyed, and every home had been broken. The explosion had suddenly taken the joy out of our lives and stolen the smiles from our faces. Old and young, everyone grieved equally for what happened to Zakhoka Delal (the beautiful Zakho). Soon, mass funerals were held, and every family cooked large meals to serve those who showed up. After the funerals, we went out in front of the mayor's office to protest and demand justice for the lives lost. Once schools reopened, all students walked for miles to the graveyard to deliver messages that we had written in class for the fallen.

No one knew who was behind the explosion. While previous bombings in the region had been blamed on the Baathist government, the Fratricide War between the ruling Kurdish parties was still ongoing, widening the list of potential suspects. Some of the locals blamed the PUK for the bomb, insisting they wanted to create instability in Zakho as it was under KDP rule. For their part, the U.S. Government had warned both regional Kurdish parties that the ongoing tensions would cost them their relief aid.

In August of 1996, to everyone's surprise, KDP leader Masoud Barzani formed an alliance with the Iraqi government against the PUK to take over Erbil. Hoping to regain control of the Kurdish region of Iraq, the former Baathist regime provided aid to the KDP to eradicate the PUK forces from Erbil, which was important to the KDP for many reasons. It was the capital of the Kurdish region, the site of the Kurdish Parliament, and the headquarters of the Iraqi National Congress (which opposed the Iraqi government). With this new alliance, Saddam Hussein launched a 40,000-man force into the northern region, which was protected by the United Nations' "No Fly Zone." This put the thousands of lives of Peshmergas and Kurdish personnel who served U.S. governmental agencies in danger. In response, the U.S. government ordered all coalition personnel to withdraw from northern Iraq.

On August 31, 1996, the Iraqi forces invaded Erbil and consequently the coalition forces and affiliated organizations (including the MCC, where my brother worked) slowly started redeploying out of northern Iraq, through Zakho and into Silopi in Turkey on the other side of the Khabur River. You might wonder whether abandoning the Kurds at that time was a strategic decision by the coalition forces, considering that their prospects for success were mixed. In 1996, the Kurds appeared to have a certain degree of autonomy from Baghdad, but unity among the Kurdish tribes and political parties was tenuous, at best. It would be hard to realize a bright future for the Kurds without having unified goals for bettering Kurdistan and ensuring a safer region for its struggling, war-weary people. The disunity among the Kurds continued to be manipulated by the neighboring powers, including the former Baathist regime.

As employees of the American government and its allied agencies, my brother and his colleagues were at risk of retaliation from the Iraqi forces if they did not leave the region immediately, as they were not guaranteed any protection against the Iraqi regime by the KDP forces in Zakho. When the coalition forces left for the Khabur River, my brother and a group of his colleagues attempted to follow the convoy across the long bridge to Silopi. However, Turkish soldiers on the other side of the bridge shot at them, forcing my brother and his colleagues to head back to Zakho, where they were captured by Kurdish forces and taken to prison for attempting to escape the region.

My brother, who was the sole breadwinner for his pregnant wife, along with his parents and siblings, was soon accused of treason. Now that we had no source of income and were associated with an enemy of the Baathist regime in Baghdad, our safety was even more tenuous. While fearfully waiting to see what would happen, we turned on the news using an old battery-operated radio, hoping to hear that the U.S. would come to our rescue. Finally, it happened. U.S. President Bill Clinton approved a voluntary evacuation of the 250 former employees of the U.S. State Department's Office of Foreign Disaster Assistance (drivers, clerks, translators, etc.) and their immediate families. The lives of more than 2,000 Kurdish personnel and their families were saved by this decision.

With all the hardship we had already endured and

would still face if we stayed, we knew moving to the U.S. was our only chance for survival. We wearily boarded the buses with our heavy suitcases, never to return. Numb, traumatized, and so uncertain what the future would hold for us. All we knew was that America was where we were headed. And ever since, not a single day has passed that I do not yearn to be back home. Motherland. Kurdistan.

CHAPTER III: FATIMA'S JOUNREY TO A NEW START

When we saw the wounds of our country
appear on our skins,
we believed each word of the healers.
Besides, we remembered so many cures,
it seemed at any moment
all troubles would end, each wound heal completely.
That didn't happen: our ailments
were so many, so deep within us
that all diagnoses proved false, each remedy useless.
Now do whatever, follow each clue,
accuse whomever, as much as you will,
our bodies are still the same,
our wounds still open.
Now tell us what we should do,
you tell us how to heal these wounds.
– *"Tell Us What to Do," by Faiz Ahmed Faiz*

Thousands of Kurdish refugees arriving in Guam in September of 1996. Photo courtesy of USAOC.

Once the announcement about the personnel and their families leaving for the U.S. became public, my brother and his colleagues were released and told to go home, start packing, and head for the Turkish border with their families. It was early afternoon and my mother was preparing lunch when we heard a loud knock on the door. I rushed to open the door and there he was, Omed! He told us to drop everything we were doing and start packing.

"We are leaving for America!" he announced.

"Wait, what?" my mother asked.

"Yes mother, I am serious! We are leaving for America."

"What about our home? Our valuables?" she asked.

"We will take whatever we can, but everything else needs to be left behind."

"Contact mati (aunt) Najat or mamo (uncle) Sherko to give them our house key and see what they recommend doing with our things," he added.

We did not know what to make of Omed's news because, in all honesty, leaving for America seemed too good to be true. We were not used to having good luck. Were we really going to the "fairytale" Hollywood land we saw in movies? We did not even carry Iraqi passports, nor had we ever traveled outside of Iraq. My mother called my aunts and uncles in Zakho and asked them to come over immediately. My aunt Najaat rushed to our house fearing a tragedy had occurred. After sharing the news of our leaving for America, my mother handed her the house keys and told her what was going on. She was happy, but just like the rest of us, she did not know what to make of the story. She recommended keeping our belongings in storage just in case the plan fell through and we had to return. She also agreed that she would wait until hearing that we were settled before making any final decisions. My mother promised that she would call as soon as we got access to a phone in the U.S. In a matter of hours, the news of leaving for the U.S. spread all over Zakho. The rest of my cousins and uncles rushed to our house for a goodbye. They helped us pack as much as we could, and we were ready to head to the border. Omed rented three taxi cabs and placed the suitcases, my parents, his wife, and all ten siblings into the cabs.

We got to the border at 2 p.m. on a hot September day and were told to stand and wait until our names were called. We waited for hours at the gate of the Khabur River bridge, and it was not until midnight that the Turkish soldiers allowed us to cross the Khabur to the presumed safety of a Turkish military camp. Of course, they received U.S. assurances that we would be in their country for a limited time. Refugee families carrying all the belongings they could started walking across the bridge. As for me, I was carrying Pambo (Reveng) on my shoulders and following my siblings. It was only when we made it to the other side of the Khabur that the fear of the Baathist regime receded and the reality that we were leaving for the great land of America began to sink in.

Altogether, the U.S. State Department evacuated 2,000 Kurds in a two-phase operation. The first phase was "Operation Quick Transit," operated by the U.S. Air Force and State Department, providing transportation to move the Kurdish refugees from Zakho to southern Turkey, and then to Guam—an immediate safe area for immigration screening and processing. The second phase, "Operation Pacific Haven," which began after we arrived in Guam, provided support for accommodating the refugees until they received immigration clearance and could move to the U.S. Being so remote, Guam was an ideal spot for the Kurdish refugees. We were not allowed to leave the island until we had the proper documentation to emigrate to the U.S.

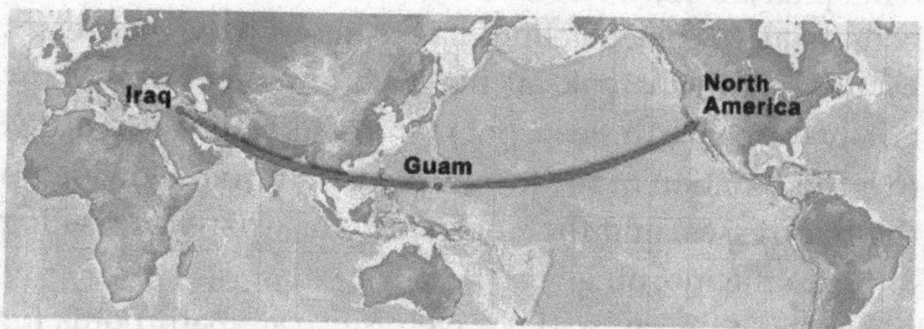

Operation Quick Transit moved the Kurdish refugees from Northern Iraq to Incirlik Air Base and then to Guam. Operation Pacific Haven cared for the refugees on the Guam island until they received immigration clearance and left for the United States. Photo courtesy of USAOC.

The call initiating our rescue came from the U.S. government, but to our surprise, when we reached the refugee camp in southern Turkey (really Southern Kurdistan), we did not see a single American. The 2,000 refugees, consisting of men, women, and children of all ages, were setting out toward an uncertain future. Many of us felt numb from our traumatic experiences. We had left all our valuables and other family members behind and carried nothing but the hope of a new settlement in America.

Unfortunately for us, the Turkish military had a long history of anger at the Kurds in Turkey for demanding their rights, and they were not pleased with being compelled to help us on American orders. Frustrated, they rudely yelled at us in Turkish to line up for inspection after we crossed the bridge, making sure we were not carrying anything sharp or explosive. Once we were cleared, they put us into military buses for the trip to the refugee base camp in Silopi. Once we reached Silopi, tents were already assembled for us on a soccer field that was guarded by soldiers in armored personnel carriers. We were given two tents plus air mattresses for the fourteen members of our household. My older siblings had to blow up the mattresses by mouth which took all night. A few members of my family were able to sleep, but many of us stayed awake due to a combination of the heat, exhaustion from blowing up the mattresses, and the uncertainty of what was waiting for us in the morning.

In the base camp, there were separate bathrooms for men and women; however, with limited water and resources, we could only manage to wash our faces and hands. At mealtimes, a truck full of bread rolls would come by the front of the tents to throw bread loaves at us like we were animals. In addition, they served chicken broth with the bread for breakfast, and the same was served for lunch and dinner. In the limited time we spent in Silopi, the Turkish soldiers became more and more agitated by our presence. They would only let us use the bathrooms at certain times of the day and our diet was unhealthy. When we insisted on the need to use the bathroom outside of the allotted times, they shouted that we should "hold it until we were on the beach," referring to the life that was ahead of us in America.

They sometimes reacted aggressively to minor disputes and were suspicious that we supported or had a political affiliation with the Kurdish Workers' Party or PKK. The PKK was, and still is, a Kurdish movement against the Turkish government that demands autonomy and Kurdish rights in Turkey. Their image is well known globally—male and female mountain guerrillas in identical olive-green baggy pants uniforms—as are the philosophical writings of their imprisoned leader, Abdullah Öcalan. Considered terrorists by Turkey, for millions of Kurds the PKK are freedom fighters who also progress-sively advocate for women's rights and the environment. The Turkish military claimed they were afraid that the PKK guerrillas would manage to find a way to infiltrate the Kurdish refugees from Iraq. To prevent this, they walked by the tents and took the young men of each family for interrogation, keeping them in custody overnight. One of those victims was my brother, Zerak.

When in Kurdistan, students would go on yearly picnics with their classmates; it is a tradition to dress in a Kurdish outfit when we are out enjoying nature. When we left for Silopi, my brother Zerak had some pictures taken of him in a Kurdish outfit. When the Turkish soldiers found the pictures, they associated him with the PKK—whose guerrillas wear traditional Kurdish clothing as their fighting uniforms. Immediately, they took Zerak away from us. My mother, terrified, ran after the soldiers and begged them to let her sixteen-year-old son go. She kept telling the soldiers that her son was too young to join or work for the PKK. The soldiers finally agreed to let him go on the condition that I would swear on a Holy Quran that my brother had nothing to do with the PKK, which I gladly did.

Not long after, Francis Ricciardone, the U.S. Embassy's chief of mission in Turkey came to the base camp to talk with the Kurdish refugees. Witnessing the unbearable conditions in the camp, he reported the situation; the American government decided to accelerate moving us to Guam, where we ended up staying for two months. The decision to move the Kurds to Guam was strategic. It gave us a "parole" status into the U.S. without the need for refugee status or visas that we would have needed if we had stayed overseas. Once the decision was made to move us to Guam, we packed our meager belongings once again. The next day, we boarded buses for a three-hour drive to the Kurdish city of Diyarbakir to prepare for the departure to Guam. The Turkish soldiers drove the buses on much better behavior, thanks to the presence of staff from the U.S. State Department as well as the American Air Force.

We reached Diyarbakir around dinnertime, and the soldiers took us to a local restaurant and told us to stay seated until it was time to leave for the airport. At 2 a.m., when we were half asleep on the hard floor, they came to take us to the airport. We boarded the long flight to Guam that would have two quick stops—one in the United Arab Emirates and the second in Hong Kong. It was our first time on a plane and so it was extremely exciting, but that excitement waned over the next seventeen hours.

While on the plane, we were not given any assigned seats—instead, they let all the families sit in groups. Soon thereafter, we heard the plane engine rumble beneath us as it started taxiing before takeoff. It was surreal. We were on our way to America!

Humorously, the concept of a seat belt was new to us, so we would be walking around the plane even when the pilot announced that we should return to our seats and fasten our seat belts. The cabin crew had not realized it was helpful to have an interpreter translate what the cabin crew was actually saying. The majority of the Kurdish refugees were Muslim, and we did not know what to make of the food served on the plane. Did it contain pork or alcohol? We also became a little restless after so many long hours on the plane without knowing our whereabouts. At the first stop, we took some solace in realizing we were in the UAE because we could read the Arabic signs through the plane window. At the second stop, new flight attendants boarded the plane, most of whom were southeast Asian, so we assumed we had to be in that part of the world.

Seventeen hours later, we finally landed in Guam! My family and I were in the first group of 792 Kurdish refugees to arrive in Guam, followed by another 1,422 refugees. Once we arrived at the airport, we were greeted by a large group of volunteers. They gave us toys, candy, and a hot meal. We spoke little English confidently, so in a nice gesture, they had "welcome" signs printed up in Arabic. What a relief! I remember the volunteers asking us to smile while they handed out the candy and toys. They escorted us through the reception and screening process, which included medical screening, customs, and an initial Immigration and Naturalization Services (INS) interview. Buses then transported us to the Andersen Air Force Base South Housing Area for our housing assignment. We stayed there for the next sixty days.

Even though my mother had made it safely to Guam with her eleven children and her pregnant daughter-in-law, she wanted a chance to voice her concern to one of the Army Generals in Guam. Once she did, through an interpreter, she told the General she welcomed the idea of continuing to the next destination once the American forces assured her that no one would take any of her children away from her. The Army General, noticing the tears coming down my mother's face, held both of her hands tight, looked her in the eye, and promised that she would make it to America with all her eleven children. He also reminded her that she would soon be home in her new country where her rights would be respected like any other citizen.

When I look back on those days in Guam at fourteen, I remember two things I struggled with at the airport: being terrified to ride an escalator and not knowing how to use a Western toilet. Our bathroom system in Kurdistan was a "squat toilet." You would align yourself exactly over the hole and squat while remaining standing. Once finished, you would rinse the floor toilet area of any mis-aimed feces until it was fully clean. Not only did they lack normal toilets in Guam, but handheld bidets as well. To most Kurds, it did not matter how much toilet paper we used; it was only after using a hand-held bidet and water to clean ourselves, that we felt satisfied.

In Anderson South, the housing office provided basic furniture and household items for our large family: cots, blankets, pillows, and personal hygiene items. We were then assigned to two and four-bedroom concrete air-conditioned duplexes. The cots provided filled the bedrooms, living room, and laundry room area to accommodate the big Kurdish households. When we arrived, the duplexes smelled like pine cleaner. After the miserable conditions in Silopi, the comforts of living in a house with air-conditioning, clean water, and sanitary bathrooms were almost too much to believe. Did we really each have a cot of our own? Did we actually have showers with clean water and healthy meals three times a day? Was there truly green grass and coconut trees outside the house? I was so excited to see a bathtub for the first time, I laid in the empty tub while my siblings laughed at me. We felt so blessed and could not thank the U. S. government enough. When a person has been deprived for so long, any simple luxury seems like a gift from heaven.

Over ninety percent of the Kurdish refugees in Guam were practicing Muslims; however, some were Christian. To meet our religious needs and ensure sensitivity to cultural, religious, and dietary differences, the Navy sent its first Muslim chaplain to Guam. The Navy and Air Force engineers built a mosque tent behind a row of duplexes facing the holy city of Mecca to enable the Kurdish refugees to worship properly. They had lovely prayer rugs lined up inside the mosque along with copies of the Muslim holy book (Quran) for those who wanted to read after praying. With limited activities on the base, many hajiiyas (a respectful way of addressing elderly ladies in Kurdish) would gather in the mosque and share religious stories.

The Air Force staff members in Guam assisted us with learning basic English, instructed cultural awareness courses, and taught some basic do's and don'ts to be mindful of once we were living in the United States. They also had varying English-as-a-second-language classes for different age groups, and we undertook those classes with enthusiasm. The classes provided structure and interest to our daily routine, ensuring we were not just sitting idly, waiting for emigration. As soon as we were done with English classes for the day, we would rush home and practice the language with each other. Many mothers would review what they learned for the day with their young children.

The Military Information Support Team (MIST) developed community centers to provide us with any information we needed. At the community center, we would find simple English language information sheets and printed classroom materials. The MIST slowly expanded our exposure to life in the U.S. by installing a twelve-foot video screen in the recreation center, where the same movies would play four to five times a day. We watched flicks such as *Dumb and Dumber, Money Train*, and *Blood Sport*. These movies helped with our English and gave us a better familiarity with life in the U.S. To help keep us entertained, they assembled a ping pong table so we could play in the afternoons after English classes. In addition, there was American-style football as well as card tables for the boys. The guys would also play soccer and basketball in the fields provided at the base. Because of our male-dominated culture, the entertainment center was mostly occupied by boys, men, and a few women, while girls were pretty much confined to the houses provided to us.

The MIST held workshops every week with translators

reviewing a cultural awareness topic and answering any of our questions. First things first—they told us what types of questions we should not ask when in America. For example, do not ask an American about their age, salary, weight, or marital status. This information was personal and not anyone else's business (which was news to us). Alongside other such culture shocks, Kurdish men were also informed that their wives might end up working, so they needed to assist with caring for their children. They also informed our parents that when disciplining children, you could not yell at them in public, but should wait until you had some privacy. Understandably, some of the men worried that these meetings might empower their women and they would no longer be the submissive housewives they had previously been. Because many of the Kurdish men defined themselves by their ability to provide and achieved a sense of control amidst all the other chaos from their position of power in relation to their wives, losing even this semblance of "order" was causing many of them stress.

While in Guam, the MIST helped us each get a Social Security card and an alien number. We had no idea what a Social Security card meant, or what an alien number was. They told us that these two cards would be our gateway to finding a job in America. Due to the prevalence of illiteracy among Kurdish refugees in Guam, and a lack of English-speaking skills, a lot of information in our paperwork needed to be fixed when we applied for a green card and citizenship. Many Kurds who immigrated to the U.S. through Guam have July 1st for a birthday, a commonly chosen generic date on the paperwork. Additionally, many married couples did not have a marriage certificate, so one needed to be created. In doing so, the MIST brought in a chaplain to re-marry the couples before leaving for the U.S.

Not being familiar with Kurdish pronunciation or the lack of some Sorani Kurdish letters in the English alphabet, the spelling of Kurdish names (when placed in the Latin alphabet) was often incorrect. Several names were anglicized and altered in pronunciation as well as spelling. For example, my name was changed from Heleen to Helen, Blend was changed to Blind, Jowan to Joan and Jiyan to Zhyan. In Iraqi Kurdistan, we use our first name followed by our father and grandfather's first names. So, my name would be Heleen Ameer Ali, Ameer being my father's name and Ali my grandfather's. When asked for a middle name, we thought the middle was the name between Helen and Ali, in other words, our father's name. So, looking at my old documents, Ameer was used for my middle name. The result combined Ali with Sairany (my father's last name) for the last name; thus, my new incorrect last name became Ali Sairany.

A myriad of agencies assisted with our emigration paperwork including the Department of Health and Human Services, the Immigration and Naturalization Service, and the Federal Bureau of Investigation. With no vaccine records and most of us not able to remember what vaccines we had been given, there was no way the healthcare personnel at the clinic could discern which we had received. Not wanting to risk sending anyone to the U.S. unvaccinated, the healthcare providers in the camp advised that we all get vaccinated with the same number of doses and types of vaccines.

With the prevalence of nutritious food in the camp and the change in our diet, almost every Kurdish refugee began to gain weight. For instance, I put on 20 pounds (9 kilograms) in the two months we lived in Guam! The MIST had given each household basic kitchenware supplies, but cooking a decent Kurdish meal was simply not possible due to the lack of Kurdish ingredients and spices. Plus, it was not ideal for the government to invest money in large cookware sets for families that would only be there for two months and leave everything behind once they left.

As such, a centralized dining room in the community center provided three hot meals a day. The MIST wanted the Kurdish women to focus on learning English, not on domestic issues. This was a struggle for most women because cooking, not studying, was one of the main tasks they performed in Kurdistan. Women and girls would spend their morning learning English and come home with food ready to eat. For the meals that were provided, the government hired professional chefs to cook for the refugees based on our dietary restrictions, avoiding pork and alcohol-based ingredients. Every morning, my brother Zerak would stand in the line to get us thirteen apples, thirteen cans of fruit, thirteen containers of yogurt, and eggs for the entire family. The same would be repeated for lunch and dinner.

Once the government personnel had a better idea of the large size of most Kurdish households, they assigned us to various states in the U.S. for resettlement. Being a family of fourteen, it made sense to settle us in a state with a lower cost of living, like Georgia. (When people ask me, "Of all the 50 States, why Georgia?" I say, "We did not choose Georgia; Georgia was chosen for us.")

We stayed in Guam from September to November and during that time, the island was under the threat of typhoon Omar. We were new to hurricanes, so camp administration representatives came to all the housing units with translators to help us prepare for the approaching storm. They brought us dry goods, candles, lighters, and anything else we needed in case of a power outage. The key to our safety was for us to stay indoors, but that did not happen. Administrative personnel became frustrated when they walked by the housing units on the eve of the hurricane and saw groups of Kurdish men standing outside with a lit fire having tea. They reminded us about the seriousness of typhoon Omar, and kindly asked the men to put out the fire and go indoors. However, after years of living under bombs while surrounded by land mines, some strong winds or rain did not seem like much to worry about.

With our two months in Guam drawing to a close, the administrative services finally told all the families the states in which they would be settling, and families started comparing one state to another. Each time we ran into a military member, we would ask them to tell us about Georgia. *What is the weather like*? *Can you buy a house there*? We were so excited to start this new chapter in our lives.

The Kurdish families were put into groups and dates for departure were assigned to each group. My family and I were the second group to leave the island. When we were preparing to leave for Georgia, we packed our belongings but included a lot of glassware and kitchen items that we collected. Our bags were too heavy, and the administrative services personnel inspected the bags and found the kitchen and household items in our suitcases that, unknown to us, were supposed to stay behind in Guam.

Once they cleared our bags, we boarded the bus to the airport. We had one more long flight ahead of us—from Guam all the way to Atlanta, Georgia, with three connections: Honolulu, San Diego, and Houston.

In Honolulu, we had a long layover. While seated at the gate with Pambo on my lap, I watched everyone. Curious children and adults would turn around to catch a glimpse of us as they walked by. It was obvious to us and them that we had come from a foreign place. I am sure that we also appeared tired, slightly terrified, and anxious. Thankfully, after all that we had been through, we were numb and too tired to care what others were thinking of us. Appearance-wise, my sisters and I were all dressed in long skirts and had our hair covered with scarves. My mother had a long gown on and had her hair covered. Some of the other women with us had their colorful sparkly Kurdish dresses on, and men had the traditional Kurdish outfits featuring baggy pants and a waist wrap.

As for me, I was mesmerized by all the tall and thin women dressed in short dresses just like the ones I had seen in the American movies. I still remember seeing a beautiful blonde flight attendant confidently walking by in a pencil skirt and bright red high heels, with three other male cabin crew members. She was laughing loudly and getting the full attention of the crew. I wondered if this was normal, since I had been raised to always lower my voice and not smile around boys. But I think, looking back, that I secretly envied her as well.

All the Kurdish families were kept together until we reached Houston and then each one was assigned a different gate number for the final leg of their destination. We found our gate and boarded our flight to Atlanta,

Georgia. We finally arrived at Hartsfield-Jackson International Airport in Atlanta at 11 p.m. on November 15th, 1996. I was fifteen. My siblings' ages in descending order were: Omed (28), Hoger (24), Jowan (22), Zhyan (20), Jehan (18), Zerak (17), Dlovan (13), Dilven (10), Blend (6), and Pambo (4).

CHAPTER IV:
HARD WORK PAYS OFF IN THE U.S.A.

"Refugees didn't just escape a place. They had to escape a thousand memories until they'd put enough time and distance between them and their misery to wake to a better day."
– *Nadia Hashimi*

A family picture taken in 1996 when we first arrived in Atlanta, Georgia.

Once we arrived in Atlanta, Georgia, we were guided through Customs without passports or travel documents with the help of the International Rescue Committee (IRC), a resettlement agency contracted with the U.S. government to provide settlement services to refugees. At the arrival gate, there was a group of case managers from the IRC waiting for us with an Arabic-speaking translator, named Mohamad. They assisted us with Customs and Protection Form I-94W Nonimmigrant Visa Waiver Arrival/Departure record. Akh Mohamad (Brother Mohamad), our translator, was a former refugee from Jordan. The case managers from IRC helped us gather our suitcases and we were driven to Clarkston, the refugee-dominated neighborhood in Atlanta.

On our way, we all looked through the windows to get our first glimpse of the streets and people. We noticed the clean and paved roads. A few fast cars then cut us off while speeding through the empty four-lane highway, which made us jump in surprise. From afar we spotted the Atlanta skyline; one of the drivers told us that was downtown, and we should explore it when we were all settled.

The building and traffic signs were all in English and nothing made sense to me. Once we arrived in Clarkston, we saw pictures of turkeys (the bird, not the country) on almost every neighbor's door. We did not understand the significance of a turkey until a year later, when we were invited for our first Thanksgiving dinner. The IRC had rented two apartments for us, a one-bedroom apartment for Omed and Shayma, who were expecting their first baby girl, and a three-bedroom apartment for the rest of our Sairany family.

Both apartments had been furnished with the basics: beds, dining table and chairs, sheets, pillows, blankets, shower curtains, towels, dishes, silverware, cooking utensils, pots and pans, as well as laundry and cleaning supplies. The apartments looked extremely expensive and fancy, compared to our mud houses in Mahala Reeta. I started exploring the apartment interior with my siblings and the furniture that the IRC had gotten us. *Could this be heaven that we were finally in*? I thought.

The bedrooms had closets built into the wall, something we had never seen before. The refrigerators were filled with food and water to last us until Monday since we arrived on a Friday and IRC staff would not be working on the weekend. Once we were in the apartment, through the interpretation of Akh Mohamad, the case managers encouraged us to get some rest and said they would meet us on Monday to talk about the next steps involved in getting settled in Georgia. Omed and Shayma's apartment was a few blocks away from ours, but they chose to stay with the rest of the family that night. We all slept in the three-bedroom apartment with our parents sleeping on floor mats.

Tired and jetlagged from long flights and making our way through multiple connections, we did not wake until 2 p.m. the following day. My older siblings started exploring the kitchen to see what was available for breakfast. They managed to fix us fried bread and tea with the Lipton tea bags that were provided. Still numb and tired from the long journey, we took the rest of Saturday off. Believe it or not, we did not even open the front door of the apartment.

Curious about our new surroundings, my siblings and

I, from Pambo to Omed, looked through the windows to watch the children in the neighborhood, who were mostly from Vietnam, Bosnia, and Somalia. I immediately noticed the spectrum of skin tones outside. I also saw both white women dressed in miniskirts, and other women wearing burkas and headscarves. I spotted a few men who walked by in their shorts while others were dressed nicely in suits for their Sunday church service (which I learned about later).

On Monday morning at 8 a.m., Akh Mohamad and the other case managers arrived with several cars to take us to the IRC office in Decatur, Georgia, a 15-minute drive from our apartment. Once there, we worked with two case managers–one to assist the younger ones with school registration, and the other to find jobs for my older siblings, five of whom qualified for employment. For the first two months after our arrival, the IRC made sure we received a $700 stipend for food and other expenses until the older children had work. Our first month's rent was also paid by the IRC. We were granted additional government assistance through food stamps for two months, given to us in books of $1, $5, and $10 food coupons.

The case managers assisted us with the top priority resettlement items: learning to drive and getting a driver's license, using the bus system from Clarkston to the IRC office and The DeKalb International Farmers Market, finding neighborhood grocery stores, and using the public payphones to make emergency calls. They also showed us where to board the school buses each morning. The older children were registered in evening English-as-a-second-language (ESL) classes, taught by volunteers, so they could improve their English after work. Those of us who were registered in the public schools took a bus to attend ESL classes in the first half of the day at the international center for the school district. After lunch, we took another school bus back to the high school to finish the day with math and science, two courses that thankfully did not require English proficiency.

I was registered in the ninth grade and my brother Zerak in the eleventh at Tucker High School. Dlovan and Dilven were registered in middle school and Blend in elementary school. Pambo would stay home with our mother and Shayma. Zerak and I commuted to school every day and then to evening classes at the Christian-based refugee resettlement agency, World Relief, for assistance with our homework. Zerak and I had always excelled in school in Kurdistan and we wanted to continue that in the United States.

Although coming to the U.S. held the key to our future, not being able to excel due to the language barrier was hard to accept. I would read my homework instructions over and over and nothing made sense. I had an English dictionary, and every word was marked with its meaning in Arabic. I would try to connect the words in Arabic to understand the homework instructions, but they still did not make sense. I asked my older siblings, who knew limited English, and they would try to help me figure out the instructions. There were times they could help, but many times I was not able to complete my homework because I could not understand the instructions. With the discipline and strict academic standards I was used to in Kurdistan, it was not easy to leave my homework undone and go to class with nothing to show my teacher.

My family was lucky; because of our wide age range,

half of us were eligible to work and provide for the other half, who would pursue their dreams of higher education. The IRC helped both of my older adult brothers, Omed and Hoger, get their driver's licenses. Omed was so excited when he passed the driving test and could not wait to show everyone his license. Hoger did not pass the test the first time but passed on his second try. Once they got their licenses, both Hoger and Omed were able to start working. Hoger's first job was at a warehouse company where he worked as a mailroom clerk. Nine months later, Omed joined him at the same company. Both of my adult sisters, Zhyan and Jowan, worked as translators for the two refugee resettlement agencies: Jowan for the IRC, and Zhyan for World Relief. My sister Jehan, who had just missed graduating from high school by one year, chose to work instead of finishing school. The IRC found her a job at a department store warehouse where she was responsible for stocking clothes.

The system that the IRC had in place worked wonderfully until my Kurdish culture started clashing with American customs. We were expected to dress in school uniforms in Iraq, our fingernails had to be cut short, and our hair had to be braided in two ponytails. My first week in high school was a huge culture shock. There were female students with long manicured nails, excessive hairdos and make-up. Male and female students flirted openly and there was constant rowdiness outside the classroom.

I asked myself, "How in the world is this allowed in a school system?" My math teacher was constantly begging students to stop talking in class. When they stopped, the teacher thanked them. Our teachers in Iraq never thanked us! We would get hit with a wooden stick for not erasing minor pencil marks from a used book, let alone talking in class.

A few weeks into starting classes, Blend was in trouble. "He is suspended because he physically hit one of his classmates," the angry teacher explained. Jowan, along with my mother, rushed to Blend's school to see what had happened. "He made fun of me, so I had to hit him," six-year-old Blend fumed to both Jowan and my mother. My mother raised Blend's hand high up and congratulated him, reminding him that he was a young man and should never let anyone make fun of him—if he did, he would be made fun of even more and be perceived as weak. According to the Kurdish idea of honor, he was right to defend himself.

In response, the teacher covered her face and thought my mother was mad. "If we tolerated hitting every time there was a verbal disagreement, we would have chaos," the teacher said.

According to his teacher, Blend should have talked to her about his classmate's behavior and the argument could have been resolved through dialogue. Clearly, there was a cultural clash between the teacher and my mother. My mother perceived hitting as necessary to prevent future bullying of her child, while the teacher was encouraging honest communication and dialogue. My mother's reaction to the situation reflected where she came from. Not that I agreed with my mother, but in Kurdistan, we seldom managed disagreements through dialogue. We often failed to acknowledge the problem and our way of addressing the issue at hand was by avoiding it, denying it even existed, or using the word Insha'Allah (God willing), meaning that it will hopefully eventually be resolved. And my mother was right! If we were in Kurdistan and Blend had not defended himself, the kids in his class would perceive him as weak and beat him daily.

Blend was not alone. The same week Kovan, who was slightly older than Blend and the child of a Kurdish neighbor of ours in Clarkston, was also sent home. I was called to translate for Kovan's family and his elementary teacher. Apparently, Kovan was using bad words and exposed his private parts when urinating on the school wall in public, something that was the norm in Zakho. Nobody had told him it was abnormal for America. We tried to coach Kovan that every time he got ready to use a bad word, instead he should say hippopotamus. After multiple attempts, Kovan got bored and said, "hippo quna data" (hippo your mom's butt) which linguistically still did the trick. As it goes, when you begin to learn a new language, it is the curse words that you are mischievously drawn to learning first.

Both of my sisters, Jowan and Zhyan, were involved in community work for their job, and had to be constantly called on to translate when a fellow Kurd was in trouble or one of the women was giving birth. On one occasion, Zhyan was contacted because a Kurdish guy, Karu, had propositioned a female undercover police officer for sex by asking her, "How much?" Unsurprisingly, he was immediately arrested, and Zhyan was brought in to explain that he did not understand the magnitude of what he was saying or that it was even illegal. In Karu's case, he saw a provocatively dressed woman that he assumed was a prostitute, without knowing it was against the law. In another case, a young Kurdish guy kept getting into trouble because he assumed any of the women dressed like prostitutes (by Kurdistan standards) *were* prostitutes. As a result, he was constantly asking women in short dresses and short shorts if they were for sale.

On a more wholesome note, my sisters were also called in to help assist with Kurdish births. These were happening, it seemed, every weekend, and my sisters were needed to translate for the women as they went into labor. As a result, many Kurdish parents named their baby girls "Jowan" or "Zhyan" out of gratitude for their assistance.

Kurdish families were notorious for being last-minute planners. My mother would remind me, "We are Muslims, and we cannot guarantee what happens tomorrow, let alone next month." Tardiness to events was favored because it showed that you were busy and had important things to worry about.

Kurds are known for our hospitality, but we are also known for showing up at people's doors unannounced and overstaying their welcome. Once a family comes to visit, they refuse to leave until extremely late. There is a Kurdish belief that if you put salt in your guest's shoes (which are left at the door when entering the home), the guests will get up and leave immediately. My sisters and I would jokingly place salt in the visitors' shoes, hoping they would leave a bit earlier, but it never worked. Once a family finally left, they would call the following morning to tell my mother that they were interested in the oldest daughter (the oldest being me, even though I was the fourth daughter in line). They would then ask for my hand to marry their son.

On weekends, the Kurdish women in the community would show up full of gossip to entertain my mother. I once heard a group of Kurdish ladies tell my mother, "Fatima, we are forced to live in a land full of fusq (an Islamic term referring to moral corruption against God)." And that was when I could not keep my mouth shut. I angrily asked why they perceived the U.S. as such. "The women show so much skin. They dress almost naked," they proclaimed. It annoyed me how "moral corruption" in the Middle East always revolved around how women dressed and performed. These same female friends of my mother had forgotten about the chaotic state we left behind in Iraq where women were covered. Clearly, covering up women did not stop the corruption where we came from. So, I had to voice my opinion in disagreement, to which they retorted that, "With so much temptation, men cannot focus, which causes chaos."

I tried hard not to roll my eyes. "Where is the state of chaos in Atlanta then?" I asked them to look around at the system and organization we were all surrounded by. One of the women had the nerve to counter that American men were simply different; they did not have the same urges as Kurdish men, so they "could handle seeing more skin on a woman."

I did my best to interject and stop the Kurdish ladies from influencing my mother. It bothered me how some Kurds in Clarkston took advantage of the public assistance programs available to them, yet they were also critical of the society that did them so many favors. I did not appreciate how they took the opportunities given to them in this country for granted and found easy ways around things. When they were caught doing something mischievous, they either denied doing it or refused to take the initiative to apologize or say, "I did not know." Such behaviors by my people put me at unease because my roots were the same as theirs and I felt the obligation to change their perception towards America. I also felt that as a Kurd, I was a representative of my entire community to Americans.

When I first came to the U.S., I began covering my hair. A hijab, or headscarf, was a new concept to many high school students, especially in the Deep South. Students in my math class would try to pull my scarf from the back to see my hair. Not knowing how to express myself well in English, I could not tell them that this was part of my faith and I could not show my hair. I finally asked the teacher, with my limited English, if I could change my seat to sit in the back of the class so no one could pull on my hijab anymore.

One day, I noticed the students in my biology class were keeping their distance from me and making rude comments about how I smelled. The students who knew my brother told him that I needed to start taking a shower because the way I smelled was unbearable. I was confused because I showered every day; however, I was not using deodorant. Nobody had told me about deodorant. Zerak was far more fluent in English than I and when he told me about my classmates' comments, I was in tears and told my family, "I am done going to school!" I did not think I would succeed with all these obstacles in my way.

For his part, my father reminded me that joy is not found in things that are easy to get. He also told me that it is not our family's habit to give up when faced with a challenge. "It's only a matter of time before you master the English language. I assure you—you will excel in your classes the way you did in Iraq," he promised. He was, indeed, correct.

Some students from my biology class spotted me in the bathroom not washing my hands after I finished and raised their eyebrows. I only used soap when I showered, a routine that I got used to in Kurdistan because of our lack of warm water and electricity. I used a bidet that I carried with me to the lady's room to wash myself, so I didn't understand why there was a need to use soap to wash my hands.

On January 11, 1997, my sister-in-law Shayma's water broke and we needed to get her to the hospital. Not having a car and not knowing how to get a taxicab, my sister Zhyan suggested that we reach out to Lilyana for help. Lilyana was a sweet, red-haired woman in her mid-thirties from Mexico City who spoke little English. Zhyan had met Lilyana in her ESL class where they practiced speaking English together. Lilyana would often give Zhyan a ride home from class and stay to have dinner with us. After every Kurdish meal, Lilyana would remind us that we used many of the same ingredients Mexicans did in their cooking. We felt that we had so much in common with Lilyana and her culture and she became a close family friend. She told us stories of when she was a little girl and how her parents would fill the car full of people to come and pick her up from school (as we did). And just like many Kurds, Lilyana was from a big household and their grocery shopping always involved buying every item in bulk (as we did).

That night, Zhyan called Lilyana to tell her that Shayma was in labor and asked if she was willing to give her a ride to the hospital. She rushed to our house to pick up Shayma and off they went to the hospital. Later that evening, Miriam, the very first U.S.-born Sairany, arrived. We welcomed Miriam with love and warmth and were so excited to be aunts and uncles for the very first time. Two months later, Shayma had to be rushed to the hospital again. Fortunately, it turned out to be happy news not only for Omed, but for us all. Shayma was expecting her second child, though Miriam was just two months old! It seemed that even in America, our extreme "Kurdish fertility" was still intact.

Once my siblings got their first paychecks, the IRC stipends stopped along with the government assistance. My older siblings supported the family while the younger ones went to school. Two years into our studies at high school, Zerak and I started applying to supermarkets to work as grocery baggers. Being sixteen, I was very anxious when we went for job interviews. While waiting for my name to be called, I turned to Hoger, who drove us to the job interview, and asked if he were certain my age would not be an issue to getting work. After the interview, the store manager told Zerak and I that we had both been hired and would be earning $6.25 per hour. The store manager told me that since, according to Georgia law, I was a minor, I would need to wear a pink name tag identifying me as such. I was happy to have a job and the money Zerak and I made went into the collective family account to help provide for everyone.

The entire concept of putting cash into the bank was new to many Kurdish families, including my own. The

Kurds from our background were not familiar with the banking system, or the process of taking out a loan, or building a good credit score. In Kurdistan, the only way you could acquire an item was by paying for it in full, upfront, in cash. Consequently, whenever we met Kurds who had been in the U.S. for a number of years and already had their own house and cars, we could not figure out how they had already earned the full amount to acquire such items. Since none of us had any experience with these matters, my sister Jowan (twenty-two at the time) took it upon herself to manage the household finances. Jowan was extremely cautious about our opening new credit cards or spending large amounts of cash without her input. We found *not* opening a credit card to be difficult, however, considering the salesperson would always inform us that doing so made the item cheaper to purchase. To us, it seemed an obvious choice. However, we did not realize that if we did not pay the credit card back on time, we had to pay interest on the amount owed. Over time, the interest would accrue, and we would end up paying far more than what we had initially thought we were saving.

Not long after my older siblings started working, we decided it was time for the family to buy a car. Unable to afford a new car, we found a used one for sale. That afternoon, as we were getting ready to make the purchase, several Kurdish families joined us to inspect the car and bless the decision we were making. This was the first car my family had ever owned. We were so excited! Hoger took us for rides to show us around Clarkston. Our favorite place to go was the DeKalb International Farmers Market. The name was a mouthful for my family, so we called the market Seeka alaama ("flag market" in Kurdish) for all the national flags that hung from the ceiling in the building. Once inside, we found all types of vegetables we needed to cook our Kurdish-style food: radishes, different colored peppers, Persian cucumbers, eggplants, zucchinis, parsley, green mint, green onion, and organic dirty tomatoes. The market also sold nuts in bulk, just like in Kurdistan, where we would weigh them and pay by the weight. Additionally, we found various types of cheeses, animal organs, spices, and herbs that served our needs. A visit to Seeka alaama every Saturday morning turned into a Sairany family tradition. Once done with grocery shopping, we would walk out of the market with enough vegetables and other food to last us for a week.

Unfortunately, Seeka alaama did not sell halal meat. Halal, which is an Arabic word for permissible, adheres to Islamic law as defined in the Holy Quran. The Islamic form of dhabiha (slaughtering animals) involves killing with a cut to the jugular vein, carotid artery, or windpipe. The animal before dhabiha must be alive and healthy. The blood is then drained from the animal through the carcass. During this process, the person who performs the act of dhabiha recites a dedication, known as tasmiya. So, for halal chicken or red meat, my family would go to the local Somalian butcher shop and buy lamb and beef in large lumps. We would chop the meat and freeze it in meal-sized portions. Other Kurdish families in our community, traveled to farms in South Carolina to buy a whole animal, brought it back to Clarkston, and slaughtered it in front of their apartment door. It was shocking for the American residents in the apartment complex to see blood in front of their neighbor's door and all the flies that came with it.

My family cooked and ate almost every organ of the animal: liver, heart, kidney, gizzards, bone marrow, skull marrow, stomach, testicles, lungs, and tongue, etc. My mother's favorite meal was the famous traditional Kurdish dish, sar u pe, which translates to head and leg (hooves), often served to guests as a sign of honor because it takes so long and is a lot of work to prepare. This meal has a high-calorie count but is delicious. The making of sar u pe usually involves multiple women, each having her own part from cleaning the head, hooves, and organs of the goat or sheep.

To prepare the meal, my mother would first remove all the hair from the head and hooves by soaking them in boiling water to loosen the hair from the skin. Next, she would slightly grill the head and hooves for flavor and begin cooking both parts of the body together in water. She then cleaned the large and small intestines (called tripe) of the animal. This process was done in advance because it took a few days to leave the tripe in water to remove the odor. Once clean, she stuffed the tripe with a mixture of chopped meat, rice, herbs, nuts, and seasonings. The tripe was then cut and stitched into pockets filled with the same rice mixture. Both the stuffed long intestine and the stuffed pockets of tripe were dropped into the kettle where the head and hooves had already been cooking and all continued cooking together.

At the dinner table, my father would hammer the head of the animal to break through the skull and get a taste of the bone marrow. Once the bone marrow was exposed, my father separated it into fourteen tiny shares so everyone around the dinner table would get a taste. Omed, the biggest foodie and most experienced of us all, could crack the skull open without a hammer, making us cheer for him around the dinner table. My mother then chopped the tongue, dipped it into a bowl of sumac (Kurdish spice), and shared the pieces with the rest of the family.

One weekend after we felt truly settled, my family and I took a field trip to downtown Atlanta to check out the main highlights. This included the Coca-Cola Museum and Centennial Olympic Park. Our first stop was to the World of Coca Cola. I was fascinated to learn that the founder of the Coke drink was an Atlanta pharmacist, Dr. John Pemberton, who created a distinctive tasting drink that was sold at soda fountains. He first created the syrup, then took it to his neighborhood pharmacy where he mixed it with carbonated water. To those who tasted it for the first time, the drink tasted excellent. I tried every flavor of Coke out with my siblings in the museum and we kept asking each other which flavor we liked the most.

We then made our way to Centennial Park for a bite. On our way, we spotted a few couples kissing and making out, and our parents immediately told us to close our eyes. Such public displays of affection were unheard of back in Kurdistan, and the idea of people kissing so passionately in public was very taboo and embarrassing for us to even witness. Consequently, for the first few months every time I saw a couple kissing in public, I would close my eyes or look away.

While at Centennial Park, we all craved something stereotypically "American." However, we did not find much "American" food available. Most of the dishes we found were from abroad. We saw cuisines from China, India, Italy, and Mexico but nothing American. I figured a big country like America must have a cuisine of its own.

Eventually, we asked someone where the "American food" was and were pointed in the direction of a place selling hot dogs and hamburgers. Excited about our first experience, we ordered fourteen hot dogs (one for everyone in the group). However, about ¾ of the way into our hot dogs, most of us began to question what kind of meat these hot dogs were made with and suspected that perhaps it was pork. We rushed to ask the women selling them and she said they were. We assumed that my mother, who was the most religious of all of us, would be extremely upset. She was, but not because of the pork. Instead, she complained that we had not let her finish the last half of her delicious hot dog before notifying her. While yes, Muslims were not supposed to eat pork, my mother was fine with consuming it before she knew any better.

Oddly enough, my family also grew to love eating Chinese food. There was something about Chinese cuisine that they found in common with Kurdish food. Every Saturday, my older siblings would treat the whole family to lunch at the neighborhood Chinese restaurant buffet. To my family, a buffet meant that we should eat as much as we possibly could in order to get our money's worth. Therefore, it was essential for my mother to have us skip breakfast that day, and we would wear loose pants. Once at the restaurant, there were countless varieties of dishes to choose from. Chicken was cooked in so many ways with different types of sauces. Various types of vegetables that we recognized, and some we did not recognize, were laid out nicely. We did not get near any dishes that contained beef because we knew it was not halal. Additionally, there was a big sushi bar section and you could ask for as much sushi as you wanted. Dessert was another story. There were cookies, different flavors of ice cream, chocolate and vanilla pudding, and various types of fruit all cut and ready to eat. I felt like I was Alice in her Wonderland.

Feeling that I needed to share my observations with someone, I started writing letters to my childhood friend and first cousin, Media, about my experiences in America. In my first letter, I talked about how technically advanced America was, but also socially isolated, explaining to her: "I no longer have to take dishes or laundry to the Khabur. We now have a dishwasher and laundry machines. We do not need to heat the water because we can change the water temperature at the sink. But I am also sometimes sad and surprised at how distant people are from each other. Everyone here is an individual regardless of their family which is good. But everyone is also busy here and you feel like you are not important if you are not busy too."

Additionally, I explained to Media in my letters how I was meeting many new people, but still felt alone, since the problems of those I met were so different from my own. I shared the contradictions I was witnessing and my frustration with having to explain all the details of where I was from. I was struck by the large wealth disparity where you would see homeless people sleeping next to luxury stores. I had also begun to notice that many dogs of middle class families seemed to live better lives than many of the children we grew up with in Kurdistan. I told her: "There are so many blonde, blue-eyed students like you here. I am one of the few with brown hair and eyes. They ask me where I am from because I look so different. I tell them Kurdistan, but they have no idea where that is. I then have to explain the whole history of Kurdistan which gets very tiring."

Being a young teen when we emigrated, I tried my best to blend into American culture while staying true to my own cultural and religious practices. I was dealing with the complexity of developing my own identity, and the added complication of finding the balance between both cultures was not easy. My parents insisted that we speak Kurdish inside the home so we would not forget our mother tongue. My parents also subscribed to the Arabic channels on television and made sure we watched the news and shows in Arabic to keep up with that language too. So, yes, I speak all three languages fluently, but each with an accent. Like many trilingual people, there are times when I end up speaking a language of my own that is a blend of all three languages in my head: Kurdish, Arabic, and English.

One thing I struggled with that was a cultural norm for a Kurd, but not for an average American, was the excessive facial hair and unibrow I had at the age of sixteen. My parents were against the use of makeup and any of us altering our facial appearance until we were in college. One day, another student asked why I did not remove the hair from my face. I was so embarrassed and asked Shayma, who was skilled in the hand threading technique, if she was willing to remove my facial hair without telling my parents. She threaded the hair between my eyebrows and removed all the hair from my upper lip and chin. She also cleaned my eyebrows without making them too narrow. Once she was done, she let me look in the mirror and I almost did not recognize myself.

Jehan, who had earned the title "spy of the family," was always looking to get Zerak and me in trouble. She immediately noticed how different my face looked and was quick to report the clandestine change to my parents. And that was when I had to admit that I removed the facial hair because kids in school were making fun of me.

I also slowly started to change the way I dressed. I would wear a pair of jeans with a nice top and cover my hair with a light hijab scarf. Without telling my parents, I would sneak a bit of makeup into my backpack to use when in school. Another challenge was not dating when I was seventeen. A male friend and classmate once asked me if I could be his date for the class prom. My response was a disappointed, "I am sorry, but I am not allowed to date."

One afternoon after classes were over, Zerak and I were waiting for the school bus when I spotted a "sister" with a hijab (the way we refer to Muslim girls who practice their faith). I was so excited to see someone besides me who wore the hijab, someone I could relate to after all those months in a school where so much was foreign to me. I asked my brother to give me a few minutes to go and drop a salaam (hello) to the sister and see whether she was willing to keep in touch with me. Zerak told me to keep an eye on the time because the school bus was not willing to wait if I ended up talking too much. I enthusiastically approached the sister with the hijab. Once I did, I spoke to her in my broken English and told her my name and how I had longed to talk to someone like myself for so long. She told me her name was Asma and she gave me her phone number so we could keep in touch. Of course, I lost track of time and did not realize the school bus had left Zerak and me behind. Zerak had begged the bus driver to wait for me, to no avail. "My sister does not speak English well. I just need five minutes to go and find her," he explained. The bus driver would not wait so Zerak got off the bus, refusing to leave me behind. Once Zerak found me, he told me that we missed the bus and asked me to be patient because we did not have a car, phone, or any way to reach our family. Luckily, Zerak remembered the way home. We ended up walking for 2 hours until we reached Clarkston.

During high school, I needed my few Muslim sisters. We provided support to one another and relief from the ignorance surrounding us. So many refugees and immigrant students in high school were not aware of their disadvantages and how bad the circumstances were. Almost all the Kurdish refugee girls in my cohort dropped out of school and chose to seek low-paying jobs as an alternative. Luckily, with the love and support of my family, I continued my struggle and was determined to stay in school. Coming to the U.S., my world had shifted completely, and I constantly needed to adjust and overcome unique disadvantages. In my case, this was to take classes and master them like everyone else. It took a lot of energy and an extra level of confidence to adjust and walk through the school hallways as the only Kurdish Muslim teenager with everyone looking at me and wondering why I spoke different and had my hair covered.

Many days when I rushed to switch books in between classes, I would find notes filled with hate and ignorant language that had been slipped into my locker by strangers. Why did they despise me when they did not know me? How was I possibly a threat to them? Would they have been kinder if they realized what I had gone through? I still cannot say for sure. This was my world, and this was how I was raised. Looking back, I ask myself why people could not have been more understanding.

My mother and Shayma were stay-at-home mothers who did not have the ability to leave the house for regular English classes. My mother had quit learning English in frustration after two months, assuming that since she had never learned to read or write Kurdish or Arabic, literacy in a new third language would be impossible. In February 1997, we were introduced to the Plotskys, a Jewish family who volunteered with IRC and were asked to teach my mother and sister-in-law English. Andi and Paul Plotsky were an accomplished couple who worked for Emory Medical School. They had two beautiful daughters, Melissa and Alyson. When Andi visited us, she would often bring Alyson with her, and she also volunteered to teach us English. Little did we know, the Plotskys would become lifelong friends who were instrumental in our resettlement journey. From the day we welcomed them into our small three-bedroom apartment in Clarkston until today, over twenty years later, the Plotskys have not missed a Sairany birthday, graduation, holiday, or wedding celebration. They have always been there for me, from helping with my world geography homework in the ninth grade, to filling out college and scholarship applications and giving me a ride to the Scholastic Aptitude Test (SAT) and Test of English as a Foreign Language (TOEFL) center. They were truly a godsend to us. As a matter of fact, we were first introduced to Thanksgiving through the Plotskys, when they hosted us and several other refugee families with whom we became acquainted over their Thanksgiving dinner table.

I admired everything about Andi and Paul, but what caught my attention most was their way of disciplining Melissa and Alyson. Andi was not inferior to Paul and Paul was not treated as the head of the household. They were equal partners, and both served as role models to their daughters. They often discussed how they should handle matters related to Melissa and Alyson's upbringing. Paul would often agree with what Andi found to be the best approach and even praise her for what she recommended. Andi had a home office where she let me work on my college essay using her office computer. She would get me started on the typing and then return to check on my progress. She would read the paragraph I typed, fix the grammatical mistakes, and share with me why certain words or phrases needed to be said in certain ways. She never made me feel guilty about the mistakes I often made. She told me that the English language was complex and many times the grammar did not make sense to her either.

We stayed in Clarkston for eighteen months before our search for a new house began. With the combined income of everyone in the family, we were able to afford a decent house in the Tucker area, a step up from Clarkston. The house that we liked, and later bought, had four bedrooms with a full basement. In the late spring of 1998, we moved from Clarkston to our new house in Tucker. We were the first Kurdish family in our community to buy a house. As part of the Kurdish tradition, when a family buys a new house, friends bring housewarming gifts. Unfortunately, almost every Kurdish family we knew in Clarkston brought us a clock for a housewarming gift. We ended up with so many clocks in the house, which was ironic considering Kurds are hardly ever punctual! Shayma and Omed shared the basement with their two children, while the rest of us and our parents occupied the four bedrooms upstairs.

We were all doing well eighteen months into our settlement in the United States. With hard work and late-night studies, my English improved tremendously. After taking an English assessment exam, the teacher at the International School I attended for half-days told me that my English was so improved that I was ready to start attending high school classes full time. In high school, however, two of the six classes I had every day were still ESL, which I attended with other refugee and immigrant students from Bosnia, Somalia, and Vietnam who spoke English at a similar level. The remaining four courses: political science, physical education, math, and science, I attended with American students. Based on the assessment exam, I was still not ready for English literature. I continued to struggle with my homework, but with the use of dictionaries and assistance from the Plotskys, I was able to excel in all my courses. I finished 10th grade with straight A's and received the highest grade in five out of my six classes.

Because of these achievements, my ESL teacher introduced me to one of her contacts at the *AtlantaJournal-Constitution* newspaper, who wanted me to write an article about how I was able to overcome the many challenges of school. After reading my story, the editor-in-chief chose "Hard Work Pays Off in U.S. Schools" for the title of my column in the newspaper.

Hard work pays off in U.S. schools

By Helen Ali-Sairany

My family used to live in a city in northern Iraq called Zakho.

In 1993, American troops came to Zakho to protect the Kurdish people from the Iraqi government.

My brother worked with the U.S. troops for almost three years as a guard, and he really enjoyed his job.

In the fall of 1997, I was going to be a ninth-grader. I was getting ready for school, buying school supplies, organizing notebooks, etc.

In the late morning of Sept. 14, I was helping my mother cook lunch. We all sat down at the table to eat.

Ali-Sairany

Suddenly, my brother opened the door and said that we were in danger. The Iraqi government had ordered all Kurds who cooperated with the United States to leave the country immediately.

We didn't know what else to do. We just packed our stuff and left.

The American soldiers with whom my brother had been working helped us and took us to Turkey. We stayed there for two days and then flew to Guam. We stayed on the tropical island for two months. Then they flew us to Hawaii, where we stayed for one night, and then to the mainland. We arrived in Georgia on Nov. 15.

After one week, my caseworker from the International Rescue Committee, the organization that sponsored my family, took me to the International Student Center in DeKalb County to test my understanding of English. I studied the language there for six weeks because my English was so bad. Then I started school at Tucker High.

In the beginning, I struggled a lot. I couldn't understand anything at all. I couldn't understand my teachers. The students helped me a lot by showing me the location of my classes. The teachers explained the chapters individually to me.

By and by, I got better. I used my dictionary to translate words I didn't know. I took the dictionary everywhere I went. I started reading children's books until I was able to read novels.

I ended the first year with a 4.0 grade point average, but my classes were all general level. The next year, I applied to the National Honor Society. I wasn't accepted because I was taking two English for Speakers of Other Languages classes and wasn't involved in any clubs.

SABIT CEKIN / Associated Press

Kurdish refugees arrive at a tent camp set up for them on the Iraq-Turkey border in September 1996.

The following year, I started taking advanced classes and participating in clubs. I was in six clubs and received many honors and recommendations from my teachers. I was accepted into the National Honor Society and Beta Club in 1998.

I am now in the top 10 percent of the junior class. I am a volunteer at Northlake Hospital and also at International Rescue Committee.

I have started looking at colleges. I want to attend Emory University and become a surgeon someday.

I have had a lot of experiences. I know what it is like to come to a new country and become a part of a different culture, different language and different people. I am grateful to all of the people who have helped me feel a part of this country.

Helen Ali-Sairany, 17, is a junior at Tucker High School in DeKalb County.

The Atlanta Constitution's column New Attitudes is written by readers ages 15 to 22. It gives young people a forum for discussing issues that affect their lives and older readers insight into the next generation.

To submit: Columns should be no more than 600 words. They can be sent via e-mail to oped@ajc.com; faxed to 404-526-5611; or mailed to 72 Marietta St. N.W., Atlanta, GA 30303.

An article I wrote for the Atlanta Journal-Constitution.

Over the course of my junior year in high school, my English improved, and I gained confidence. I did not want to use the fact that English was my third language as an excuse. I worked longer and harder to overcome the language barrier. For example, using my dictionary to read a page would take me two to three times longer than the average American student. In my junior year, I started enrolling in advanced classes. That year, I was accepted into the National Honor Society which was a huge accomplishment for me. During my senior year, I enrolled in all advanced placement (AP) college-level courses. And I was not focused only on grades. Alyson Plotsky, who was also in high school, suggested that I get involved in school clubs in preparation for my college applications. I joined honor clubs and got more involved in the community. With every small success, my self confidence continued to grow, and I slowly started to raise my hand and participate in class discussions—a far cry from the younger girl who used to wash the family dishes in the river.

During my senior year, Andi Plotsky and I started visiting colleges in the area. We narrowed our search to two schools, Emory University and Agnes Scott College. Emory was my top pick. With both schools being private, I knew I needed to work hard and get scholarships to pay my way through college. With help from Andi and my high school guidance counselor, I learned what was needed to be accepted—good grades, a solid personal statement, extracurricular activities, and a good SAT score.

I knew that being accepted to Emory or Agnes Scott would not be an easy process, but I was learning to have faith in myself and my story—coming to the U.S. as a refugee with nothing. And that was what I chose as a topic for my college essay. I shared my story on the college admission applications at both Emory and Agnes Scott. Rather than talk about how I excelled in my course work or how I was the ideal candidate for the rigorous course load offered at both institutions, I wrote about my vulnerability and my family's struggle trying to fulfill the American dream. I talked about my goals as a young refugee girl in America because at that point, reaching my goals was all I could talk about.

I had good grades and was involved in extracurricular activities, yet my concern was my SAT score, specifically the section on evidence-based reading and writing. The evidence-based reading and writing portion were comprised of two tests, one focused on reading and one on writing and language. I do not remember my exact scores, but I knew I did not do well in reading and writing. The exam was timed, and I tried my best to complete the reading. However, I was only halfway through when they called, "Time's up." With my low score, my college counselor recommended that I consider applying to a community college because my current English proficiency was not going to get me through Agnes Scott or Emory. I hated to hear my counselor's lowered expectations, and I knew deep within myself that I would succeed. I had to prove my counselor wrong because lowering my sights was exactly the opposite of what I had envisioned for myself all those years. I refused to doubt myself or listen to my family who would shout, "We told you so!" when I did not meet their expectations. I had to tune out all the negativity that surrounded me.

I received a rejection letter from Emory. However, not long after I was rejected from Emory University, I received a letter from Agnes Scott College offering me admission to their incoming class of 2004. As soon as I read the letter, I shouted the good news to my family and started translating the letter to Kurdish for my mother. I called Andi and Alyson to share the exciting news. My siblings and I celebrated that night with Hoger treating us all to ice cream at the local Dairy Queen. After finishing the fall semester of my senior year with straight A's and having an acceptance letter from Agnes Scott College, it was time to take a deep breath and celebrate the holidays with my family.

Music and dancing are integral to our culture; in fact, it is our way of life. It is through music and dancing that we Kurds protest, fight for our rights, excel through life, find a spouse, hold gatherings, picnic in the mountains, and raise a family. As a child in Kurdistan, I remember watching the different dances from each village of Kurdistan, each with its own unique variation and name.

For New Years' parties, Kurds dress in traditional Kurdish outfits to celebrate, with women's dresses being particularly colorful. Thankfully, we knew a few Kurdish refugees who could sing and play Kurdish musical instruments. Jowan, in her work at the IRC, was tasked with developing activities for the Kurdish community, one being the New Year's celebration. I remember Jowan intentionally meddling with the start time of the party knowing that Kurds were notoriously late showing up to events. She had learned that if she said the party started at 7 p.m., Kurds would not show up until 8 or 9 at night. However, if she said the start time was 5 p.m., then the party could really start at 7 which was what she intended all along. We had so much fun dancing until late at night at those parties organized by the IRC with the Kurdish band. In the traditional Kurdish style, we danced in a big circle holding each other's pinkies (called govend by Kurds). Typically, at a party, a few inquiring mothers would spot me for their sons, and the next day, calls would be made from those mothers asking to pay us a visit in Tucker.

Being the tallest girl in the family, I was always mistaken for the oldest sister. With our involvement in the Kurdish community, the new Kurdish families for whom we would translate knew the Sairany family had girls of marriageable age whom they could pursue to marry their sons. During my two decades of living in the U.S., I have seen many changes occur in the Kurdish diaspora in America. Unfortunately, one phenomenon that has not changed and continues to puzzle me is the institution of arranged marriage, though in theory, I recognize that in some cases people may benefit from a little matchmaking.

The vast majority of Kurdish families I know, including my own, choose arranged marriage over marrying for love. Many young Kurdish men fear educated and independent girls because they are "harder to control." Oftentimes, families return to Kurdistan to find a young dutiful girl for their son instead of an educated woman in the U.S. who is used to a different life here. Once they find a girl back home, they propose, have her become engaged to their son, and start the paperwork to bring her to America. The same happens with Kurdish girls. A girl's parents bring her back to Kurdistan to find a suitor who is less educated and far less experienced about the challenges of living in the U.S. for their daughter.

Some arranged marriages happen in the form of a direct exchange to avoid naxt (the bride price), also known as a dowry. The naxt varies according to the wealth and social status of the family. Exchange marriages work as follows: if one household head gives a daughter or a sister to another household as a wife for their son or brother, they expect a wife for their son or brother in return. In certain cases, the arranged marriage exchange will involve three families where family A gives a daughter or sister to family B, family then B gives a daughter or sister to family C and family C gives a daughter or sister to family A. If this sounds unfair to the brides, that is because it is, as their desires are hardly considered if at all. It also makes women seem more like items to barter than human beings with their own dreams and desires for their life. Of note, some revolutionary Kurdish institutions have developed the idea of Jineology (science of women) to study and fix issues such as this in our society—but I digress.

Once married, if a woman becomes a widow, she usually stays with her in-laws. If she has young children, she may marry one of her brothers-in-law, who then becomes a father to the children of his deceased brother. Most Kurdish marriages are monogamous, but that is not to say that polygamous marriage does not exist. The Islamic faith allows a man to marry up to four wives at one time if he fulfills the Islamic obligations towards each wife. The husband is responsible to provide for each wife and the children produced by each, including a house, food, and clothing. In addition, the husband is obligated to give equal attention to each wife.

The Kurdish mothers who visited us would ask me or Dilven, who was four years younger, to perform certain tasks to make sure we were healthy—cracking open nuts to be sure we had solid teeth, serving tea and sweets so they could see if we had any deformity or limp when we walked, or engaging in conversation to ensure that we were shy and modest, not controlling or bossy. All these tasks made Dilven and I extremely uncomfortable, considering we had three older sisters who were more marriage appropriate. Kurdish parents are famous for choosing the youngest and most attractive female in one's family for their son. The maturity or education level of a girl often does not matter. The marriage conversation is always initiated by the female heads of the households, who also take care of all the naxt negotiations and asks in terms of nishani. The men only get involved once both families agree. Ironically, the result of these customs is that it is women, not men, who are the 'guardians' of this patriarchal model.

The thought of even marrying a Kurdish man from my community had not occurred to me. I was focused on starting college and I had always assumed the Kurdish families who visited would consider my older sisters. My mother would do her best to explain that I was only seventeen and there were three sisters ahead of me before she could consider me for marriage. However, the mothers still insisted on wanting me instead to marry their sons. That was when my mother pushed back and said that I was focused on going to college and marriage was not on my agenda. The mothers promised to let me go to college and pursue my dreams while married to their sons. At times, the same family would stubbornly make multiple attempts, hoping I had changed my mind about marriage.

When it came to marriage, my parents made it clear that the decision to accept or decline a marriage proposal was mine because ultimately it would be me living with the individual. However, they made it apparent to all of us, that whoever we chose to marry must first be Kurdish and second Muslim. To me, this felt like an unjust decision the family had made for us because most of the Kurds we knew did not pursue higher education, and those who did were not interested in a girl like me with a strong will.

Growing up with six boys in the family, I was nicknamed Aysha Kurani, meaning a tomboy. I loved dressing up like a boy and would sometimes go to the extent of beating up boys who dared to harass Zerak. There were times they would stop arguing with Zerak when I got in the way because they viewed themselves as men, and it is not honorable for a man to argue with a woman. My brothers teased me about the marriage proposals I received from those Kurdish families, which of course annoyed me. After every proposal, my brothers would tell our mother, “Next time a Kurdish family calls for Heleen to marry their son, just tell them you do not have a daughter, you have a police officer.”

While at school, I could joke with my male classmates without serious consequences, even about issues like a marriage proposal. But within the Kurdish community, I had to tone down my comfort with talking casually to men. A man’s affection towards a woman is seen as a sign of weakness among Kurdish men, something I never understood considering the romantic depth of the Kurdish and Arabic languages. I seldom remember my father showing affection to my mother in front of us. It made me wonder how the eleven children all came about! My older brothers always treated us with seriousness. At seventeen, I started to notice how differently non-Kurdish men treated their wives in public. In Kurdish culture, there are no public displays of affection, for instance.

I also noticed how American men would do small flirtatious gestures with their wives or assist with the child-rearing. Some even changed their children's diapers in public, something that was total blasphemy in the Kurdish culture. Did I really want to be with a serious man all my life? Or did I want to be with an American who often expected chemistry and physical contract prior to marriage? Or perhaps I wanted a little mix of both worlds? Sometimes, I felt as though I wanted to date like an American girl where I would be loved with no commitment to marriage. While other times, I found myself a mirror version of my mother, arranged marriage with a Kurdish man I hardly knew. Every time I imagined myself on one path, I yearned for the other, a feeling that never made sense to me and would chase me throughout my adult life.

CHAPTER V:
A REFUGEE WITH CONTRADICTIONS

Growing up as a refugee in America, I experienced two things.
The first opened me up to the difficulties of adulthood.
The second reinforced the fact that for someone like me—
a female refugee, a minority, a Kurdish-American—
there were limits.

Agnes Scott College, Decatur, Georgia.

The summer between my graduation from high school and the start of my freshman year of college was an exciting one—I was the first Kurdish female from my community to attend college and I had secured enough scholarship money to pay my way through Agnes Scott. Also, I had recently been promoted to cashier at the supermarket and that came with a pay raise to $7.50/hour. As I finished high school, I had so many questions running through my mind: *What should my college major be? What activities should I get involved in? Where and how would I finish my homework?* One question others often asked me was, with Agnes Scott College being all-girls, was I worried about finding a man to date?

"No! I am not," I kept explaining. Why would I be worried when I knew I was not allowed to date anyway? After all, according to my family, any man I wanted to marry had to be a Kurdish Muslim.

I could not have been happier to start college. Agnes Scott was a Presbyterian-based institution in Decatur, Georgia. Each day, I took the train from Avondale to the Decatur transit station to reach campus. On my return trip, the Avondale station was across the street from the IRC office, where Jowan worked. Once at Avondale, I would call Jowan and she would pick me up so we could ride home together.

Agnes Scott's campus had about thirty buildings, including a gorgeous red brick-and-stone Victorian building that had won national awards for its design. I was fascinated by how beautiful the campus was. I took photos of it to show to my cousins back home in Kurdistan and bragged about how picturesque it was. The college put a lot of time and energy into the week-long orientation for incoming freshmen to get us ready for the next four years. I had a chance to meet with advisors for information about the various science majors. I toured all the laboratory facilities and met the science professors. I was also assigned an older "Scottie" sister. She was two years ahead of me and would check to make sure I was adjusting to college and had everything I needed for the first year.

During orientation week, I registered for five classes: English literature, calculus, general college physics, chemistry, and biology. Each of the three science classes had an accompanying lab every week. When the semester started, I was in lab from 2 to 5 p.m. every Tuesday through Thursday. I did not have much of social life at Agnes Scott because I was not allowed by my parents to live in the campus dormitory. This was frustrating because I felt as though I was missing out on real college life and evening activities. I was only on campus to take classes and complete my science experiments. The breaks between classes and labs would be spent in the writing center getting help with my writing skills for the English literature class. While in high school, I was often told that my college years would be the best days of my life. Now that I look back, my college experience was not that different from high school. As soon as I was done with my labs and classes, I would take public transit and meet Jowan at Avondale Station or have one of my brothers pick me up outside the campus to drive me home.

The first few months of classes were a huge adjustment, considering that the standards were much higher than high school. The curriculum at Agnes Scott was extremely rigorous. At that time, Agnes Scott was ranked No. 1 among national liberal arts colleges on the list of

Most Innovative Schools in *U.S. News & World Report* and second nationally for Best Undergraduate Teaching. After four years in the United States, I was still catching up on my reading speed and writing skills, which meant that the course work was even harder for me. My English literature professors would often give me a few extra days to work on my essays with a tutor at the writing center, which I really appreciated.

Over the years, most Kurds who were initially assigned to settle in Georgia had relocated to either Nashville or Texas. The city of Nashville is considered the "Kurdish capital" of the U.S., since over 10,000 Kurds reside there. Many have become an integral and vibrant part of that community. Some of these families managed to preserve their cultural practices by living in an insulated bubble at the expense of their children. Most had their sons married to female cousins back home.

My family started thinking about moving to a place where there were more Kurds and a more diverse community. Most of Omed's and Hoger's friends, with whom they kept in touch, lived in Michigan. Those friends recommended that my mother and older siblings visit Michigan to explore the community.

While in Michigan, our friends took my mother, Omed, and Hoger to Detroit, a city that had a large population of Iraqi refugees. Once they saw the community and all it had to offer, my family fell in love with the Middle Eastern vibe they got in Michigan. Ann Arbor had an Islamic public school system up to high school, which was a key determining factor in my family's move to Michigan. My parents did not want my younger siblings to assimilate completely to American culture and realized that having them attend an Islamic school would be ideal to preserve their faith and cultural practices. I did not feel strongly about this decision by my parents, but I disagreed. I had attended a non-Islamic high school and did not change one bit! In my opinion, my siblings should have been allowed to attend non-Islamic schools just as Zerak and I had, to better prepare them for life in America.

No Christian American students could attend the Islamic public school. The school was strictly for students from Muslim households. All the little girls, including Dilven, were required to cover their hair and were often separated from their boy classmates. The curriculum covered the basic courses like world history, geography, math, and science. However, the topics that were contrary to Islamic teachings, like Sigmund Freud's ideas on sexuality and Charles Darwin's theory of evolution were not discussed, which automatically narrowed my siblings' way of thinking.

By now, we had gone through countless transitions and moves between cities, countries, and even continents. I was emotionally exhausted. I had hoped the family would be settled by this time so we could start feeling the joy of stability in our lives. However, not long after their visit to Michigan, the decision was made to relocate the family there. At eighteen, I took a firm position that I was not making the move to Michigan! I had worked so hard to get into Agnes Scott and receive scholarships to pay my way that I was not ready to give up everything and start over again. Telling my parents this was very emotional for me. But they understood and decided to leave me, Zerak, Jowan, Zhyan, and Hoger in Georgia with my father, while my mother went to Michigan with Omed and the rest of the family.

It was difficult for everyone when my mother and half of my siblings moved to Michigan. We had never lived apart, even when we had to leave Kurdistan. Jowan and I took on the extra responsibility of cooking and cleaning the house in addition to working and my taking a full course load at Agnes Scott. However, not long after my family moved to Michigan, my younger siblings were struggling with the new school system and the rough winter days in Ann Arbor. They started to miss Georgia. My older siblings were not able to find the jobs they had hoped for in Michigan, and eventually my family realized that the move there had not been a smart one. At the end of the academic year, they returned south to Georgia.

That same year, Hoger, who was twenty-eight by then, was entertaining the idea of getting married. His best friend had recommended he marry his younger sister, Jehan. Of my brothers, Hoger was, by far, the most rational and social. He valued family and relationships and had gone to college and lived on his own in Mosul for several years. He was quite handsome and often called the "brown George Clooney" by friends. Several Kurdish girls in the diaspora who were highly educated had shown interest in Hoger, and we were in support of his marrying someone of his intellectual level who already lived in America. However, Hoger perceived the Kurdish girls in Atlanta to be too westernized. To him, this meant they were more open to talking to other men, dressing indecently, and more likely to stand up to their husbands, which he did not find to be marriage-worthy.

Unfortunately for him, Hoger had to wait until he got his citizenship and apply for a U.S. passport before he was able to leave the country. Once he had the necessary paperwork, the decision was made. Hoger and my mother got ready to return to Kurdistan to find him a wife. Before takeoff, my mother called our relatives back home to share the news of their visit. As soon as the news made it to Zakho and Erbil, every family member in Kurdistan needed a favor. Hoger ended up with a long list of items they wished him to bring with him: technology gadgets including cameras and DVD players, T-shirts, vitamins, jewelry, perfumes, etc. My cousins, aunts, and uncles asked my mother and Hoger for everything they could possibly think of and my mother did not have the heart to turn anyone down. The next thing I knew my mother and Hoger ended up with six large suitcases full of goods to take back with them to Kurdistan. Right before departure, Hoger bought a video camera so he could record all of us and the fancy buildings in our city in order to show them how nice and developed America was.

With no airport in Erbil at the time and Kurds not having access to Iraqi Kurdistan through Turkey, their only way of returning was through Syria. One thing worth mentioning is that every Kurd who returned to Kurdistan had to pay extra for the overweight suitcases. Most Kurds who left through Guam came from large households and every family member living in Kurdistan needed goods from the U.S. that they could not acquire there.

When they finally reached Syria, Hoger and my mother spent a few days in Damascus and from there they made their way to Qamishli, located in the Kurdish part of northern Syria, now called Rojava (Western Kurdistan) where they had to hire a motor canoe to cross the Tigris river into Iraq. From there, my uncles and cousins were waiting to receive them and their suitcases.

The first few days after their arrival was overwhelming. My female cousins all showcased for Hoger, hoping that he would ask one of them to marry. As much as this might sound strange, marrying a first cousin in Kurdish culture is totally normal. Hoger, however, had Jehan in mind and wanted to see what she looked like. When my family visited Kurdistan, they often left for a whole month since it took a few days to reach Zakho and another three days to return. The same six suitcases that they brought would, over the weeks, fill back up with Kurdish fabric, spices, gold, souvenirs, and gifts from aunts, uncles, and cousins for us all upon their return.

Someone like Hoger, who lived in the diaspora, could marry a girl from any family living in Kurdistan. Hoger found Jehan to be a good fit. The whole family, including me, had concerns because Jehan came from a family with a higher socioeconomic status. Jehan had never lived abroad and did not understand the struggles of living in a country where everything was so different from what she knew. Plus, Jehan had never experienced poverty as we had, nor was she on the same intellectual level as Hoger.

Since Omed was married with children to look after, Hoger had spent more time making sure we were doing well in school and that our needs were fulfilled. He would often drive me to the mall and pick out clothes he thought would suit my age and body shape. Hoger thought the world of me and often bragged about how smart I was. When I was admitted to Agnes Scott, he committed to giving me a ride to and from Agnes Scott whenever Jowan was not able to pick me up. On our way to class, he would drive by BMW and Mercedes dealerships and remind me, "You will graduate with a degree and one day own one of those. Just do not forget about me when you do." During our rides, he would also turn the volume up on his stereo and blare Kurdish songs by Zakaria Abdulla. Because the lyrics of the songs described women's breasts as pomegranates, I would always get bashful hearing him sing the words. Hoger and I were the same exact height and I often accompanied him to shop for Jehan's engagement gifts. The most memorable outing was when Hoger and I went shopping for her engagement ring and the lady at the counter thought I was his fiancée. I was all smiles, and the lady asked if I was excited. To this day, Hoger teases me, asking if I am still excited to be engaged to him.

Unlike Omed's wedding, Hoger's had to match Jehan's expensive taste. Jehan asked for way more gold and her nishani (bridal gifts) was much more than what Shayma had. For Jehan, every gifted item had to have a designer brand name. As for the wedding, everything had to be rated with a certain number of stars, including the photographer, videographer, wedding venue, and even the cake. Any of our gifts that were not to her liking, she would criticize and refuse to put them on. She also refused to share the same house and neighborhood with us, so Hoger had to get a separate apartment for her.

Once Hoger married Jehan, his life and relationship with the family were consumed by Jehan. Anything that did not exceed her expectations was criticized by her and her family. Regardless of what Hoger had to offer, it was never as good as what she used to get from her father and brothers, including the wedding ceremony, jewelry, gifts, the house, and furniture. It bothered me to see how unappreciative she was of my brother, yet no one in my family dared to stand up to her. I tried to stay out of it, considering I was occupied with college and planning for pharmacy school. However, when her criticism involved me and my values, I had to stand up for myself.

I was likely the only one of my siblings who never held anything back, especially when it came to my principles. Coming to the U.S. at a young age, I grew up believing in hard work and being self-made. When I was criticized by someone using her father's name for status, it was hard not to push back.

Following Hoger, Jowan and Zerak later returned to Kurdistan to meet and marry their significant others. Of all my siblings, Zerak was the only one who married a second cousin, someone that my mother had chosen for him to marry because she was related to my mother. As strange as this may sound, during one of the visits to my uncle's home in Erbil, they forced my female cousin, Dilkhwaz, to sit across from Zerak in a room and then asked Zerak if he would take her for a wife. Zerak, although uncomfortable, agreed, and they were married in a matter of weeks. Instead of one wedding, Zerak ended up with two: one in Erbil and a bigger one in the U.S. when his wife finally managed to immigrate over.

My brother Dlovan was also pressured into an arranged engagement with our seventeen-year-old cousin, Sayran. My mother was the mastermind of all these arranged marriages, and she was also the one who set the standards for an ideal wife, which were: youth, attractive looks, colorful non-brown eyes, and submissiveness. When Dlovan went back to Kurdistan with my mother, he was introduced to Sayran and asked to check her out. Sayran, just like Dilkhwaz, was not allowed to finish high school because girls were meant to stay home, and it was the responsibility of the husband to provide for them.

Dlovan, only twenty-one at the time, agreed to my mother's choice for a wife and proceeded to get engaged to Sayran in a small celebration where the two exchanged rings. After his engagement, Dlovan returned to the U.S. immediately to work on Sayran's immigration paperwork and bring her to America. However, things quickly fell through. Sayran's father agreed to proceed with the marriage under the condition that Dlovan take Sayran's brother to America also. Knowing this was not going to be possible, Sayran's father used this as an excuse to end things with Dlovan so they could keep the dowry that Dlovan had given Sayran on the engagement day.

The arranging of all the marriages by my mother made me feel uneasy. The thought of marriage would run through my head every now and then, but I did not want to get involved with a cousin nor was I interested in arranged marriage. So, I knew marriage would have to wait in my case. I was not against the idea so long as I acquired a professional degree of some sort and started making a living. Plus, I was still undecided about my college major and had my mind focused on either dental, medical, or pharmacy school after graduation.

To my father, nothing was more important than having his eldest son (Omed) educated because one day, he would be responsible for providing for the entire family. From his perspective, this made sense when you considered the limited opportunities available to women in Kurdistan. However, my father did not prefer his sons to his daughters. In fact, he wanted all his children to be educated and make good use of their education.

To an average family in Kurdistan, if you were not a lawyer, engineer, or doctor, your degree was simply not good enough. They valued degrees that involved technical skills more than those that involved the humanities such as drama, philosophy, or history. So, when I chose pharmacy in my junior year of college, my father asked if pharmacy school was as good as medicine. I told him that pharmacy was medicine! "Will you still be called a doctor?" he asked.

"Yes, babu (dad), in pharmacy school I will get a doctorate and people will call me a doctor."

With his concerns squelched, my father was immensely proud that for the very first time, a child of his was going to pursue a graduate degree and carry the title of doctor.

On the early morning of September 11, 2001, the terrorist attacks by al-Qaeda on the World Trade Center and Twin Towers changed the scope of personal life in ways I could not have imagined. The tragic day itself brought back memories of the car bomb market explosion I had experienced as a child, and repressed trauma surged back up to the surface as I cried for the victims and their families. The attacks also punctured the presumed safety I felt I had in America. I realized there was no such thing as a country free of terrorism.

To make matters worse, to many angry Americans, there was no distinction between the Muslims who caused the attack and those that didn't. This great country that had welcomed me with open arms in 1996—after all my traumatic experiences in Iraq—became uncomfortable aggressive towards me. I was called a terrorist and linked with the masterminds of the 9/11 attacks based on the assumption that we somehow shared the same beliefs, a notion as absurd as presupposing that most Christians agree with the Ku Klux Klan who similarly pervert the Bible's teachings.

Because I was wearing my hijab, strangers would stop their cars and throw trash at me, call me names, and shout, "Go back to where you came from!" These racist encounters happened on a near-daily basis, some small, others blatant. I started to worry about my own safety and if someone would physically harm me or a member of my family. I shared my concerns with my siblings and told them I was worried about taking the public transit system because of these racist encounters.

My mother recommended that I remove my hijab. I refused because removing my hijab meant that I was giving in to the false narratives and letting bigotry win. In fact, the persecution made me feel even more attached to my hijab. I was ready to tolerate racist comments and keep my hair covered for as long as I could. However, with this determination came a huge responsibility. While wearing my hijab, I had to work extra hard to demonstrate how my faith meant peace and not terrorism. I would go out of my way to show kindness and love. One encounter I had was with a sweet little (presumably Christian) girl at the supermarket. I was working in the bakery department and when I handed the girl a cookie, she thanked me and said to her mother, "Mommy! I got a cookie from the Virgin Mary."

Her mother looked up to see me. Suddenly, her facial expression changed. She angrily returned the cookie, grabbed her daughter by the hand, and stormed away from the bakery.

In the aftermath of 9/11, the Dean of Student Affairs at Agnes Scott held an urgent meeting with all Muslim students and advised us to avoid using the public transit system. Faculty members, as well as volunteers from the campus, would take turns driving me home on days one of my brothers could not pick me up. I was overwhelmed by the love and support I got from everyone on campus, and it truly made me feel that this was the America that had welcomed me with open arms previously.

Soon thereafter, I was introduced to a Southern Baptist minister who had assisted a few Kurdish families to come to the U.S. through Guam. These families had told him how goal-oriented and accomplished I was, and he asked to be introduced to me. It felt strange to get an email from this minister whom I did not know but who complimented me and wanted to meet me. I thanked him for his kind words but asked why he wanted to meet.

He emailed me back to tell me that he was stunned to learn that an accomplished young lady like me had fallen for an "evil" religion like Islam that promotes the killing of innocent civilians.

Not sure what to make of his response, I shared the email with the Dean of Students at Agnes Scott. The Dean informed me that his words were offensive and asked if she could handle the matter on my behalf. And I thankfully never heard from him again.

I seldom talk about my faith and the impact it has had on my growth in America. Coming from a patriarchal culture and society, I would say that my faith granted me the right as a woman to fight for what I believed in. It is hard to believe that the God of any faith, including Islam, Judaism, or Christianity, would encourage the suffering or killing of innocent civilians. However, there are people within each religious group who choose to interpret and practice their faith differently. We have a verse in the Holy Quran (5:32) which says that if you kill a person, not in retaliation of murder or to cause mischief, it is as if you have killed all mankind—on the other hand, saving a single life is like saving all mankind.

Clearly, the deranged members of al-Qaeda or similar groups do not adhere to this advice.

Just like anything in life, I believe your attitude defines who you are. If your mindset is strict, then your way of practicing your faith is likely to be strict. If you are tense and angry in your approach, your practice of your faith will also be angry and tense. I did not think it was fair for that minister to condemn all practicing Muslims for the brutal act of a few terrorists whose victims also included Muslims in those towers. But it seemed, following the 9/11 attacks, that as an identifiable Muslim, I now had to answer for every crazy, extreme, or misguided supposed follower of Islam in the world—and there were over a billion followers.

Friday afternoons were my usual work time at the supermarket. One Friday after classes, I asked a classmate for a ride to my job. I did not see the need to call my family to tell them I was headed to work because Fridays were my usual workday. I also did not carry a cell phone for my family to reach me. Failing to hear from me and not knowing my whereabouts, my family feared that something serious had happened to me. My mother sent four of my brothers to look for me on the college campus and in the Decatur area. As I entered the store to begin my shift, the intercom was sounding, "Helen, if you are in the store, please come to customer service."

I rushed to customer service and they handed me the phone. It was my mother, who was in tears. She asked why I did not call to tell her I was headed to work. She wanted to see me immediately to make sure I was fine. The store was about a seven-minute drive from where we lived, and my boss excused me for a quick break to check on my mother. Hoger was already outside the store to pick me up. Once we approached the intersection near our house, my mother, in her Kurdish gown, was outside waiting for me. This shows the impact that the 9/11 attacks had on all Muslim American families, including mine. After this incident, my family decided to get me a cell phone. They made it clear that the phone was for emergency calls only, so I would not be distracted by texts and calls with friends. I was excited to finally have a cell phone and used it to talk with my mother and siblings throughout the day to let them know my whereabouts.

One evening, I had to stay late on campus for a guest speaker event featuring Angela Davis. Attending the event and writing a paper about it was part of a psychology course assignment. Earlier that day, I told my mother I would be coming home late in the evening. Not remembering I had called, my mother had left me three angry voicemails for being late. I skipped the book signing by Angela Davis and rushed outside to listen to the voicemails. My mother was not only mad at me for being late, but she also went to the extent of threatening to stop me from continuing college! Terrified by those voicemails,

I asked my friend Alexis to give me a ride home. That evening, Alexis and I rushed to my house and arrived around eleven. Fearing my mother's reaction, I asked Alexis to come into the house with me. Alexis, through translation, told my mother that we had an important event for class that had made me late. Hearing from Alexis reassured my mother that I was late for a good reason. She finally calmed down and started serving Kurdish tea and sweets.

Later she noticed Alexis rubbing my back and pulled me into a corner to ask me if Alexis was a lesbian. I honestly had no idea and did not know how to address this embarrassing question at the time, so I waited until the following day to ask Alexis myself.

Never having had a friend from the LGBTQ+ community, I was not sure how to talk with Alexis without offending her. So, I figured I would ask her if she had a boyfriend. I reasoned that was a safe question because if she was a lesbian, she would tell me she did not date boys. So, I asked her if she had a boyfriend and she answered, "I do have a boyfriend, but I am open to dating either."

I was now even more confused and asked her to explain. "I can have intimate feelings for both genders," she added.

I then asked, "So you can sleep with both?"

She laughed hard and said, "Only one at a time. If I happen to be dating a guy, then I will sleep with him. And if I was dating a girl, then a girlfriend it is."

I was not 100% certain what she was trying to tell me, but I think I was a little closer to understanding the back rub that my observant mother had noticed the night before. It was also an interesting window into how much

I had been sheltered sexually that it never occurred to me that she could be bisexual.

People on campus were bewildered to see that Alexis, a member of the LGBTQ community, was best friends with me, a practicing Muslim girl in hijab. It never occurred to Alexis or me until many years later that we both had one thing in common. We both grew up being rejected for things that were outside our control, and we both strove for a sense of belonging.

For my own safety, I had to stop working at the supermarket and was offered a job at the campus bookstore. I felt safe in the bookstore, and friends and professors stopped by frequently to check on me. I loved working there and the freedom I was given to decorate the store's mannequins and window displays with my color and fashion taste. I got a lot of compliments on how I could mix and match colors to captivate the customer. I would also play Kurdish and Arabic music on the bookstore stereo even though my friends teased me about playing it.

The downside of working at the campus bookstore was I would be without a job during the summer. Since I was planning to attend pharmacy school after I graduated from Agnes Scott, I wanted to spend some time working as a technician in a pharmacy. I asked Zhyan to drive me to local pharmacies to ask if they had any openings for a pharmacy technician. Finally, a pharmacist at a local CVS asked me to return to discuss a job opportunity. When I returned for the interview, the pharmacist greeted me and asked me several personal questions. Instead of telling me about the job opportunity, he lectured me about the United States constitution and Christianity. I had a bad feeling that this person thought I was pro-al-Qaeda because of my hijab. I excused myself because the discussion was not going anywhere, and politely shook his hand. He held my hand tightly and in a threatening voice said, “In America, this is how we shake hands.”

When I got into the car, Zhyan noticed how pale I looked. I told her about my encounter with the pharmacist. Being protective of me, she wanted to go into the store and tell the pharmacist that what he did was not professional or ethical and he could get fired. For my part, I just wanted to go home.

The following day, I had another interview that Zhyan offered to drive me to. This job was for a front desk receptionist at a private clinic run by a Muslim couple. I felt my chances of getting a job would be better there as I assumed they would be more accepting of my hijab. However, the couple informed me that they were not comfortable with my running the front desk in my headscarf because I would “scare off all the patients.” To make up for the offensive remarks, the wife who helped run the clinic asked if I would be willing to take care of her mother at home instead, a suggestion that angered Zhyan, who then grabbed my arm and rushed me out of the place.

Such actions were typical of Zhyan, who was my most protective sibling. I always saw Zhyan as the leader of the family who followed up on her words, and her wisdom resonated with me over the years. She also had many talents, which included being the best cook in the family, an innovator with amazing creativity, and having an indomitable will, which made her tough as a rock. Despite holding a full-time job, she finished her bachelor's, master's, and doctorate degrees.

As for me, I was still struggling to find a job. A friend of mine, an undergraduate at Emory, was working in the neurobiology lab at Emory Medical School. She called me one day to tell me the lab needed another technician. They were paying $9 per hour, which was significant, considering I was making only $7.50 an hour at the supermarket. With my friend's connections at Emory, I was able to start working there immediately. To get to work, I rode to the Decatur station with Jowan and caught the Emory shuttle from Agnes Scott to Emory Medical School. After two months of working in the laboratory, I realized I was not happy running experiments all day, but at least the job helped me realize I wanted a job that involved human interaction. While at Emory, I was introduced to the head of the Department of Middle Eastern Studies, Dr. Mahmoud. He asked if I was willing to work as a research assistant to transcribe Arabic videos into English transcripts. Suddenly, I went from unemployed to holding two jobs. I would transcribe for Dr. Mahmoud partly at home and a few days a week at the university library.

I was in the library one day when a man named Ali introduced himself to me. He was tall, handsome, and polite. Wearing a hijab at the university campus was equivalent to carrying a sign saying that I was Muslim. After 9/11, wearing a hijab was a huge responsibility because whatever I did, people associated my actions with the entire Islamic faith. This was exhausting because I was human and susceptible to making mistakes just like anyone else. The fact that people associated my flaws with my faith was upsetting.

Ali asked where I was from and what brought me to Emory since he did not remember meeting me at any of the Arab Student Club meetings. I told him that I was not a student at Emory but working with Dr. Mahmoud for the summer. I was nervous talking with him and finally told him that I needed to leave because of my workload. Ali then asked if he could have my phone number. "I am sorry, but I do not carry a cell phone," I responded.

He asked if he could visit me again in the library. I told him I was busy, but we could have lunch one of the days I was on campus.

I later learned Ali visited the university library almost every day looking for me. One day, he finally spotted me on my way to the cafeteria and asked if he could join me for lunch. As we were eating, Ali shared that he was half Lebanese and half Iranian and was intrigued by me. I told him that we could be friends, but there was no way I was going to get involved in a relationship with him. He agreed that we should not rush into what we should call each other but asked if I would keep an open mind. Over the course of several months, Ali and I became close. He was easy going and more of a friend than a boyfriend. I told him about my background and that my family would not allow me to date or marry someone of his ethnic background. Clearly, Ali and I had feelings for each other, but we were not ready to make a commitment nor were we ready to fight for the feelings we had. I wanted to believe that Ali could be a man who meant everything to me: affectionate, loving, and impactful enough in his love to make me rearrange my priorities.

Then Ali called me once while I was at home and my brother Zerak caught me talking to him. He immediately began berating me as a "whore" for having a boyfriend.

"How can I be a whore?" I asked. "I have never even kissed a boy!"

I tried to explain that Ali and I were just friends, but to no avail. Zerak went into a crazy rage that prevented him from comprehending anything I was saying. He then began pulling me by my hair down the hallway to the living room while accusing me of bringing shame to the family.

His accusations made my family frantic. Would I become the girl in the Kurdish community with a bad reputation? They all began yelling at me and questioning my true intentions. All I could do was sit in the corner of the living room with my knees pressed against my chest confused and scared of what would happen to me as many paranoid thoughts ran through my mind.

After the beating and insults, as punishment, my family took my phone away and threatened to withdraw me from Agnes Scott. Tragically, I blamed myself for how they reacted and felt I should have known better than to give a boy my telephone number. It is strange, looking back, at how I made excuses for their abuse because of how much I loved them.

I immediately cut off all contact with Ali.

When Alexis—who I considered to be a best friend as she was always so sweet and understood my problems—heard about the Ali situation, she recommended I run away. But I knew that was not an option. I did not want to disgrace my family by having them tarnished as the family that made their daughter flee the household.

Alexis sympathetically tried to explain to me that their reaction was not acceptable, but I did not listen and just explained to her how I needed to hold out until I finished Agnes Scott. The sad reality was that since Zerak was the older male in the family, his abuse was seen as justified and in defense of the family's "honor." In Kurdish culture, the "purity" of the woman is of paramount importance to the reputation of the family. If the woman is perceived to taint her "purity," she has to be eliminated from the family just as cancer has to be eliminated from the body. Over the years Zerak often hit me and made disparaging comments about my applying makeup, or even liking boys. He was "the son" (carrying the family's honor), while I was "the daughter" (seen as a risky burden).

During the fall semester of my junior year, I finally chose my major. After taking two psychology classes, I knew I loved human psychology, so I decided on psychology first. In addition to psychology, I excelled in the sciences, so I chose biology as a second major. I also decided to apply to pharmacy school. To meet the requirements for my major, I had to take a psychology course each semester, and there was only one available for me to take—the Psychology of Sexuality, a taboo topic that we never discussed at home.

I was torn between my course requirements and the amount of explaining I would need to do when my family discovered I was taking the course. I remember meeting with the course professor, Dr. Jennifer Hughes, who is now a dear friend of mine, to share my concerns about the course content. When I had a question but was too embarrassed to ask, Jennifer encouraged me to write my question on a piece of paper and slide it under her office door. She promised to get back to me via email. I also hid the book from my family and covered the images in the textbook, so when I was seen studying, the images in the book showed no signs that they were about sexuality.

The most uncomfortable part about the course was when controversial topics were discussed through a case presentation. Following the case, we would be asked if the sex was forced or voluntary. The girls in class would then comment. Some would even go to the extent of talking about their own experiences. Dr. Hughes assigned questions and had us work in groups to share our opinions. I was afraid to express my opinion, fearing how my naïve takes would be perceived by my classmates. For example, one question was at what age should people stop practicing sex. Having no perspective on this topic, I naively put down forty-five.

In a very non-judgmental way, Alexis explained that people should practice sex as long as they wanted to, and she thought forty-five was way too early for people to stop having sex. I felt that I had said something I was not supposed to. I could not think of a reason why I picked forty-five; maybe because my cultural upbringing made me see sex as an act connected to procreation rather than pleasure, and I did not conceive of women having children past their child-bearing age. Nevertheless, it revealed how I was not properly educated on human sexuality.

We had to complete a semester-long project that counted for 25% of the course grade. I met with Dr. Hughes to get permission to do my project on the cruel and sexist practice of Female Genital Mutilation (FGM), which was still rampant in many parts of the world, including some rural areas of Kurdistan. She gave me the green light to proceed with the topic. I picked FGM because the practice bothered me, and I wanted to bring awareness about it to the women in my class. Many girls who went through FGM suffered from extreme pain and lack of orgasms in their married life. FGM was imposed on them without considering the long-term consequences to their health and psychological well-being. The procedure involved the cutting or removal of some or all the female clitoris and external genitalia in order to control a woman's sexuality by limiting her sensations during intercourse. Most families feared that if they failed to have their daughters and granddaughters cut, they might expose them to social exclusions or that they might be overly promiscuous since sex would then be too enjoyable.

Many people assumed that men were the main enforcers of FGM; however, it was usually the elderly women who kept the tradition alive. The grandmothers were the ones who passed the suffering that was inflicted on them on to their daughters and granddaughters. Various non-sterile sharp instruments were used to remove the clitoral hood and glans, the inner labia, and outer labia. The procedure varied, depending on the "circumciser" (mutilator). Some were close to the vulva, leaving a small hole for the passage of urine and menstrual fluid, and the vagina was later opened for intercourse and childbirth. As you can imagine, this procedure had many complications depending on the extent of the cutting and the type of instrument used, including chronic pain, infection, and difficulty urinating and passing of the menstrual flow, which could induce fatal bleeding.

Once I was done presenting my project, my classmates immediately wanted to know if I had been cut. I explained that I was not, and told them I was lucky because my father was educated and in the healthcare field in Iraq when my sisters and I were young, so he did not want an old lady using an unsanitary sharp instrument on any of us. They wanted to know if anyone in my family was cut, and I started to get a little uncomfortable with the personal questions about the topic. “Most of my maternal aunts and cousins who lived in the rural areas were,” I responded. Everyone was fascinated by the presentation, but shocked to learn that FGM was still happening in some parts of the world.

I chose to major in biology and psychology because I wanted to learn about human beings and the role each organ played in shaping human behavior. When I took the course on the psychology of sexuality, it was my first exposure to understanding human behavior from a secular perspective. Everything we learned in school while in Kurdistan had to be in line with the teachings of Islam. Any concepts that were contrary to Islam were usually skipped over. I started to realize that you could not avoid sexual urges merely by mentally repressing those thoughts. Sex and having feelings for another person were part of human growth. However, this was not something we often talked about in my culture or family. This was when I started to question everything I had been taught over the years.

At the age of twenty, I came to realize that my cultural upbringing would not work, at least not in America. Toward the middle of that semester, Jehan spotted my psychology of sexuality textbook in my room and asked me what it was. I told her that it was part of the requirements for my major and begged her not to tell our mother about the class, because there was no way she would understand. That was the first time my sister and I had an honest conversation about sex. She asked about the class and the content that was covered. I was nervous while trying to share my assignments and course materials with her. She asked if the course materials were appropriate. I told her that everything we talked about was academic and research based. On her way out of my room, she promised not to tell anyone in the family about the course.

In college, I also learned about child psychology and the role of cognitive and social support in healthy growth through Jean Piaget's theories. I then began to think about my own early life experiences, where I had to compete with my ten other siblings for my parent's attention and how restless I would get in the process. I had believed that each achievement would gain me more of the nurturing attention that any healthy little girl needs from her parents, but it often did not come.

While this restless urge to succeed and get accolades gained me attention and praise from outsiders as the "smartest" child of eleven, it was ineffective with my parents. I realized that when you grow up in a state of turmoil where survival and security become the first precedent, your parents expect you to grow up fast and not waste energy on seemingly superficial desires, such as wanting to be praised and be told how proud of you your parents are. I realized that, as a child, I was never once encouraged to show my vulnerability. In fact, it was discouraged as it was seen as a weakness that could endanger myself or my whole family. During war, there is no space for tears, toys, and enriching colors, and life can become mechanical.

I then wondered how in the world I could ever be mentally balanced with all that I had gone through!

In my social psychology course, we discussed how bullying can have a detrimental impact on a child's healthy growth. It dawned on me that my family never appreciated this fact. Instead, just like any other Kurdish children, we were often disciplined through beatings and child abuse. The whole concept of positive reinforcement was never applied to us. As a matter of fact, if you did not do what was expected of you, you were beaten by your parents. So, it was not surprising that when I learned about the "Diagnostic and Statistical Manual of Mental Disorders" from the American Psychiatric Association's manual, I immediately began diagnosing myself and my siblings with most of the mental illnesses I read about.

I have always been a risk taker. One of the biggest risks and joys I found at a young age was traveling. At times traveling was not possible because I did not have the proper documents and, at other times, my family did not let me travel on my own. The spring of my junior year in college, I wanted to get my driver's license, but I did not know how to drive. The chaplain at Agnes Scott and her daughter offered to teach me. One day, on a trial drive, I told the chaplain that exploring the world was a dream of mine. Since coming to the U.S., I had never been outside the country because I was not a citizen with the proper documents to leave and return. And after 9/11, it was risky to travel while wearing a hijab and not having proper documents.

In 1998, I only had a green card that identified me as a legal resident of the United States. The chaplain told me about an interfaith pilgrimage that was partly sponsored by Agnes Scott and encouraged me to participate. Every year, a group of volunteers from Jewish, Christian, and Muslim communities embarked on a three-week pilgrimage to a country that had suffered years of tension over differences in religious practices. They had previously gone to Turkey, Israel, and the West Bank, and their next plan was for a pilgrimage to Andalusia and Morocco.

I was fascinated and beyond excited to participate. Jowan was against the idea of me traveling alone, but I was not going to give up. Jowan, as the oldest sister, was overly protective and would always hold us to our cultural rules and restrictions. However, I did not see exploring the world as something that was wrong when it came to our cultural rules. After many meetings with my family, they finally agreed to let me go on this trip. Jowan hesitantly applied for my travel document while I held a fundraising event to collect money for the pilgrimage. Everything was going well until the Spanish Embassy in Washington, DC said they could not grant me a visa on time because I was still a green card holder. Extremely disappointed, I told the chaplain about my visa issue, and they selected another candidate to replace me on the pilgrimage. I had to hand over the funding I had collected.

Not giving up just yet, I looked for other opportunities to study or do service abroad. The following year, I learned about the Hubert scholarship—in honor of an alumnus of Agnes Scott—for community and service work abroad. This time, I wanted to get the scholarship and go to Syria to teach English to young girls in Damascus. Damascus was an ideal spot because I spoke Arabic and would blend in easily. The scholarship committee selected me, and I was recognized at the Agnes Scott Awards Ceremony. I had assumed that my family would be supportive, considering how hard I worked to win. However, this time the family stood in my way. I started to feel isolated and felt my family was always between me and my goals of making a difference abroad.

Instead of refusing the scholarship, I created a service project of my own through the International Rescue Committee (IRC) and held classes about a healthy diet and planned parenthood for young Somalian mothers. I already knew that the IRC held ESL English classes for the mothers, and I wanted to take advantage of this opportunity. The scholarship money was spent on supplies and transportation services to take them to grocery stores and review nutritional facts about the food items they ate. After three months of teaching these classes, I was surprised to learn how limited their knowledge was about contraception and selecting healthy food items for their families. They exposed me to their diet, and I would tailor their meals to make good use of the healthy options available to them in the local stores.

Following 9/11, the Bush Administration began talking about invading Iraq. Even though al-Qaeda claimed full responsibility for the attack, and they were based in Afghanistan, the U.S. government chose to bomb Iraq as well. In November of 2001, an excerpt from a memo by Bush's Defense Secretary Donald Rumsfeld listed many reasons as a justification to invade Iraq such as: Saddam's moves against Kurds in north, U.S. discovery of Saddam's connection to the Sept. 11 attack, anthrax, and the dispute over the WMD (weapon of mass destruction) inspections.

In January 2002, President Bush then began the groundwork for an invasion of Iraq, which he called a member of the "axis of evil," declaring, "The United States of America will not permit the world's most dangerous regimes to threaten us with the world's most destructive weapons." In addition, the Bush Administration pushed for international backing to invade Iraq. Failing to get the support it needed from the U.N., the U.S. and the United Kingdom launched an invasion of Iraq in 2003.

Shortly after the invasion, the U.S. intelligence agencies failed to find any weapons of mass destruction or evidence linking Iraqi's former regime to al-Qaeda. At that point, the Bush and Blair Administrations began to shift to secondary rationales for invading Iraq. Arguments such as "Saddam Hussein had violated human rights and gassed his own people in Iraqi Kurdistan" were used for justification. This was true, of course, but the U.S. had been aware of this fact when it happened back in 1988 and refused to declare it as genocide or stop the regime back then because Iraq was a strategic ally against Iran. I had been living in America for eight years by then and had learned how the U.S. government often put American interests ahead of the human rights of those Iraqi citizens. I learned that politics was ugly and much different than what the average American felt about those living in other parts of the world who were less fortunate.

The U.S. had sadly supported Saddam Hussein during the 1980s when he committed some of the worst human rights abuses against the Kurds. A document by the National Security Archive released in 2003, showed that the U.S. government provided military as well as financial support to Saddam Hussein during the Iran-Iraq war with the full awareness that Saddam was using chemical weapons in Kurdish villages, as well as against the Iranian military. It was clear to most Kurds, especially those who had had experiences like ours, that the Bush Administration purposely falsified evidence to justify the invasion of Iraq. Yes, Saddam was evil, but his evil was nothing new. In fact, it was why he had been strategically useful to America in the 1980s against Iran. We, therefore, rallied against the war; however, our actions did not change things. The war eventually happened.

As a twenty-year-old who had experienced traumatic incidents and displacements in northern Iraq because of my Kurdish identity, I was shocked to see the American news cover the human rights violations by the former regime of Iraq for the very first time. It was disappointing that after so many years, the Bush administration was acknowledging that what we Kurds experienced was indeed a human rights violation, but only doing so for political gain. I wanted the opportunity to ask Bush and his political advisors where they were when urgent help was needed to stop these violations. My people were gassed. Young men were buried, burned, or shot in Anfal because they were Kurds. Instead, thousands of Kurdish children died of starvation due to the economic sanctions supposedly imposed on Saddam Hussein. In fact, those sanctions were forced on the most vulnerable civilians in Iraq.

In the summer of 2003, my siblings, Hoger, Zerak, and Jehan, chose to join the military forces as interpreters where they could make a lucrative salary due to their Arabic speaking skills. They asked me to hurry and finish college so I, too, could join and make a six-figure salary. But I had my mind set on graduate school and was not interested in being deployed overseas nor in joining the military as a translator for a war I opposed. I had worked hard to make a life for myself and was not ready to let go of all that I had accomplished.

Not long after my siblings were deployed to Iraq, the horrific scandal of Abu Ghraib prison became public. To me, the Abu Ghraib scandal was one of the most painful cruelties the people of Iraq had to endure after they overcame the atrocities of Saddam Hussein. As previously mentioned, my own father had been held at the same prison years earlier by the Baathists, so this scandal really struck a chord with me.

Abu Ghraib, a prison complex located twenty miles west of Baghdad, was first opened in 1950 by the Baathist regime and used by Saddam Hussein as a maximum security prison where there were abhorrent living conditions, not to mention torture and executions.

Abu Ghraib gained international attention in this scandal when personnel from the United States Army and Central Intelligence Agency committed several human rights violations against the male and female detainees. This included physical and sexual abuse, torture, rape, sodomy, and murder. The abuse started in the early fall of

2003, but it was not until the death of one of the detainees that it got the attention of the Army in Abu Ghraib district.

I asked a friend of mine in the U.S. Navy to explain how something horrific like this could possibly be committed by those who had sworn to uphold the U.S. Constitution, which I admired. He explained that, as military personnel, they were discouraged from interacting with locals in Iraq. "We were told Iraqis were the masterminds of 9/11. We were asked not to interact with civilians. Anyone we encountered in Iraq was an enemy. We were told these people were after us. We were brainwashed." When photographs of the women detainees were made public, there was outrage.

According to Huda Al-Nuaima, a college professor at the University of Baghdad, many of those female detainees have disappeared since they were released from Abu Ghraib. Al-Nuaima said one detainee who was raped and made pregnant by a U.S. guard was later killed by her family in an "honor" killing, a practice not unusual in the Middle East since it was believed that rape brought shame to the entire family. As a Kurdish-Muslim woman, I understood how the stigma of being raped by an American soldier was culturally unbearable. This explained why not a single female came forward to talk about her experiences in the U.S.-run jails and the abuse endured during the invasion in 2003. The American soldiers who committed these crimes not only failed the Iraqi people but their own country and values. I knew the U.S. military was better than this, as my own life as a child was saved by a Marine, so I felt incredibly sad at such a betrayal of American principles.

Hearing the news and stories from home brought so much pain and sadness to my life. The images coming out of Abu Ghraib haunted me. How could this happen to vulnerable detainees in their own country? I felt hopeless since there was nothing I could have done to save the Iraqi people or my Kurdish people from the abuse they endured under Saddam Hussein and later the United States Government. Kurdish refugees in Georgia were often reminded that those who suffered in Abu Ghraib were likely the Arabs who celebrated the atrocities committed by Saddam against Kurds (thus somehow making it justifiable). I found this reasoning to be nonsense. The Iraqi detainees did not deserve this. No human did.

In the summer of 2003, I began applying to pharmacy schools. I knew that when I finished my degree, I would go back to care for the underserved in the Kurdish region. I applied to one local and two regional schools of pharmacy. My family did not want me to go to a school that was far from them, so we decided I would apply to a school in Georgia, South Carolina, and North Carolina. That way I could stay with the family or visit them often.

The admissions offices were impressed with my applications and chose to move forward with interviews as early as August of 2003, even before seeing my Pharmacy College Admission Test (PCAT) scores, which I was scheduled to take in the fall of 2004. My mother and Omed drove with me to North and South Carolina for pharmacy school interviews. When my mother and I went to the interviews, we received strange looks from almost everyone on the campus. The interviews went well, and I answered every question with all the passion I had. Since I spoke with an accent, the members of the interview committees asked where I was from.

"I am from northern Iraq," I responded. I figured they would not know where Kurdistan was, so I chose to say northern Iraq. Two faculty members told me the committee would decide on my admission that week or wait until they received my PCAT score.

I waited two weeks and there was no answer from the schools where I had interviewed. I finally called one of the faculty members who interviewed me. He promised that the letter would go out that week. If I did not hear by the end of the week, I was to call him back and he would let me know about my admission. I was certain I would receive an acceptance letter, as I figured there was no way the school would reject me without knowing my PCAT score. However, to my surprise, when I received the letter, it stated that due to a large number of applicants, they were not able to grant me acceptance.

I wondered if that was the real reason for my rejection. As it was still summer, it did not seem possible that the school had a big pool of applicants for the following year. To make it worse, the faculty members had said they would wait for my PCAT score (but did not). All in all, I was rejected from all three schools that I applied to and was completely devastated.

In early October of 2004, I went to take my PCAT exam. When I talked with some students who interviewed at the same schools, I learned that their admissions were on hold pending their PCAT scores. I did not understand why these schools had rejected me without waiting for my PCAT score. I suspected that my hijab played a factor. After the exam, I shared my story with a few trusted faculty and friends at Agnes Scott College. I considered suing these schools for possible discrimination, but I was told that if I did, it was unlikely I would ever get admitted to another school. The prospective pharmacy schools would look at me as a difficult candidate who would be willing to sue them if I did not like their decisions.

On January 20, 2004, I became a naturalized citizen of the United States. I still remember this day as if it were yesterday. There was a long wait until I was finally called by an immigration officer who asked me questions about U.S. history and the founding fathers. The officer told me that I had passed the exam, but I had to be patient because the ceremony was not until that afternoon, four hours later. It took eight long years to get to where I was, but it was worth the wait, and I was grateful. I was about to become a citizen of a country that would give me the right to vote, the right to run for office, and the right to be self-made.

When I entered the ceremony room, it was full of candidates from every part of the world: Cameroon, Nepal, Bosnia, Brazil, Ghana, South Korea, India, Bhutan, and Malaysia. Some had their family members record or take pictures to remember this special day.

When the ceremony finally started, we were asked to raise our right hands and everyone's cameras started flashing. After a lengthy oath, I heard lots of cheers and claps. We were told that we were now the citizens of the

United States. I was so excited and started waving a little American flag that I had. We were asked to recite the Pledge of Allegiance with our right hand over our hearts facing the American flag. Pledging to the flag, I had a feeling that I am still unable to describe. Pledging allegiance meant freedom of expression and living and working freely as a Kurd, not worrying about being arrested or kidnapped because of my identity. It also meant a sense of obligation to serve both America and the country that had borne me, Kurdistan. And finally, it meant I could hold a U.S. passport and travel freely to any part of the world as an American.

My sister, Jowan, chose to postpone marriage for as long as she could and turned all her focus and attention on helping manage our household when we moved to America. To do so she managed all the family finances from the day we arrived in Atlanta. For years we had to give her everything we made, and she earnestly stashed away the family's money while limiting each of us to $20 a week for personal items. Any amount beyond that required an explanation; we had to convince her why we needed more money. As a result, when we did buy our first modest house as a family, Jowan managed to pay off the entire thing in only two years with our savings, surprising all of us and relieving us that we were now loan-free homeowners.

However, by this time Jowan was in her late twenties, and the family was frantic about her still being single. In an attempt to get her married, my family had her return to Kurdistan once or twice a year, hoping she would find someone. In the winter of 2004, Zhyan, Jowan, and our mother went back to Erbil for Zhyan's marriage. At Zhyan's wedding, our oldest second cousin, Hatam, who was a few years older than Jowan and a legal resident of the United Kingdom, saw Jowan. He told his family he would like to marry her, but she turned his offer down. My devout but also superstitious mother sought help from both a religious cleric and a magician to see if someone had put a magic spell on Jowan to stop her from marrying. A patient Hatam waited for two years and did not give up trying until my mother jokingly told Jowan that if she refused to marry Hatam, she was going to marry him herself. After many attempts, and the involvement of both families, Jowan finally relented and agreed to marry him.

For his part, Hatam had escaped the harsh conditions of Iraqi Kurdistan at the same time we evacuated the region. Hatam's maternal grandmother was my mother's half-sister. Unlike us, Hatam failed to find a safe pathway to leave the country. Instead, he joined thousands of the country's top intellectuals, healthcare providers, and scientists who escaped through Turkey, where he made his way to Bodrum. Once in Bodrum, he paid a Turkish human trafficker to board a small inflatable boat with a dozen other refugees and no life jackets. Once the sun set and the waves settled, the trafficker sailed the overcrowded boat through the Mediterranean Sea to the shores of Greece. From Greece, Hatam went to France, Germany, Belgium, the Czech Republic, and the Scandinavian countries hoping one of these countries would give him residency status. When he was on the verge of losing all hope, and fearing he would be deported, friends recommended that he seek asylum in the UK. There he was finally able to obtain residency status. Like my brother Omed, Jowan and Hatam also soon settled in Colorado (Kurdarado). They now have three adorable children: Shad, Soz, and Shiyar. Thankfully, Jowan has softened up over the years and she is no longer the harsh financial disciplinarian with her husband and daughters.

A friend wanted to introduce me to a Kurdish friend of hers named Rebin, who was living in Kurdistan. She thought Rebin—an open-minded physician—and I would make a great couple. I told my mother I wanted to meet Rebin and get to know him. I later learned that Rebin's father was politically connected. We corresponded by phone and email and he sent me poetry with sweet words, words I never had anyone say to me before. My mother recommended that I give Rebin a chance because he checked all the right boxes: Kurd, Muslim, highly educated, from a good family, and rich. But for me, those were not the only prerequisites for true love.

When Rebin learned about my citizenship, he was quick to ask if I was willing to return to Erbil so we could meet in person and get married. As a U.S. citizen, through a fiancé visa, I would be able to get Rebin to America within six months.

To me, that sounded like the right next step considering I had been rejected from pharmacy school and had nothing else planned. Rebin, who had slowly integrated himself into every detail of my life, contacted my family to explain he was serious about marrying me.

In May, I graduated from Agnes Scott College with a double major in Biology and Psychology. I was excited to be done with college but anxious since I did not have plans for graduate school, nor a job lined up after all the years of hard work. What was I to do with my double major now? For the first time in my life, I felt I had let down every person who had believed in, encouraged, and pushed me forward. I had failed my father who always dreamed of having his child pursue higher education and become a doctor. I could not explain what had happened. I had always overdone things, I had gone above and beyond, especially when it came to graduate school. I was in despair.

My mother encouraged me to take some time off and return to Erbil, visit with cousins I had not seen since 1996, and meet this mysterious Rebin who claimed to have fallen in love with me.

In August of 2004, I joined my brother Hoger on his return to Kurdistan to see his family who lived in Zakho. Jowan and Zhyan were against the idea of my going back to Kurdistan because they were suspicious of Rebin's true intentions. It was hard to accept what Zhyan and Jowan were telling me, since they had both returned to Kurdistan to enter arranged marriages with their prospective husbands.

Hoger and I reached Zakho at four in the morning, where we stayed with Hoger's in-laws for several days. Through the grapevine, my presence in Zakho became known. Amusingly, almost all our male cousins thought I was back to marry one of them. At a family picnic in the mountains of Zakho, all the male cousins tried to get my attention so I would choose one of them for a husband. To an average uneducated young man in his early twenties, it was a dream to marry someone like me because I could serve as a way of reaching America. However, in my view, cousins were siblings, and I could not have any romantic feelings for someone I shared a family relationship with.

When Rebin and his family visited us at Hoger's in-law's house in Zakho, I saw him for the very first time. He was a short man with hazel eyes. Rebin and his family were dressed in black when they visited us, and he later told me his father had been assassinated by a suicide bomber in Erbil. The next day, Rebin's family invited us to the famous Malta restaurant in Duhok city for lunch, a thirty-minute drive from where we were staying. Malta was located on top of a hill with a beautiful view of the city. This lunch invitation allowed Rebin and me to be alone for the first time and talk face to face. Once we were done with lunch, Rebin asked Hoger if he could meet with me alone in the park of the restaurant. The families stayed in the restaurant while Rebin and I walked together to the garden. It was extremely awkward to walk with a man who was so much shorter than myself, since I could not even look him in the eye. He told me about the instability in the region and how many physicians, himself included, were trying to leave the country. I sympathized with him about the situation and his father's death. We exchanged rings and became officially engaged, but as we did, I couldn't help thinking that this man who had sent me such lovely poetry did not look or sound excited to see me.

After a week-long stay in Zakho, Hoger, his wife, and I rented a car and drove to Erbil where we stayed in a hotel.

One afternoon, Rebin's mother called Hoger to invite us to lunch while Rebin was in Baghdad. While we were at their house, Rebin called to say that he wanted to return to Erbil for a day and have me leave for the U.S. so I could start on his paperwork.

I pushed back! I reminded him that I was there to visit with my cousins and see Kurdistan. He seemed to be fine with my decision to wait a while before returning to the U.S.

After lunch, Rebin's mother and my sister-in-law took me to the Qaisari bazaar, the biggest historic bazaar in Erbil, where we walked through a maze of narrow paths between shops under a roof of corrugated metal. We walked through countless alleys until we reached their family's goldsmith shop where the owner offered us a seat. They brought us complimentary Kurdish chai in little teacups from one of the local tea houses. The head goldsmith brought out sets of gold to show my sister-in-law and Rebin's mother. They asked if I liked what they were showing me. In the Kurdish culture, it's customary for the bride to receive gold as part of her dowry from the groom, but I was clueless. I told them to pick whatever they thought appropriate. The women settled on a Kurdish belt, a gold necklace and earring set, and a few other pieces that cost roughly $12,000.

The next day, my brother, sister-in-law, and I spent some time in Erbil and visited a childhood friend in Shoresh. We did not return to the hotel until midnight. When we arrived, we found Rebin waiting for us outside the hotel. He asked Hoger if he could meet with me alone. Hoger was quite uncomfortable at his request this late at night and hesitantly left me alone with Rebin for ten minutes. Once we were alone, Rebin was extremely angry and asked why I made his mother spent $12,000 on gold jewelry. I explained that I had not been involved in the whole negotiation process. Feeling guilty, I told him that his mother and my sister-in-law negotiated a price they felt to be fair. Hoger returned and asked if there was anything he needed to know. Rebin immediately changed the topic, told Hoger that he was looking forward to seeing us the next day, and left.

Not long after that, Rebin left for Baghdad. That was the last time I saw him. I obtained a temporary phone so Rebin could call when he was in Baghdad, but he never did. The warm, sweet Rebin that I had known in letters had changed for absolutely no reason that I could understand. Two weeks after our "engagement," I visited his mother to say my goodbyes to her. She asked if she could keep the engagement ring and have Rebin bring it with him to the United States.

At that point, I was totally confused about how things were being handled by Rebin and his family, so I decided to visit Rebin's brother and ask for his guidance. I told him that I had not heard from Rebin since the engagement and that my ring had been taken by his mother. "I have been calling Rebin for the past two weeks, but have not heard from him," I added.

Taken by surprise, his brother suggested I move on because Rebin was obviously not serious about the relationship. He told me that Rebin had been in touch with his friends in Erbil and Rebin had stopped answering my calls. "Rebin is probably feeling bad and is not able to confront you to end things," his brother said. He apologized on behalf of his family.

I later learned that through his political connections, Rebin had been promised a diplomatic post at the United Nations in New York. That meant that Rebin no longer needed me to get to the United States. On my way back to the United States, I got an email from Rebin. His brother had asked him to contact me. Rebin's email explained that we had rushed into the relationship. He then told me about his post at the United Nations. He said he did not want to commit to a long-term relationship until he knew his whereabouts in the United States. He wished me luck and wrote that he felt confident I would find someone better in the future.

I landed in Atlanta feeling terrible about myself. At twenty-two, my life had turned completely upside down and I felt I had failed at everything I had hoped for: no job prospect, rejected from several graduate programs, and dumped by a man who tried to manipulate my emotions to make his way to the United States. I coped with the depression by losing my appetite, which left me frail. My mother, not knowing what to do, said how guilty she felt for supporting my return to Erbil and not letting me apply to programs outside Georgia. She and my siblings reminded me how silly it was of me to feel so down considering I was still young.

"Heleen, get your act together and start applying to programs again next year. Forget the South, you can study anywhere you want," my mother said.

I then realized that I could not continue feeling this way because I felt discriminated against. I also could no longer grieve for a man who never took me seriously. I knew I was stronger than racism and was not going to let discrimination stop me from attaining my dreams. I had come too far to let go of my ambitions.

I slowly got back to my routine in Georgia. I accepted a temporary job teaching Arabic to a group of Army Rangers at Fort Benning. I lived at Fort Benning for three months, where I would spend ten hours a day with twelve Army rangers teaching them about the Islamic faith, Middle Eastern culture, and the Arabic language. With the images of Abu Ghraib still fresh in my mind, I felt an obligation to bring as much awareness as possible to the Rangers before their deployment to Iraq. It took me a while to open up to my students. I took them on field trips to Middle Eastern grocery stores where we shopped for dolma and cooked it together. We reviewed the various religious practices in Iraq, and I took them to a mosque in Atlanta, so they could experience the Friday sermon and prayer. Over those three months, the Rangers became my support system. With their sense of humor and energy, they lifted my mood every day and made me forget all the pain I'd felt in Erbil. They said they were impressed by my hard work and confident that schools outside the South would be honored to welcome me into their program.

I soon started applying to pharmacy schools again. This time, I applied to schools in Boston, California, and New York. The first interview I had was with Northeastern University in Boston, Massachusetts. Northeastern had started a Doctor of Pharmacy program the year I applied, and they only accepted students with a bachelor's or a master's degree. The program accepted fifteen students from 600 applicants. My family encouraged me to remove my hijab for the interview, so I would not be judged for my headcover. However, the hiring committee at Northeastern chose to interview over the phone and granted me admission to their incoming class of 2010 one week after the interview.

The day I received the most beautiful news of acceptance into my dream program, I thought a miracle had happened. I did not even finish reading the letter before crying, "Oh my God! Look at this!" as the rest of my family did their best to remain calm.

"Heleen, what is going on?" my parents asked.

"Oh my God, Babo, oh my God, Ouda!" I shouted. "I got accepted!"

In sharp contrast to the joy of my acceptance, in the late spring of 2006, something tragic happened to my family. My sister, Dilven, was taking college classes at DeKalb Community College. One afternoon, I was scheduled to pick her up after class. However, I waited for hours in the car and Dilven did not show up. When I tried to call Dilven, her cell phone was off, and I started to worry. I parked the car and looked for Dilven in every building, but she was nowhere to be found. I called the campus police and was told that Dilven had left the family. I called my family to share the sad news and was asked to return home.

We reached out to Dilven's friends, and they all refused to share anything about her whereabouts. My mother was in tears, but the police told her that there was nothing anyone could do. Dilven, who was nineteen at the time, had chosen for herself. The next day, I went back to her school to talk to her hoping she would change her mind and return home. However, when the campus police saw me, they warned me about returning to the campus because Dilven had filed a restraining order against our family.

In some ways, all of us could see this coming. Dilven was, and still is, the prettiest of all the sisters. Because of her beauty, she always got the most attention from others, both in Kurdistan and in America. Fearing that her attractiveness would bring her problems, my parents and siblings were always extra protective of her, and I am sure that control everyone exerted only further pushed her away. Dilven and I had also grown up more as rivals rather than sisters. She was four years younger and far more Americanized. She was eight when we emigrated to the U.S. and less influenced by the culture in Kurdistan I had been raised in. The U.S. was the only home country she had ever known. My family had always compared her accomplishments to mine and would use that comparison to belittle her, which bothered her a lot. The classic family cliché was that she had gotten the "looks" and I the "brains," which was unfair to both of us, but more so her. Dilven wanted to have her own identity and did not want to have to measure up to my accomplishments. She hated math and science and was not interested in anything technical. Her heart and free spirit were instead interested in art and photography.

However, those skills did not mean much to my family. My family had always feared Dilven would rebel. My mother had once taken Dilven back home to Kurdistan to see if she would like to marry someone, but that did not go well. My older siblings would question her actions and even hit her when she stood up for her beliefs. I believe her decision to run away was made when my mother tried to bully her into an arranged marriage to a Kurdish man who was interested in her. Ever since Dilven ran away, my mother liked to remind us that Dilven had taken a piece of her heart with her. She never wanted us to talk about Dilven or discuss her whereabouts because her news brought my mother a lot of pain.

A few weeks after Dilven's disappearance, one of our neighbors saw her at a diner in the neighborhood. Dilven had taken her hijab off and was now working as a waitress to provide for herself while taking classes. Our neighbor mediated a conversation between Dilven and the family and she decided to maintain contact with a few conditions. She wanted to work and refused to marry any Kurdish man. Not long after her return, Dilven told me that she was in love with a Pakistani American man from Connecticut named Nazim. She had met Nazim at a concert where he was playing guitar. Nazim was twenty-eight years old when he proposed to Dilven, who was twenty. Dilven insisted on marrying Nazim and said she would run away again if we opposed her marriage. We later learned that Nazim had asked Dilven to return home because his parents would not accept him marrying a girl who had run away from her family. Nazim's parents visited us several times and the families both agreed to have Dilven and Nazim perform Nikah (a religious marriage contract). Dilven had already packed her things and asked to leave with Nazim, a move that took my family by surprise. By then, nothing could stop what Dilven had planned for her future. We all wished her the best of luck because that was all we could do.

As I was getting ready to leave for Boston, I received a call from Childspring International, saying they needed an Arabic translator for Baby Noor's family. Childspring, an Atlanta-based charity, helped sponsor Noor Al-Zahra Haider's trip from Baghdad to Atlanta, where she would get the healthcare she urgently needed at Children's Healthcare of Atlanta. Known as "Baby Noor" to millions of Americans in 2006, the three-month-old baby girl had the double misfortune of suffering from a life-threatening defect known as spina bifida and being born with the disease in a war-torn land. Spina bifida, a congenital defect where the spinal cord does not develop properly, had caused fluid accumulation in her brain and paralysis from the waist down. The doctors in Baghdad had told Baby Noor's family that their daughter would be wheelchair-bound for the rest of her life and a burden to her family, and it was better to let her die.

When I arrived at Children's Healthcare, I was introduced to Noor's grandmother, Khala Soad (Aunt Soad) and Noor's father, Haidar, who was my age. I told them that I was also from Iraq and was there to serve as their translator. I spent three months with Noor and her family and was involved in every step of Baby Noor's care, so Soad and Haidar could be well informed. The doctors at Children's Healthcare performed several surgeries to realign Noor's spine and close her spinal cord. They inserted a shunt to drain the excess fluid that had accumulated in the outer membrane of Noor's brain. After the surgeons finished, they met with Noor's family and told them everything went smoothly.

Soad looked me in the eye and asked me in Arabic, "Do you think Noor would be able to walk in the future?" I translated her question to the surgeons. "I'm not here to take away hope. Time will tell," the surgeon responded. Not 100% pleased with the response, Soad nodded and said, "Insha'Allah khair" (God willing it will be good).

At that moment, I failed to see the human element in their response. As the surgeon conveyed the news, a touch by one of the surgeons would have given Soad more assurance for her precious granddaughter. Everyone who cared for Noor had good intentions, but they failed to understand Noor's destiny growing up in Iraq as a broken little girl in a broken place. They also failed to understand the judgmental society to which this girl would return and the impact it would have on her.

Soad kept a scrapbook and collected all the newspaper articles about the famous Baby Noor. Every morning when I got to the hospital, she would pull out a new article from her book and ask me to read it to her. For couple of months, I was fortunate enough to get to know Soad better. Soad was the backbone of her family and the reason Baby Noor came to America. She told me about the U.S. airstrike and how a tank rolled over the kiosk where she sold groceries. One cold winter day, American soldiers burst into her home on a routine raid. They searched every room looking for the male family members. She knew that it was her chance to bring Noor to the attention of Americans then. Not knowing how to communicate with the soldiers, she started exposing Noor's back with the tumor to the soldiers.

One can assume that Baby Noor's ailment was the

byproduct of the brain drain Iraq has experienced over two decades of war, economic sanctions, and civil conflict, causing a mass migration of intellectuals and medical professionals. While the initiative by the U.S. military was to be applauded for escorting Baby Noor and two members of her family out of the country to seek immediate care, one shouldn't forget the hundreds and thousands of other Iraqi children that had been deformed, handicapped, and even killed from war and instability.

As I sat in the back of the room where Noor was being cared for, and with the media waiting outside to update the American public, I could not help but envision our futures. Many Americans think that bringing refugees like me and Baby Noor to this great country will put an end to our sufferings. However, what they fail to understand is the forever trauma that we will live with for having to leave our land and loved ones due to war. The trauma to adjust to a new place, culture, and people that are so difficult for our body and mind to comprehend.

One morning while I was performing my translation duty, I met Noor's host family. They would often call when they did not understand what Soad wanted. Once they found out I had plans for graduate school in Boston, they wanted to connect me with one of their friends in Boston, named Mercede. They told me that she would be a good point of contact to have in Boston. The family contacted Mercede via email that same day to tell her about me and my plans for studying at Northeastern.

Mercede, an elegant Persian lady in her mid-fifties, came to the United States from Iran for her studies. She was a board member at Bayridge, an all-girls independent residence and cultural center in the Back Bay. Bayridge provided off-campus housing for unmarried university women in undergraduate and graduate programs at the various universities in the area. Mercede shared that she had stayed at Bayridge when she was a graduate student and about my age. Bayridge had a unique atmosphere that enhanced serious study with opportunities for cultural and personal enrichment in a supportive family-like environment. When I contacted Mercede asking her for a housing recommendation, she immediately recommended Bayridge. She asked that I come to Boston to visit Bayridge. I also wanted to visit Northeastern and meet some of my prospective professors.

After three months of translating for Soad and Haidar, they told me how homesick they were and how much they wanted to return to Baghdad. However, Noor still needed care. They had the option of staying or leaving Noor behind with the assurance she would be returned to them once she was done with her recovery. They chose to leave Noor behind and returned to Baghdad. They were followed by Noor's return several weeks later. My interaction with the family and role as interpreter stopped when they returned home. I lost touch with Baby Noor but watched the news to keep up with her progress.

I booked my flight to Boston where I planned to spend three days with Mercede in July of 2006. I instantly fell in love with the city, its history, and Northeastern. I knew living in Boston would change my perspective on the world moving forward. I learned that Boston was known for its intellectual reputation, which originated from its many universities. I loved how the writer Mark Twain once wrote about Boston, "In New York, they ask, 'How much money does he have?' In Philadelphia, they ask, 'Who were his parents?' In Boston, they ask, 'How much does he know?'"

CHAPTER VI:
LIFE IN BEANTOWN

"So, here you are. Too foreign for home, too foreign for here. Never enough for both."
– Ljeoma Umebinyuo

Northeastern University, Boston, Massachusetts.

I had decided to remove my hijab when I started pharmacy school in Boston. This decision came after many days of deliberation and the conclusion that how I practiced my faith was nobody else's business. There was no need to expose my faith to others by wearing my headscarf or letting others know that I was a practicing Muslim. Boston was going to be a start of a new chapter in my life.

My departure for Boston felt as if I were just starting as an undergraduate. As already mentioned, when I studied at Agnes Scott, I did not have much of a social life. For the first time, I was going to live away from my family and on my own. My mother, siblings, and I packed two suitcases full of items we felt that I would need, including new clothes. In addition, my mother baked non-stop the week before my departure, so that I could have home-baked goodies in case I got hungry while studying. I left a week before classes started to get situated in Boston. All my siblings gathered at my mother's house to bid me goodbye. Once I got in the car with Omed, who was driving me to the airport, my tearful mother threw a cup of rice at the car as we drove away. Throwing rice symbolizes rain, which is said to be a sign of prosperity and success.

In two hours, I had landed at Logan International Airport and realized taking off my hijab was not as simple a decision as I initially thought. It meant that I needed to be ready to give up the only Heleen I knew—unraveling twenty-three years of myself. Feeling guilty (perhaps irrationally) for not having my hair covered, I rushed to one of the bathrooms at Logan and put my hijab back on. Once my hair was covered, I felt a sense of relief and got a call from Mercede. She was at the baggage claim to pick me up and drive me to Bayridge. My psychological tug-of-war on whether to wear the hijab or not would have to wait for another day. At that point, I settled on the comfort (or crutch) of having it.

Bayridge was located in the Back Bay and had various housing options. With the high cost of living in the Back Bay, I was only able to afford the cheapest option Bayridge had to offer: a small room with a bed, desk, and tiny closet. Before I left home, my family allowed me to open a personal bank account and order checks for my personal use. My siblings also let me keep a few of my own paychecks from the last few months of work to cover my housing costs while in Boston. In addition, they bought me a brand-new laptop for schoolwork, so for once in my life I finally felt I was adequately prepared.

Mercede was quick to tell me about the severe winters in Boston and recommended that I get a pair of rain boots. She also shared the importance of having a thick puffer coat for those rough winter days. Bayridge was within walking distance to Northeastern, so I knew I did not need to rely on the subway system (the "T") to get to class every day. I was provided with breakfast and dinner daily and was responsible for my own lunch. Being the only Muslim in the residence, the chef made sure that my dietary restrictions were respected.

Living alone in Boston changed my perceptions. For the first time, I could leave my house whenever I wanted. I was solely responsible for my own finances as opposed to my college days when everything was paid for by the family. I had to get a federal loan to help pay for school. Growing up in the Kurdish culture, a loan was something to be avoided at all costs. So, for me to get a thirty-thousand-dollar loan from the government annually was not an easy decision.

The start of pharmacy school was hard. I took all the rigorous courses needed for the first year, plus a graduate course on cultural disparities in healthcare. I did not work during the first semester, so that I was able to get a feel for life in Boston, adjust to the graduate school workload, and see how it felt to live on my own and rely on myself for everything.

While in Bayridge, I met some impressive young professionals and students from around the world. They lived in the Boston area for post-graduate studies or to do medical research in some way, shape, or form. Dinners were my opportunity to network with these professionals and students and hear their amazing stories. But what caught my attention the most was how nicely some of the girls would dress on Friday evening to meet their dates, something I had never experienced. My Friday evenings were usually spent in my room, where I would lounge around in my pajamas, call my family to fill them in on my life, and study for the upcoming week.

I remember Anna, a twenty-one-year-old junior at Boston College who was from Barcelona. She would put on makeup and a pair of high heel shoes that made her look unbelievably tall for her Friday night dates. She was madly in love with a research fellow at the Massachusetts Institute of Technology (MIT), named Sebastian, who was from the Czech Republic. Anna was from a wealthy Catholic family, while Sebastian was living on the stipend from his fellowship. When Anna's mother visited, Anna asked us not to mention Sebastian in front of her mother, knowing she would never approve of him. This made me realize that it was not just my culture and religion that had restrictions on whom we could date and marry.

Five weeks into classes we had our white coat ceremony, a symbolic observance that stressed the importance of the dedication required to pursue a career in healthcare. We had an inspirational keynote speaker and then the Dean put a white coat on each one of us. The school celebrated 125 incoming P1 (first year Doctor of Pharmacy) students that evening. We were asked to repeat the oath of pharmacy. Of those 125 students, only fifteen would eventually go on to graduate with a PharmD degree and I would be one of them. We were called the graduate PharmD students because we already held either a bachelor's or a master's degree. Also, we were expected to take a few graduate courses in addition to the PharmD course load. After the ceremony, we were invited to a reception with family and friends. Unfortunately, no one from my family was able to be present to celebrate with me, but the fourteen other students in my graduate PharmD program had become a surrogate family over the past few weeks.

Northeastern University was and still is nationally known for its co-operative (co-op) program, which is a paid internship that students participate in between semesters. I remember faculty members telling me that Northeastern graduates were far more prepared than those from other colleges of pharmacy because of the co-op program. "When our students graduate, they already have two to three pharmacy experiences on their resume," they explained. Two months into my schoolwork, I met with my adviser to figure out where to do my first co-op. I found out that it was not necessary to stay in Boston for the co-op and I could return to Atlanta for my internship and stay with my family. Factoring in how much money this would save, along with my homesickness, I was quick to let my advisor know that I wanted to do my co-op in Atlanta. My advisor contacted the head of recruitment at a retail pharmacy chain in Georgia, and they arranged for an internship position for four months at a pharmacy in Lilburn close to where my family lived.

The week before I left for Atlanta, my mother called to see what Kurdish food I missed the most so she could cook for me. My favorite meal was always the red bulgur wheat that she cooked with tomato paste alongside her salad with sumac. My mother reminded me how easy red bulgur was to make. "You should ask for a more difficult meal," she said. I spent two weeks with my family to enjoy the holiday before I started my internship.

I arrived at 8 a.m. to start my work at a retail community pharmacy in Lilburn with my white jacket, ready to apply the one semester of knowledge I had acquired at Northeastern. By then, I knew the top 200 drug names and their indications and how they impacted the human body. The first person I met was my mentor, Dr. Anahita Smith, and two technicians that I called "lifesavers." Anahita taught me many lessons from her ten years of experience in the pharmacy. I worked long hours, anywhere from eight to twelve-hour shifts, and I was tasked with every job responsibility a pharmacist would have except for signing off on prescriptions, since I was not licensed yet. Anahita let me spend a couple of hours a day in the aisles, hoping that I could assist patients with their questions about over-the-counter drugs.

It did not take long to learn how frustrating a retail life could be for so many pharmacists. I witnessed a lot of anger and impatience from patients, especially when it came to health insurance claims and the burdensome bureaucracy of the U.S. healthcare system. At least half a dozen patients a day would come early for their monthly refills and become angry at Anahita and me when insurance did not pay for their early refill. There were times I could hear patients shouting at the drive-thru window. I tried my best to explain why insurance would not cover their early prescription refill and if they refused to wait, they would need to pay out of pocket.

The extent of multitasking required by an individual pharmacist at a retail community pharmacy is unimaginable. We did everything, from managing angry patients in the drive-thru, dealing with third-party insurance claims, counseling patients, inputting hundreds of prescriptions daily, and answering countless numbers of calls from the physicians—some disapproving of the decisions we made for their patients. One day, as I was finishing counseling a patient, the drive-thru bell kept furiously ringing. The next thing we knew, the patient at the drive-thru was hitting the window with both hands, screaming for help. It was so frightening, we all dropped the tasks at hand to give this patient immediate attention.

One Friday, I was ten hours into a twelve-hour shift, already worn out from an excessively long and stressful day. As luck would have it, I then had an encounter with a male patient who was adamant about having me counsel him on Viagra (used to treat erectile disfunction). Viagra is one of the top 200 drugs in retail, so I knew enough to counsel him. I told him not to combine Viagra with similar drugs and I listed the names of those drugs for him. I warned him about some of the side effects he should watch for and to seek emergency treatment if those side effects appeared. He then asked if I could demonstrate how Viagra worked. Noticing that I was starting to blush, Anahita jumped into the conversation as she realized the patient was looking for more than health counseling. Later, as we were wrapping up the day, our last patient arrived for an early refill prescription of opioids. Although he showed signs of being in pain, Anahita told me we could not grant him an early refill even if he was willing to pay for the pills, because opioids were a controlled substance. The patient lost his temper and started belligerently accusing me of being a racist for not giving him his pills. We managed to have the store manager escort the patient out. Thankfully, we did not need to call the police. After a twelve-hour shift, I was both mentally and physically drained. I walked to my car and could only think about how I would have to go through similar experiences the very next day.

The most disturbing thing about working in a retail pharmacy was not being able to use my clinical knowledge as a pharmacist to provide the care needed to the countless number of patients in my community. As pharmacists, we are taught to be gatekeepers of medication safety. Every prescription medication we fill has benefits but also the potential to harm a patient. However, the retail system I was a part of did not allow me to be the kind of pharmacist that I was taught to be. I did not feel I was given the necessary tools to perform my duties as a healthcare provider. I was part of a broken system that put my life and a countless number of my patients in danger by placing unreasonable work volume and expectations on us. I did not think working for twelve hours non-stop with no breaks to deal with a countless number of stressful demands by the corporate office, patients, and physicians was safe for the well-being of any pharmacist.

My four-month internship was approaching an end, and I could not be happier to be done with the stressful life of retail pharmacy. Anahita, like any good mentor, asked me for my honest feedback. I shared how impressed I was by her leadership and how good she was at stepping in during stressful moments. Maybe it was due to my lack of experience, but I told her how I felt. She shared that retail was overwhelming for a lot of pharmacists. “Many pharmacists leave the retail setting a couple of years into the practice because of overload and burnout,” she added. Since I was just starting pharmacy school, I was worried and asked Anahita if I was going to be okay.

”Helen, retail might be the higher-paying job opportunity right out of pharmacy school, but it is not the only job option out there,” she explained. Anahita drafted a wonderful recommendation letter for me and topped it off with a farewell party. She also asked me to keep in touch and offered to keep me in the system so I could work part-time at her pharmacy when I visited my family in Lilburn if I so desired.

I returned to Boston for the summer semester and found a one-bedroom apartment across the street from Bayridge. I continued working at a retail pharmacy in Boston to make the extra money I needed for food and rent. Summer semester went well, and I excelled in my classes while working part-time. For the fall semester, it was time for my next co-op experience. Because the housing cost was reasonable and the internship was paid, I decided to stay in Boston and work at the Dana Farber Cancer Institute, which is a Harvard teaching hospital. The work and environment were much more enjoyable than the retail setting. I worked in the chemotherapy room from 9 a.m. to 5 p.m. every day and could be with friends in the evenings. I also agreed to work at Dana Farber every other weekend to make money to cover my book costs.

Ironically for someone assisting in others' care, health insurance was something I was not able to afford, and despite working hard to stay as healthy as I could, it was not always possible. One morning on my way to Dana Farber, I felt a slight pain under my arm. I figured the pain would fade in time, but it kept getting worse. When I checked under my arm, I saw an egg-sized abscess. The pain and pressure caused by the infection radiated into my chest. I needed to go to the emergency room but was afraid of the medical bills I would have to pay. I remember meeting a friendly young woman named Zara from Romania who lived in my building. She was a dermatology fellow at Brigham and Women's Hospital. I thought I could ask her to look at the abscess and see if she was willing to help.

I knocked on her door to explain my concern. She invited me in, examined my underarm, and told me that I had an ingrown hair. She noticed that I was a bit feverish and told me I needed a minor procedure to drain the abscess to relieve the pain. "Helen, you have to take care of this immediately or the abscess will continue growing and your pain will get worse."

I shared my concern about not being able to afford the care I needed. I asked if she was willing to help me drain the abscess and save me from the emergency room costs. She said, "But I am not licensed to practice in the U.S." I understood where she was coming from, so I offered to cut myself if she was willing to merely observe and make sure the incision was in the correct place. I was desperate for help, so she agreed to be present when I drained the abscess and offered to clean the incision. She had several scalpels from her practice in Romania and let me borrow the one she thought to be most appropriate. The pain was extreme as I pressed the scalpel against my skin. She encouraged me to press harder until I was able to open the abscess. As soon as I did, the puss exploded from all the pressure built up over time. Zara then stepped in, cleaned my underarm, and wrapped it with a bandage. I then took some ibuprofen to help with the inflammation and pain. She offered to stop by my room the next day to check on me and continue cleaning the wound.

The next day, I woke up feeling better. I felt I was ready to get back to work now that the pressure was relieved from my underarm. As usual, I walked 45 minutes in the snow to Dana Farber. My supervisor thought I was out of my mind to come to work after what I had gone through, even though I did not tell her that I made the incision myself. She sent me home immediately and told me to return when I was fully recovered. After a few days, my underarm healed, and I was ready to get back to my regular routines. The irony was not lost on me; while I was training to help others in the medical field, I feared going to a hospital since I had no health insurance. Such a dichotomy made me see the necessity of giving everyone universal healthcare coverage.

My fourth semester at Northeastern University was extremely hard, which did not help my stress level. I was taking five courses and working on the weekends. There were days when I woke up with a migraine headache and my jaws clenched. I would take a few ibuprofens, grab a cup of coffee, and run to my courses. The headaches continued and I started worrying about the number of ibuprofens I was taking daily. A clinical oncology pharmacy specialist at Dana Farber invited me to a social event to meet the Middle Eastern community in the Boston area. That evening, I met a couple from Iraq. The husband was an orthodontist and his wife a pathologist, and we bonded over dinner. The husband noticed that my teeth looked flat from clenching and grinding while asleep. I told him about the headaches and how worried I was about taking ibuprofen every day. "The headaches are from the tension of grinding," he hypothesized, and he recommended I get a nighttime mouth guard, but the cost of care remained an issue. So, he offered to build me one at no cost. I could not thank him enough. I did not know how many more times I would get this lucky to get healthcare for free. I was advised to seek therapy to assist with the stress I was experiencing. "And physical exercise is always a huge help," he added.

My mother mailed me her pills for stress that had been prescribed for her. I received the package only to discover it was benzodiazepine. We were taught to counsel patients against sharing pills, especially a controlled substance. However, since I was desperate to get my stress under control, I had no choice but to try them. After the first two pills I took, I was unable to function at full capacity. I immediately threw the pills away and realized I was doing myself more harm than good. I put on my running clothes and walked to the Charles River, about twenty minutes from where I lived. I started jogging and then slowly ran for 3 miles (almost 5 kilometers). Immediately, I committed to running that distance every other day and soon turned it into an everyday activity. After a couple of months of daily running, I felt my energy level rise and my comprehension improve. Another benefit was an improved appetite. It felt so good to run that I would run even when it was raining or snowing.

My stress level continued to improve as I started to keep myself busy with student organizations and activities. I ran for office and became the chapter Vice President of the American Pharmacist Association Student Organization. Part of my responsibility was to involve as many students as possible and develop activities on behalf of the chapter. One thing that came to mind was the struggles of pharmacy students in the Kurdistan region and how the resources and books they used were old and outdated. The first activity I took on was a book drive to collect books and journals for Kurdish colleges of pharmacy. With the support of the chapter advisor, other pharmacy students, and the Harvard College of Medicine, we collected two containers full of textbooks and medical supplies for students overseas. During my limited free time between classes and studying, I went to Longwood Avenue where Harvard Medical School and several teaching hospitals were located to ask for donations of books and journals. However, I did not have enough funding to send the shipment overseas.

In the summer of 2008, Northeastern University

funded my attendance at a Summer Leadership Institute in Washington, DC. While there, I decided to meet with the leadership of International Relief and Development (IRD), a nonprofit organization that focused its operations in regions struggling from conflict, Kurdistan being one. IRD's mission was to reduce the suffering of the world's most vulnerable people, including war victims. I presented the plea of the Kurdish people and made a case to IRD to fund the shipping of the medical textbooks and supplies to the medical and pharmacy school in the Kurdish region of Iraq. The IRD agreed but said that I needed cooperation from people in the region. The easiest way was first to get the containers to Mosul, the nearest city to Duhok, and my contacts had to then be willing to get the supplies from there.

Through this initiative, I developed many contacts in the Kurdistan region, including the Ministry of Health, Higher Education, and most deans of colleges of pharmacy and medicine. I started gaining recognition in my own community from the Kurdish professionals in North America and Europe for the work I was doing to help students back home. Of all the universities I contacted, the University of Duhok in Kurdistan agreed to collaborate. The Vice President of the Office of International Relations contacted me to tell me that his office was willing to send people from the university to get the supplies from Mosul. In our spare time, we used a classmate's car to move the supplies and books to IRD's warehouse outside Boston. This process lasted months until the shipment left and was delivered in Mosul, a two-hour drive from the University of Duhok.

Weeks went by and I did not hear a word from the

university. I decided to write an email to the vice president to see if the shipment was delivered. I got a response back to my email, but only to show how disappointed the university was that the books and supplies were used and not new. In my reply, I told the vice president that a "thank you" would have been more than enough and that we were insulted by their response, considering this initiative was run by full-time financially-strapped pharmacy students trying to help their fellow Kurdish pharmacy students overseas. We had made it clear to them that we were collecting used and new books from the hospitals and sources where we had access. We were aware the books were at least one to two years old, but that was far better than relying on older outdated sources.

While at Harvard, I was introduced to Dr. Kamiar Alai who was just finishing up his master's in public health there. We were introduced to each other by Dr. Kamal Artin, a Kurdish psychiatrist who thought that Kamiar could assist my book drive and any future initiatives I had for Kurdistan. After several meetings where Kamiar treated me with the utmost respect, we became close friends and I started to look up to him as a champion and role model to craft myself after.

I soon learned Kamiar was not only a provider but an HIV specialist and an activist with his brother, Arash Alai, whom I later met as well. Both brothers worked together to develop HIV education for providers in Iranian Kurdistan, also known as Rojhilat (Eastern Kurdistan). They loved Kurdistan just like any patriotic Kurd would when given enough resources to make a change. As part of their initiative, they bravely promoted sex education to younger boys and girls in a society where such a topic was taboo and not discussed publicly, which only created a range of bad health outcomes, since young people still had sex but with no proper education regarding it. Arash went on to explain how the young women in Rojhilat were lost in a society where most of them never experience an orgasm during their lifetime, and men likewise never fully understand their sexual desires or those of their wives. As a result, most of the couples are hungry for real sexual passion, but they are too afraid to speak about it. Arash and Kamiar had traveled to Rojhilat (Northwestern Iran) numerous times but soon went missing. I later learned both were imprisoned as de facto hostages in Tehran by the Iranian Government, accused of being CIA spies.

Knowing the Alai brothers, I knew they had no place in the CIA spy business. The two were down to earth Kurdish healthcare professionals like me who strived to get all the training necessary in order to advance Kurdistan and serve the needs of their people. I could not help but witness yet another Kurdish talent go down the drain, like my father. The Alai brothers were specializing in a topic that was extremely difficult for a conservative society to comprehend, and I know their Kurdish identity further complicated their advocacy work.

"Traveling—it leaves you speechless,
then turns you into a storyteller."
— The Travels of Ibn Battutah

After finishing a stressful semester, a few classmates and I planned a three-week trip to Italy and Egypt as I had never been abroad other than going back to Kurdistan. By then, I had made it through two years of pharmacy school and successfully finished two internships at Northeastern as well as a one-year term as the Vice President of the American Student Pharmacy Chapter at Northeastern. I was ready to explore the world and felt I had earned an adventure. Our travel date was approaching, and we needed to book our flights and make housing arrangements. Unfortunately, the friends who initially agreed to make the trip had a change of heart. I was by myself to figure things out.

I was disappointed that my friends did not follow through on their commitment to travel with me; however, it ended up being a blessing because it prepared me for many more journeys exploring other far-off places on my own. After many days of serious thought, I decided to travel on my own. I had heard great things about both Italy and Egypt, and it was going to be a dream come true to see a part of both Europe and Africa, considering how disappointed I was when my previous plans to travel to Spain and Morocco fell through.

I booked my tickets for a month, planning to spend a week in Italy and three weeks in Egypt. I had no idea where to stay or what I would do. Fortunately, when I was doing the book drive, one person who had been impressed by my passion for wanting to help students in Kurdistan was a young Ph.D. candidate named Mason, who was half Kurdish and half Iraqi Arab. Mason provided a lot of guidance with the book drive and we became good friends. He had a cousin, Leena, who lived in Rome whom he contacted on my behalf. Leena did not speak Kurdish but spoke fluent English. She and I started emailing back and forth, and she offered to let me stay with her in Rome and ended up guiding me through my travels in Italy.

Italy, unlike any other European country, can be overwhelming at first. The towns and cities were all stunning and it was so easy to get around. The locals took their style very seriously. I was told that Italy gave every single girl a boost of self-esteem because of all the young Italian men who tried to flirt with you. Walking in the city center of Rome, I saw all high-end brand name fashions from all around the world. While in Italy, I made a commitment to myself to try gelato in every flavor. So, I would have a gelato after each meal and sometimes two in the afternoon. I started exploring the fountains first and then other historical sites. I saved my visit to the Forum, Colosseum, and Vatican City for last. Leena and I planned to have dinner together when I returned to her apartment on my first day. After that, she would wait for my return each day to hear my stories, including my daily crushes on the charming young bus drivers who would drop me off outside her apartment. I would tell her things and she would laugh with me for hours. She agreed with everything I said, but she found it amusing to hear about her culture from a non-Italian.

Leena asked my thoughts about Italian men. I told her I thought they were aggressive when compared to American men. I thought the compliments and flirtations were excessive, but again I was brought up differently. I would simply ignore the "ciao bella" (hello beautiful) and everything else the Italian boys would try with me. Once, an Italian local who knew I was foreign, approached me and tried to grope me. Thankfully, my skills from a self-defense class I took at Agnes Scott and my daily running came in handy. As he got close to me, I bent my knee and hit him in his groin. I then ran as fast as I could to the bus station.

While in Italy, I planned a full-day visit to Florence. Once in Florence, however, I extended my stay, remaining there overnight and taking the train to Venice the next day. I called Leena from Venice to let her know that I would return to Rome in the next couple of days. The artwork in Florence was unparalleled and I found some of the finest leather and jewelry in the world. On the train ride to Venice, I met two sisters from Austria who were also going to Venice for a day trip. They let me accompany them, and we became friends. I have kept in touch with them over the years since. We strolled through all the narrow alleys and were intrigued by the smelly canals of Venice. Curious, we stopped at a mask shop in the city center. We wanted to try the expensive masks on but were not allowed unless we were serious buyers. I talked with the shop owner, and he eventually let us try on the masks. While doing so, he asked me about my ethnic background and where in Iraq I was from. I told him I was from the Kurdish region. He then asked, "Where in Kurdistan?" I told him that I was born in Erbil and he then started speaking to me in Sorani. My jaw dropped. A Kurd in Venice?! I asked if he was from Erbil. He nodded and said he had emigrated from Erbil around the same time as my family had and lived in Venice ever since. What a beautiful addition to my day. Indeed, Kurds can be found everywhere in the world.

The three-hour gondola ride in Venice with the two sisters and the handsome gondolier singing for us was like a dream. At the end of the ride, the gondolier started making out with the older sister and I closed my eyes. The younger sister told me to relax, that her sister was merely having fun. At sunset, the three of us headed back to the train station. The sisters got off the train in Florence, where they were staying, and I continued back to Rome. I did not get back to Leena's until midnight. For my last day in Rome, I slept in and spent the rest of the day with Leena. We went out that afternoon to enjoy my last helping of gelato before she dropped me at the airport for my flight to Cairo.

Of all the countries I have explored, Egypt continues to be my favorite. They say if you drink from the Nile, you will come back to Egypt. Maybe it is true. I have never felt such a bond with a country as I have with Egypt. I grew up watching Egyptian media, so I was familiar with the culture and Egyptian Arabic, a dialect that is close to my heart. As a child in Erbil, I watched Egyptian movies and comedy shows with my mother and aunts, so I knew all the famous actors from that country. As soon as I landed at the airport and heard the locals speaking to me in Egyptian, my heart was filled with joy because it brought back all the beautiful nostalgic memories from my childhood.

I landed at the Cairo International Airport at 1 in the morning. I picked up my suitcase from baggage claim and went outside. I was expecting Nader, a friend of mine originally from Egypt who was studying abroad at Northeastern, to pick me up at the airport. Nader's alarm did not go off and he was delayed in picking me up. There were hundreds of cab drivers there pushing me to take a ride with them. They noticed how worried I looked, and a few offered me their cell phones to call a contact in Cairo.

I thanked them and kept waiting for Nader. Two hours later, Nader and his best friend, Maisara, finally arrived. I looked terrified and as they rushed to get my suitcase, Nader kept apologizing and saying how horrible he felt about not showing up on time. They drove me through downtown Cairo, and it looked and felt like 10 a.m. rather than 3 in the morning. Indeed, Cairo is a city that never sleeps.

We arrived at Nader's house, and they had the whole first floor ready for me. This was where his grandparents usually stayed. Nader and his parents stayed on the second floor. I remember sleeping very well and not waking up until 10 a.m. Once I awoke, I went to the second floor, knocked on the door, and was welcomed by Nader's mother, who was an Iraqi Arab from Baghdad. She seated me at the dining table in the kitchen and had the maids fix me breakfast. Nader's father soon joined us to give me a very warm welcome. He assured me that I would enjoy my stay in his country. Through our discussions, I learned Nader's parents were both Northeastern graduates, where they met. His father soon had to leave for work, but kindly told me to let him know if I needed anything.

While I was in Cairo, people were getting ready for the holy month of Ramadan. Just as Americans decorate their houses for Christmas with lights, Egyptians decorate their houses with Ramadan lanterns and light the candles at night. Nader's mother arranged my travel to Luxor, Aswan, and all the other places that I wanted to see before Ramadan. "The whole city shuts down during Ramadan because of fasting," she explained.

Maisara offered to give Nader and me a ride to the majestic Pyramids of Giza that day. Maisara, who was very funny, kept reminding me that Egypt was the mother of civilization as I rode a camel, went to see the Great Sphinx of Egypt, and visited other sites. When we approached the gate of the pyramid, there were only two ticketing options: Arab tourist and non-Arab tourist. The non-Arab tourists had to pay more than the Arab and Egyptian tourists. Maisara, with his sense of humor, recommended that I let go of my patriotism for the moment to save money. I told Maisara that I was from the Kurdish region of Iraq, but it was not fair to assume that I was Arab. He suggested we speak Arabic and pretend we were from Iraq. So, I told the agent at the ticket counter that I was visiting from Iraq and paid the fee for an Arab tourist. Once I got my ticket, Maisara continued to tease me about how I sold my identity for a cheaper ticket.

Seeing the pyramids was a dream come true. Maisara and I went deep inside one of the pyramids only to find an empty tomb. Maisara recommended that I get on a camel and have the guide walk me around the pyramids. The scariest thing about a camel ride is when the camel gets up headfirst. I almost fell over, but the guide said to hold on tight because the camel then raises his back up.

Some of the biggest highlights of my visit to Egypt were: the famous Khan El Khalili bazaar in old Cairo, a flight to Luxor to see the Valley of the Kings, the Karnak and Hatshepsut temples, a river cruise to Aswan where I saw the Abu Simbel temples, Philea temple, the unfinished obelisk, the citadel of Salahadin, the Azhar school, and the tombs of many religious icons. I also went to Khan El Khalili a few times to buy gifts for my family. But perhaps my favorite part of the trip was spending time with Nader and Maisara in the tea houses in the old city and listening to the music by the Egyptian legend, Um Kalthum.

I wished I could have stayed longer in Cairo but fall semester classes were about to start and it was time for me to head back to Boston. On my last day in Cairo, Nader and Maisara took me to the airport and wished me safe travels. The second my plane took off, I started thinking about other countries I wanted to explore. One of my friends once warned me about traveling: "It is an addiction, and the addiction always starts with the first trip." I think they were right.

As soon as I landed at Logan Airport, I called my mother to tell her that I was back in Boston. I sensed sadness in her voice and asked if things were all right at home. Things had not been going well for as long as I could remember as my mother resented the many years she lived under my father's strict rules. She resented her father who married her off at such a young age. She resented the fact that she had to live in a country that was so foreign to her and that it had caused the estrangement of her daughter Dilven. She felt my father had failed her in so many ways. My father made my mother take on all the household responsibilities. Jowan, Zhyan, Hoger, and Omed were all married by then and had their own homes and children to worry about. My younger siblings needed guidance now that the older siblings were gone. However, my father did not seem to care. "Dai guri, your father has left the house," my mother shared, weeping over the phone. I begged her to stop and reminded her that we all knew this was long overdue. With my father and older siblings out of the house, my mother felt she no longer had any support in looking after my younger siblings. My parents had been on and off for years because they never got along. My father, especially after his second imprisonment, was abusive to my mother and us. He often left the house and then returned and then left again and then returned once more. We knew Dad was not a father we could rely on, which hurt, as it seemed he had been altered beyond repair by outside forces.

My mother also failed to find fulfillment in keeping in touch with her loved ones from Kurdistan. She was disappointed because she felt she was being taken advantage of. Every time she called her siblings, it was becoming customary for them to ask my mother for cash, a daughter to marry, a sponsorship for one of their sons to immigrate to the U.S, and to ship them various goods. By living in America, our relatives from back home were under the false impression that we were loaded with money and living this fabulous "Hollywood life," not knowing that we had to work long hours to make the minimum wage to pay a countless number of bills and the mortgage. If we refused to help them, they would then make us feel guilty for supposedly having abandoned them back in Iraq, even though every single of them wanted to do the same.

When we were still in Zakho, my mother would often consult a sheikh (religious cleric) about my father's jealousy and temper and always hoped that the sheikh would tell my father to ease up on my mother and their children. Unfortunately, the sheikh, without fully giving my mother a chance to elaborate on her concerns, always blamed my mother for my father's jealousy and temper. The sheikh also avoided eye contact with my mother and reminded her that a woman should dutifully honor her husband and family and never question or complain about his rulings. He added that my mother should feel blessed for her suffering because that would add to the balance of her good deeds on the final day of judgment.

As we grew older and exposed our mother to the proper teachings of Islam, she thankfully realized that what the sheikh had told her was not necessarily correct. The translation of the Holy Quran is subject to multiple interpretations and many times the interpretation was dictated by men in the Middle East, who often used religion to their benefit. Seeing how religious men back home had taken advantage of the illiteracy and financial dependency of women like my mother, I was even more determined to seek higher education, explore the world, and work to be intellectually and financially independent. I did not need to rely on some cleric to interpret what I needed to do, as I knew science and psychology were my key to understanding and guidance through life.

Unlike my mother, most of my sisters and I, with exception of Dilven, waited until we finished our studies and landed a dream career before we thought of marriage. Jowan married at the age of thirty, Zhyan at twenty-eight, Jehan at twenty-nine, and I was in my mid-twenties and still single. My mother would often remind me how when she was my age, she already had multiple children. She would emphasize this point when she learned I did something that was not to her liking. I understood where my mother was coming from, but I also knew early on that I did not want to get married early or live a life similar to that of my siblings.

Growing up, I watched my mother obsess about keeping our home clean, and she insisted on doing everyone's laundry. And if she was not cleaning, she would be cooking or baking. Her cooking style was always very intensive and a true labor of love, which she preferred to do alone. My mother especially did not trust my cooking. My hands were not meant for cutting and chopping meat because "I was too into paper and pencil," she would dismissively remind me. Chopping vegetables and deseeding pomegranates for her signature salad were the only culinary chores she would trust me with. However, as I chopped the veggies, she would repeatedly remind me to dice finer, and my result was never satisfactory. Since she derived so much satisfaction from preparing our meals, she was not a fan of eating out at restaurants. She also felt guilty paying for meals when she felt her cooking was better and at a fraction of the cost. We once treated our mother to kebabs at a nice Persian restaurant. She loved the ambiance, atmosphere, music, hospitality, and even the food. Yet, when she saw the price on the final bill she loudly exclaimed "What! This is too much! The food was not worth this!"

Although she was my rock, it would be a lie to say that my mother was always easy to deal with. From the time I was a teenager, we began arguing about everything and she would constantly remind me how stubborn I was. Whereas my other siblings would sugarcoat their words with her, I was much more blunt, which caused more friction. While she was proud of my performance at school, that was pretty much it, and she constantly complained about my fashion taste, phone calls, guy friends, messy room, and books I would leave scattered about the house. I often screamed at her to give me my personal space, which she never did. That is something a Kurdish child learns early on—that privacy does not exist around your parents, regardless of your age. Each time I would slam my door in anger to signify that she had hurt my feelings, she would remind me how ungrateful I was for all of the sacrifices she had made for me, causing me extreme guilt. Perhaps most painful of all, she would then remind me that as punishment for my not appreciating her, I would have a daughter who would mistreat me the same way. After each fight, she would not talk to me for days, until I would eventually come up to her and apologize while kissing both of her hands.

Being a single mother of half a dozen young children was hard on my mother, especially in a country where everything was still so foreign to her. Perhaps the only thing that kept my mother sane while living in the U.S. was her Kurdish TV box that gave her access to the Kurdish channels so she could keep up with the news from back home, and the daily phone calls she got from each of her children to tell her about their lives. She would hear news about the U.S. from the same channels, but it was always a day or two late. My mother did not care about the urgency of the news if it was delivered in a language she understood. She had also gone from having her children by her side in the afternoons to watching overly dramatic Turkish-subtitled soap operas all alone while sipping on her afternoon chai.

I would call my mother after classes every day to learn what had happened on one of her shows. At times, she would ask for my guidance on a medical complaint she had. Over the years of living in the U.S., my mother had put on quite a bit of weight from eating an unhealthy diet and not walking to the bazaar as she used to in Kurdistan. When she presented herself to me with back pain or an upset stomach, I would often remind her to cut back on eating fried food or to walk twenty to thirty minutes every day in the neighborhood. My mother was never happy with my response, especially when I reminded her how she needed to watch her weight and cut back on eating three large meals. She questioned my credibility and that of my pharmacy school for not having a better recommendation for her chief complaint.

Because my mother spoke no English, she often had one of her eleven children attend her doctor's appointments with her. Being the only child in the medical field, it made sense for me to accompany her when I was home. She would first talk to me about her complaints and then I would interpret what she had conveyed to me for her medical provider. If she happened to be happy with the doctor for that visit, she would pray for him or her in Kurdish. Many times, the prayers my mother made had to be translated into English, which left me in a very awkward position. Once when her provider was a young man, she prayed that he would soon find a beautiful wife. Upon hearing my mother, I could not help but laugh at how awkward my mother's prayers would be if I translated them to her doctor. He then looked at me and asked if he could know what my mother had just said. Embarrassingly, my mother would even go to the extent of praying that I end up with a handsome gentleman like the doctor.

While my mother was worrying about setting me up

with a husband, my sister Jehan was finding one of her own. Working back in Ramadi, Iraq, Jehan had met and fallen in love with a white Italian-American named Leigh who was a government contractor at her base. I was working on a busy weekend when I received an out-of-area call. It was Jehan! She called to inform me that Leigh had proposed to her and she wanted to share her excitement. Although I was very happy for her, I was also extremely worried at how the family would take this news, considering how they were still hurt from "losing" Dilven after her marriage to an unapproved husband. I knew some of our siblings would not approve and this would bring tension to the family. It is an unfortunate fact that when you marry a Kurd you marry their entire family and sometimes their clan as well.

Unlike the rest of us, Jehan had darker brown skin with two big brown eyes. Because of this, she had low self-esteem because she was never approached by Kurdish men or families to consider her for marriage. As the saying goes, beauty is in the eye of the beholder, but to most Kurds, beauty was being fair-skinned and curvy; and the very thin Jehan was everything but. By Western beauty standards, Jehan had a perfectly toned body, yet to Kurds, she was "shaped like a boy," since she lacked wide hips and large breasts.

Like Dilven, Jehan rebelled from our strict family rulings. When we came to the U.S., the hijab was imposed on both Jehan and Dilven (unlike me who did it willingly). Coinciding with their independent streak, anything the two of them asked for was typically met with the reply that, "Only bitches (or whores) would want that," to shut them up. Early on, my family tried to arrange Jehan's marriage to a first cousin of ours. Naïve at the time, she agreed, until my father objected to the marriage because he had a personal conflict with the groom's mother. Jehan was heartbroken and forced to break things off to please my father.

What I feared most did eventually happen. The family objected to Jehan's marriage, but just like Dilven, Jehan was determined to proceed with her decision to marry Leigh anyway. As her punishment, Jehan was not only disowned by most family members, but her husband's race was altered so the Kurds in Georgia would not look down on us for our sister marrying a white American. As part of this ploy, my mother would tell her Kurdish women friends that Leigh was Lebanese, and his name was Ali. To his credit, Leigh was so kind and genuine to my mother that she gradually accepted him, and over the years he slowly became my mother's favorite son-in-law. Of note, Jehan and Leigh achieved a happy ending and now have a beautiful ten-year-old daughter that they named Aveen ("love" in Kurdish).

Ironically, at the very same time Jehan announced her marriage to Leigh, Dilven's marriage was on the rocks and having difficulties. At the age of twenty, Dilven needed guidance and found herself lost for agreeing to a marriage she was not prepared for. She and her husband were quite different, and she discovered she was not ready to cope with her husband Nazim's drug habit, controlling nature, and his mother's micromanagement. She decided to walk out of the marriage at the age of twenty-one. Nazim had reached out to me about helping to have Dilven return to him, but with my school and workload, I declined. I now feel extremely selfish and guilty for not doing more for

Dilven when she needed me, which may have led her to seek out that failed marriage. I feel ashamed for not being there for her like a loving older sister when she was lost and trying to figure out what to do with her life. Dilven, like any immigrant girl, was lost and escaped one proverbial jail only to walk into a different kind of prison, not realizing it until she was already stuck and married.

We were soon back on campus for the fall semester of 2008. I was twenty-six years old and excited to have discovered a new passion—a love of traveling the world. However, I could not deny that every now and then, I felt a sense of emptiness in my life. Despite my age, I had never dated or even expressed my feelings to a man. One late night, I was on my laptop re-writing my notes from class and listening to podcasts from some of my therapeutics courses. Once I was done studying, I happened to be checking emails and I got a Gmail chat message. I wondered who would be messaging me this late at night. It was Mason! He wanted to know how my trip went and if Leena had been a good host in Rome.

That one-time chat with Mason turned into a nightly conversation. As soon as I finished studying, I would wait for him to get online to talk to me. At that time, I was relationship naïve, and I did not know what I wanted nor was I comfortable starting the conversations. I knew companionship brought me joy, but I was not interested in getting physically involved with anyone. I felt that was something holy and should wait until I was married. Over the next few months, Mason and I started getting closer to each other. Mason was open to having relationships and had dated a countless number of girls. As for me, I had no experience with relationships, and I was still a virgin.

To my simple mind, I was ready for a relationship and whoever I was going to meet had to be "Mr. Right," which in my case meant a Western guy with Kurdish roots. This was the perfect ingredient to fill the gap in my life. I started telling everyone that any man I end up with had to have the right ingredients for "Mr. Right," as in someone who was a Kurd like me, but born or raised in the West and who had loosened up over the years in terms of the cultural and fundamental practices. These same "Mr. Right Ingredients" meant that he was as torn as I was between two different worlds: the West and the East, and thus he would understand and relate to what I was experiencing.

These mixed ingredients in my imaginary Mr. Right meant that we would be splitting up the house chores, he would respect my boundaries and space, he would want to venture out into the world with me, and we would cherish our Kurdish values and our friends. This same Mr. Right would understand how Kurdish culture sometimes meant more drama than a Shakespearean play. He would not be appalled to see me react to things that were culturally okay and suggest I seek counseling for getting overworked over what my mother had done. He would understand that regardless of what happened, my mother would always be right, and I had to beg for her forgiveness. This Mr. Right would know how Kurds came from an emotional culture, one that may seem loud, aggressive, strange, and irrational to many—but one that survived thousands of years of attempted annihilation and so was forged in the crucible of oppression, a culture wrought with the coping mechanisms people developed to maintain their sanity.

Mason sounded like the perfect Mr. Right Ingredient for me. Mason's father was a diplomat for the former Iraqi regime. So, his parents moved with Mason from one country to the next depending on where they were assigned to serve. Mason did not speak a word of Kurdish even though his father was a Kurd. He grew up in a Shiite family but did not have a good sense of what his faith meant. He was born in Baghdad and raised in the West, but he loved Kurds. Mason was in a long-term relationship with a Catholic girl from Rome, but his parents opposed his relationship, which eventually left him heartbroken. His parents were firm for Mason to find a soulmate from his roots. I was so convinced about Mason being the right ingredient that I started fantasizing about the activities we would be doing together–going to movies, cooking together, and even attending concerts.

As a woman who was forced into an arranged marriage at age thirteen to a stranger fourteen years older, my mother did not appreciate how I perceived Mason. To my mother, being married is all that mattered. Yet to me, the conflicted Kurdish/ American, what attracted me to Mason was more than marriage. Perhaps he was equally conflicted over his identity. Perhaps he reminded me of my own struggles without him verbalizing it.

Undeterred, my mother reminded me about the importance of being married, having a partner to care for me when I was sick, and having children to give me the feeling of motherhood. I knew for a fact that I wanted a married lifestyle far different from that of my mother and siblings. I was not interested in marrying just to have a husband. I wanted an equal partner who would be my best friend. I had grown up to believe that marriage, like any relationship in life, was a contract where both partners had to commit to their part of the agreement so the relationship could prosper. If either partner failed to commit and expected the other partner to live with his or her failings, then one partner was likely to get fed up and the relationship would eventually fail. Due to shame and societal judgment, it was usually the woman who, for the sake of her children and society, sacrificed her career and dreams to put up with the failures of her partner.

I was raised to be independent. However, when it came to marriage, my parents expected me to go through the traditional process and for my family to have the final say. This contradiction left me confused and I was perceived as being rebellious for telling my family how I felt. My family expected to know the man. They wanted to meet him and ask him tough questions. Did he practice his religion? Did he drink or smoke? Was he in good health? Would he be able to provide for his family? When it came to marriage, my family saw me transitioning from being my family's property to my husband's property with little say on my end. When I chose to make my own decision on such a personal matter, my family felt as though I was belittling our cultural values and rejecting their "duty" to evaluate a potential partner.

I made plans to visit London during the spring break of 2008 to meet Mason. After three days of visiting, we were having coffee at a coffee shop in the famous Trafalgar Square in London when he abruptly surprised me with a kiss in public. He told me that even though we were different in so many ways, he felt we had a strange bond and he could not resist keeping in touch with me. The feelings were mutual—I could feel the rush of hormones and chemicals running through my body, but I was at a loss as to how to respond to him. At the same time, I knew this magical unrealistic moment I was living with Mason would bring me pain and sorrow in the days and months to come. I could almost hear my mother's voice and I feared I would not be able to fulfill the role of the girlfriend he had envisioned due to my strict upbringing. He held my hand and asked if we should continue exploring London together, and for a moment I felt the whole world belonged to me and was my oyster. Was this the normal life other people experience? Those who did not know lives of pain, war, and abandonment?

After spending a week in London, it was time to head back to the States. Mason dropped me at the airport, and I took a direct flight to Logan International. I landed late on a Sunday afternoon and once home, I went to bed and did not wake up until 3 in the morning. When I woke up, I started feeling the pain of loneliness. I cried from feeling the despair of liking a man who was an ocean away and knowing that I could never be his ideal girlfriend. I had to dry my tears, unpack my suitcase, and get ready for classes later in the morning.

Following my spring break trip to London, I had to finish my last semester before starting a year of rotations in Boston. Mason and I kept in touch for months after my return from London. Unfortunately, our differences became more apparent and added so many complications to our communication and relationship. To try and overcome these complications, Mason decided to spend a week with me in Boston to see if there was a way that we could resolve our differences. I wanted to hold on to him figuratively, but I just knew he could never be mine physically. He begged me to open up to him, but something was holding me back. Every time he kissed me, I felt caught between my love and desire for him and the guilt I felt about my culture and faith. Mason could not understand my feelings and did not appreciate my religious and cultural values. It felt as if trying to resolve our differences was just beating a dead horse. My girlfriends were bewildered to see me return to my room at night, while my supposed boyfriend slept in a hotel room by himself. "But he came from London to spend time with you and you guys should spend the night together," they would remind me. They forgot about my strict Kurdish upbringing and the fact I was unable to become sexually involved with him.

To complicate my life even further, I received a devastating call from Omed to tell me that my father had been diagnosed with lung cancer. I cried for hours and did not get out of bed until late in the afternoon. My mind was now elsewhere, and I started showing up to my rotations unprepared. My academic performance was in jeopardy and my adviser told me that I needed to either pull myself together or postpone the rotations to the following year. I knew postponing was not an option, so I had to work hard to get my act together—but first I needed closure and had to end things with Mason.

Pharmacy school, like any professional school, requires

students to complete clinical rotations in their last year of training. At Northeastern, we were assigned to six, six-week rotations with a one-off rotation. Every six weeks I was assigned to a different site for training until the year was over. My first rotation was in the retail pharmacy setting, which I was not looking forward to but decided to approach with an open mind. The experience was no different from the internship I had done at the retail pharmacy in Atlanta where I had to resolve insurance claims and deal with impatient patients.

Following my rotation in the retail pharmacy setting, I interned for six weeks at the Department of Public Health followed by a twelve-week rotation at Tufts Medical Center. Once I was done at Tufts, I interned at a pharmaceutical company for six weeks and ended my rotations at the Demick Diabetes clinic. While at Tufts Medical Center, I practiced in the Cardiac Care Unit, where most patients were waiting for an organ transplant. While on rounds, we would meet patients and sometimes over the next few days, would learn about the passing of the patient. It was mentally hard for me because I developed a bond with my patients on a personal level.

Knowing my father had cancer, it was hard to care for my patients while keeping my emotions in check. I gave 100% to each patient and would be depressed once I learned the patient had died. Most patients I encountered were desperate for an organ transplant. However, before patients could be listed for an organ transplant, we had to interview them to make sure they would be responsible for their health once they received one. I once overheard a patient's excitement about a holiday weekend. To this patient, a holiday weekend meant a lot of partying and drinking, which would hopefully result in numerous car accidents and the availability of organs. This patient hoped he would be one of those lucky recipients of an organ that would get him out of the cardiac care unit. I realized both how precious life is and how blessed I was to be in good health, but also how people are complicated and can be deserving of mercy without being good-hearted themselves. Desperation can truly muddle one's moral certitude.

I enjoyed the six weeks interning at the Massachusetts Department of Public Health. I loved the spirit of the public health service and the advocacy work involved in advancing pharmacists' patient care service. I also liked my rotation at the Demick Diabetes clinic.

My last rotation was at a pharma company where I had to promote the sale of their products by presenting the evidence of their efficacy. A few weeks into the internships, I failed to find fulfillment in what I was doing as a student. As far as I was concerned, I wanted to live a life of public service and I knew that type of work at a pharma company was not suited for me. I did not want to be a salesperson. I wanted to help alleviate suffering.

After six rotations in different practice settings, I realized I was most fit to serve in public health service and advocacy. In December of 2009, I learned about a fellowship opportunity at the Food and Drug Administration (FDA) and decided to apply. They called me for an interview, and I arrived wearing my hijab. They greeted me with respect and asked if I had any flexibility in removing my hijab. I was not sure what flexibility meant considering the hijab was part of my faith. They told me that they were not able to proceed with the fellowship interview because if I was accepted, I would be a public servant and could not have anything covering my head. I asked how covering my hair to fulfill my religious obligation was a barrier to serving the country and the needs of patients. They apologized and told me that this requirement was an institutional policy and there was nothing they could do.

Determined not to let my hijab stop me, I was now even more tenacious. I knew I could serve in so many ways and my rejection from the FDA fellowship was not the end of what I was passionate about. For example, I knew I could always return to the Kurdistan region of Iraq to meet the needs of the underserved population and refugees there. During my off rotation, right before graduation, I made plans to visit Kurdistan.

It felt a bit strange that for the first time, I was returning to my homeland as an independent twenty-eight-year-old woman. The plan was for me to stay with Baci (aunt) Soad, who had been one of our interpreters in Guam. She was a single woman in her 60s and a U.S. citizen who had returned to Erbil after living in the United States for more than thirty years. She was the only person I knew that I could trust staying with while in Erbil.

As soon as the plane landed at the Erbil International Airport, I became emotional. I never thought the day would come when I would land in Kurdistan at our own international airport. The feeling was surreal. Everyone on the plane took off their seat belts, stood, and removed their carry-on luggage from the overhead bin while the plane was still taxing to the terminal. Once out of the airport, I saw Baci Soad waiting for me in a cab. On our way home, we picked up kabobs for dinner. As soon as we finished, the craving for a Kurdish chai kicked in. Baci Soad had a Kurdish soba, which was an oil-burning stove that she used to warm up the living room, where we also slept. She also had a two-piece teapot. The first teapot is used to boil the water and the second teapot brews the tea using the steam from the first. She let me get a good night's rest and did not disturb me until I awoke on my own the next morning.

Baci Soad and I went to the Qaysari Bazaar so I could get a phone card. When we reached the mobile phone shops, there were dozens of booths offering the service of unlocking cell phones and selling phone cards. While we waited at one of the shops, a young boy brought us two Kurdish chai in small teacups on a tray. I offered to pay, but the shop owner refused and told me the tea was a courtesy for customers. As I was drinking my chai, Baci Soad became angry at a man in the shop for staring at me. She reminded him that if I were his sister, he would not want a male stranger to stare at her that way. I started to get uncomfortable as the encounter escalated and the shop owner had to intervene by apologizing and asking the man to leave his shop.

That same morning, we got an internet card so I could access my emails while in Erbil. We then walked around the Qaysari Bazaar to buy items for lunch. She took me to the butcher shop where the animal carcasses were hung, and the butcher would cut any part of the animal body for sale. Baci Soad asked for one kilogram of boneless meat. I found it ironic that, in the same line of butcher shops, there were stores where they kept shoes in display cases, and had meat exposed to the air.

One of the items Baci Soad did not want to miss when in Qaysari was the maasti marr (yogurt made from goats' milk) which is only available from March to August. "There is increased competition from manufactured and daily imported yogurt, however, customers are still loyal to local yogurts from the villages and mountains of Kurdistan," she explained. The quality of maasti marr is unparalleled. However, educated locals like Baci Soad were a little concerned about the fat content. They sold maasti marr in plain buckets with no labeling or nutritional facts. I helped Baci Soad carry the bucket of maasti marr to the main street where we tried to hail a cab to head home. Once I started waving my hand to stop a cab, Baci Soad warned me not to do that again, as the cab drivers in Erbil were not used to women waving their hands at them. "It is usually a male member or an elder that stops the cab and a girl simply gets in. If you do that again, they will mistake you for wanting to flirt with them," she reminded me. It was so hard to believe that a simple hand gesture to stop a cab could be so different across the ocean. I kept my opinion to myself, and we got into the cab and drove home for that day.

After a delicious lunch, I finally logged onto my email account and let my contacts know that I was in Erbil. I scheduled meetings to visit hospitals and meet the deans of colleges of pharmacy. Almost everyone agreed that the region needed young faculty who lived in the diaspora to return and assist in teaching students. During my stay in Kurdistan, I split my time between three main cities in the Kurdish region. I was so touched by the kind hearts of the people in the region. Everyone I visited insisted on buying me a present, offered to show me around, and gave me a warm welcome.

In one of my meetings, the Ministry of Health—who happened to be a distant relative of my mother's—asked if I could spend some time with his daughters in Hawraman. I wanted to see Hawraman and felt this was my only chance, so I welcomed the offer. The next day, the minister sent a car to Baci Soad's house to pick me up. We drove to Sulaymaniyah, a two-hour drive from Erbil. Throughout the drive, the minister talked about the beauty and history of Hawraman. He told me about the Hawrami dialect, culture, and of course my distant relatives. He was quick to remind me about the talents of the Hawrami tribe, adding that they were known for their artwork, creativity, music, and medicine. "This is partly because we eat a lot of walnuts here in Tawellah," he added. He then popped open a walnut for me and showed me how a loose walnut looked just like a brain. The minister spoke half Kurdish and half English to make sure I was following along. Once we reached Sulaymaniyah, I was amazed by the villa where the minister and his family stayed. He introduced me to his three daughters who all spoke Hawrami, a dialect that was completely foreign to me. The minister's wife, a gynecologist, returned home after her clinic hours.

The family invited me to dinner at Komalayati, a membership-run restaurant and popular spot for all the rich families of Sulaymaniyah. The place was incredibly fancy, and the food was amazing. The daughters introduced me to their friends and made sure they all knew I was from America. I noticed the change in their facial expressions as soon as they heard the word *America*.

The friends took a countless number of pictures with me and invited me to their houses. For a moment, I felt like a Hollywood celebrity. I could not be that impressive and was not sure why they were so intrigued, but then again perhaps I would have done the same as a youth in Zakho.

While in Sulaymaniyah, the minister arranged for a two-day trip to Tawellah, the birthplace of my paternal grandfather. Tawellah is a mountainous town, where all houses are made from mud and built on three mountains that face each other. The mud houses were engineered in a way where the roof of one house served as a yard for the mud house built above. To see my grandfather's house, we had to do some serious climbing. I never met my grandfather, but I knew he was completely detached from his family in Tawellah and I was to discover the story behind that detachment during my stay. My grandfather, who was engaged to a first cousin through family arrangements, moved to Erbil for a work assignment. In Erbil, he met my maternal grandmother who was a widow and mother of a daughter. For my grandfather, it was love at first sight. He broke his arranged engagement, angering not only his family but the whole Hawrami clan. Consequently, his family and the town disowned him and seized his property rights in Tawellah.

After a delicious barbecue lunch, we walked to Awesar, located on the border of Iraq and Iran and a picnic hub for locals in Tawellah. While at Awesar, there was a defined line separating Iraqi Kurdistan from Iran (or Rojhilat, what Kurds consider to be Eastern Kurdistan). I spotted many signs bearing skulls and crossbones indicating landmines and danger to anyone attempting to cross the invisible line, which was sad to me as this was really an imaginary line dividing two areas of Greater Kurdistan.

We then continued our walk into downtown Tawellah to meet my distant cousins. I spotted coke bottles full of homemade pomegranate syrup for sale. The cousins told me about the whole process of making pomegranate syrup, a product specifically made in Tawellah. Pomegranates became ripe for picking in autumn and the syrup was made immediately after picking the ripe ones. One of my cousins had a factory that made klash, an old traditional Kurdish shoe usually worn by men for the Kurdish New Year or other celebrations. Most craftsmen making klash shoes are from the Hawraman mountains of Kurdistan. Klash is believed to have first been worn by Zoroaster, founder of the Zoroastrian religion, which also has ancient connections to the Kurds and various other faiths practiced by Kurds. My cousins charged about 100 U.S. dollars for a pair of klash because of the intense manual labor involved in making them. The shoes had soles made of cotton fabric and goat hide and my cousins showed me how the klash were intricately handmade. They delicately passed the cotton threads between their toes before connecting them to a small machine in the shop that wrapped the threads together, helping them form the sole of the klash. The upper vamps of the klash were then made with knitted wool thread.

My cousins asked how long I was planning to stay in Tawellah. I was sad to tell them I was leaving the next day but promised to visit them the next time I was in the region and to keep in touch until then. The following day as we were having breakfast which included quince jam, walnut pizza, and cardamom chai, one of my cousins knocked on the door and presented me with a pair of female ballet klash that he handcrafted overnight to take home with me. I was just in awe when I saw the klash and how cute they looked. I thanked him and told him how special the gift was. I promised to wear them for my graduation to honor his labor in making them and he asked me to send them pictures when it occurred. We left Tawellah and I felt as though I left a piece of my heart with those kindhearted people—new relatives who cared for me and that I never imagined I would meet.

On our way back to Sulaymaniyah, the minister and his family offered to make me a Kurdish outfit to wear for graduation with the ballet klash. We went to the oldest qaysari in Sulaymaniyah to find a lovely piece of fabric that could be tailored for me to take home. We went to countless fabric shops, and I was mesmerized by the beautiful colors of Kurdish fabric. As usual, at every fabric shop we entered, the shop owner had the teashop next door serve us complimentary tea with sweets, and they would bring down rolls of fabric to open in front of me to make sure the material was to my liking. After the fifth roll, we agreed on the fabric. We then went to the bazaar where the tailor took my measurements and told me the dress would be ready in twenty-four hours.

Before I left Kurdistan, I visited my father's relatives in Zakho and Duhok. I spent a few days in Duhok to see the region and the university. While there, I met the Vice President of International Relations with whom I had corresponded about the book drive. He introduced me to the President of the University, Dr. Esmat Khalid. Together, they told me the school of pharmacy was transitioning to an American-based system and they needed faculty to assist with the transition. They were willing to provide me with housing and a salary that was comparable to what I could earn in the U.S., and it all sounded great. I said I needed to talk with my family about the job offer and would email them an answer once I was back in the United States. Dr. Khalid explained that there was no rush, but they would need me to join the faculty for the fall semester of 2010.

After my meetings in Duhok, I got into a shared cab, and off I went to Zakho, where I visited my paternal aunts and uncles for a few days. They were so happy to see me so mature and independent. I told them I was thinking about returning to work in Duhok and I could immediately see the frantic look on their faces.

"You must have lost your mind," said one of my uncles. "Heleen! You are too Americanized and would not do well in the male-dominated society of Kurdistan," they explained. They discouraged me from returning. I learned that they had reached out to my parents to get the idea of returning to Kurdistan out of my head. I was aware of where they were coming from, but I also wanted them to give me a chance to explain my reasoning. I had an urge to serve and who was better to serve than the displaced refugees in Kurdistan? For my cousins, childhood friends, aunts, and uncles, the culture in Kurdistan had not changed. The major change that had happened over the many years was me. For the very first time, I felt I was a foreigner in my own country. They were preserved in a time capsule, while I had gone off to become a new person and return with new ideas about what was "normal."

Later that week on my way back to Erbil, I had a dinner date with my childhood friend, Brwa. We connected after so many years through Facebook. Our friendship dated way back to my days in elementary school in Erbil. We talked about all the years I had been away and how the culture had evolved when it came to women and their roles in society. I told Brwa I was thinking about returning to serve my people and wanted to get his opinion. Brwa was taken by surprise, joking "If you return, I might just have to marry you." Brwa agreed that living in Kurdistan as a single female would be hard and I needed a male companion. He then asked if I was willing to give him a chance to be that companion. I did not expect him to bring up the idea of marriage or dating seriously, considering we had been friends for so many years. I thought about how different Mason had been and that maybe I should consider someone from back home who would appreciate where I was coming from. I respected Brwa and our families had been friends for many years. However, this complicated matters even further, because now I not only needed to think about returning to serve, but about marrying a local who had a tribal background. I was not sure I was ready for so many changes all at once. With my graduation four weeks away, I told Brwa I needed time to think about how I wanted to proceed and was open to the idea of us keeping in touch and talking more.

I was afraid to tell my family about Brwa because the news would have scared them and they would have thought he was like Rebin, with the intent of using me to make his way to America. Brwa, who was a year older than I, had recently finished his master's degree in information technology. He worked for the KRG part-time and taught information technology at the University of Salahaddin. He took pride in his tribal background but insisted he was open-minded about women's roles because he went to Baghdad for his college degree, which had broadened his outlook of the world. However, when it came to marriage, it became evident that he needed the blessing of every one of his family members.

As I left Kurdistan, I also felt I had abandoned a part of my heart in the region. On my way back, I stopped in Istanbul for a few days to experience the culture and indulge myself with Turkish food. To me, Istanbul had the perfect mix of Eastern and Western culture and was the only city in the world where one could have a European experience intermixed with Islamic grace. The city was also home to several million Kurds who were forced to migrate there in the 1990s after the Turkish military burned down thousands of Kurdish villages as part of their attempt to defeat the PKK.

I returned to Boston, ready for graduation. My mother, Jowan, and my sister-in-law attended my graduation. I was the first in my family to graduate with a higher degree and the first to be called Dr. Sairany. My family was proud of me receiving my doctorate. However, there was still a lot of work to be done. Immediately after graduation, I had to start studying for my board exams. I applied to the Georgia State Board of Pharmacy for licensure to practice.

While studying, I received a call from Brwa. He sounded down, and I asked if everything was okay. "The two of us will not get anywhere with our relationship," he replied. I did not know what that meant so I asked him to clarify. He told me that his family was not open to the idea of our getting married because of how Americanized and independent I was. His family was afraid I was too strong-minded and would not acclimate to the traditional practices in Erbil. His family was also worried about my age, because I was in my late twenties and only a year younger than their son. They were concerned that I would not be submissive enough because I was both more educated and more worldly than he was.

I could not help but laugh at their flimsy excuses. I remembered my grandfather from Tawellah who stood up against the wishes of his family and tribe for the love of my grandmother. I told Brwa his family had legitimate reasons and he should be mindful of their concerns. He asked if I was upset. Why would I be upset about losing someone who was not willing to fight for me? I ended the call feeling firm about where I stood but also tearful. I asked myself, what lessons were there in my encounters with Mason and Brwa? I was too naïve for a relationship with a Westerner and too Americanized for a Kurd. With my upcoming licensing examinations, I did not have time to grieve or cry or even think about how confused I was. The one thing that mattered was to pass my licensure exam. I had come too far to fail.

CHAPTER VII:
STUCK BETWEEN TWO WORLDS

You ask me about that country, whose details now escape me,
I don't remember its geography, nothing of its history
And should I visit it in memory,
It would be as I would a past lover,
After years, for a night, no longer restless with passion,
With no fear of regret.
I have reached that age when one visits the heart
merely as a courtesy
– *"Let Me Think," Faiz Ahemd Faiz*

Kurdish uncles in a tea shop in Erbil, Iraq, carrying the weight of the world on their shoulders. Photo courtesy of the Kurdish photographer, Ranj Abdullah.

What concerned me the most about returning to the Middle East after all my time living in the United States was whether I could still be part of the land where I had been born. Was the cultural umbilical cord severed beyond repair? No native could ever imagine the problems refugee families face as they adjust to a new culture, language, and people. In my case, being expelled from my own land was also traumatic. Growing up, I tried to blend in with American culture as much as I could without losing my own traditions. That meant celebrating Thanksgiving, eating apple pie, and joining school clubs. Unfortunately, there was only so much I could do to assimilate without being tagged as the "wanna be" white girl, and conversely, only so much I could hold on to without being referred to as "fresh off the boat."

I had to weigh the choices I made for myself carefully to determine if they would work or have negative repercussions. I was now a twenty-eight-year-old single, first-generation immigrant with multiple failed quasi-relationships (by American standards). I felt lost, not knowing where I belonged. Since I came to the United States, I had never felt American enough nor Kurdish enough. At Northeastern, the Persian students argued with the Arab students over my identity, claiming that I was more Persian while the Arabs thought Kurds were closer to being Arabs. My classmates often asked if I was either Persian, Spanish, Lebanese, French, Turkish, Italian, or Brazilian. They even went to the extent of initially speaking to me in all sorts of languages. I grew up so desperate for belonging that I began accepting any suggestion I would get from people. I also liked the fact that I passed for so many nationalities and it gave me the sense of being a world citizen. But after a while, this feeling of wanting to belong somewhere made me feel as though I belonged nowhere.

After my visit to Kurdistan and my last phone call with Brwa, a false dichotomy started to haunt me. Was I an American or a Kurd when it came to cultural norms? This sort of cultural depersonalization is complicated to fully express for someone who has never felt it, but if you have, you know immediately what I am describing.

Being brought up in America taught me many beautiful things. It taught me what it meant to be a Kurd. It taught me how to fight for my rights. Being brought up in America also taught me that I was not of lesser value because of my identity or gender. With hard work, persistence, and strong faith, I was able to get into top schools, fundraise, travel the world, give talks, protest, challenge governors for my rights, and shout as loudly as I could for the causes that meant so much to me. My upbringing in the States also taught me that making a change is not impossible, no matter how many obstacles exist. Through my studies, I learned that I could change anything I did not like, provided I maintained respect for others' opinions.

Yet, I also had hopeful visions for Kurdistan, such as eventual relaxation of a strict culture, one free of judgmental and tribal practices, double standards, and men's superiority over women. In the last few years, I had heard so much about how the region was progressing, and I was hoping there would be an end to these practices. Like any Kurd growing up in the diaspora, I had always missed home and dreamed of going back to serve. Now that I had finished school, I hoped that I could return to where it all began to be a part of the promising changes that the region needed.

Would it ever be possible for me to be part of the home I had come from and be assertive about the values I had embraced in the West? There was no way I could know the answer without taking my chances and returning.

Three months after graduation and having acquired the necessary training (and after some serious thought), I decided to return to my motherland to provide first aid care to refugees who escaped conflict to find refuge in northern Iraq. I felt a deep sense of obligation to help and serve others regardless of their backgrounds. To do this, I decided to risk my career as a new graduate and move back to the Kurdistan region of Iraq.

To do so, I emailed the President of the University of Duhok, Dr. Esmat Khalid, to accept his job offer to join the faculty for the fall semester of the 2010 academic year. For verification of my credentials, he asked me to have my diplomas authenticated at the Iraqi Embassy in Washington, DC. I mailed my diplomas to the embassy even though this request seemed a bit strange. The diplomas soon came back stamped by the embassy, but the ink had bled through the paper and damaged the appearance of the diploma. I was disappointed, considering how hard I had worked for these pieces of paper and how the embassy had mishandled them.

My family was concerned about my decision to go back and my safety. My parents were particularly worried that I was not ready for the move and that the locals might take advantage of me. They were afraid I would be disappointed in the bureaucratic system back home and return to the U.S. heartbroken. Their reasoning was that if I did not go back and have my nostalgia ruined, Iraqi Kurdistan could retain its romantic veneer for me; they believed if I saw it up close through changed eyes, I would grow to resent its true reality.

Despite this, I was determined that I was going to be part of the desperately needed change in the region and felt confident that I would prove my family wrong.

I landed at the Erbil International Airport late at night and was picked up by Jowan and Hatam. Jowan, who had returned to Kurdistan a month earlier, was working as a senior advisor to the president of the Kurdistan Parliament. She was granted this position thanks to a dear friend who was married to the deputy president of the Parliament (which I later realized is typical of the usual nepotism). Jowan and Hatam had a five-year-old girl, Soz, and a three-year-old boy, Shad. They moved back to Kurdistan because they wanted Soz and Shad to grow up in Kurdistan with a better appreciation of their religious and cultural values. Jowan loved the benefits she received for being a senior advisor and appreciated the flexible work hours, which allowed her to spend more time with her family (something that had concerned her when she lived in America). For his part, Hatam was in the real estate business and also doing well.

The next day, I was picked up from Jowan's house by the university's driver, who drove me straight to Duhok University. My housing was not ready, so the university put me in a hotel for a week. It was Ramadan and the whole city was pretty much shut down during working hours. I had to eat iftar (meal after sunset) outside, while my suhoors (meal before sunrise) were provided by the hotel. Hearing the call to prayer at sunset in Duhok and joining the community for iftar felt bittersweet.

I had reconnected with my cousin, Media, after all these years. Unlike me, Media was a physician, a married woman, and had a son (notably with blue eyes like her). When I visited, we had a lot of catching up to do. I met her husband who was a police officer. Media was sharing a three-floored house with her mother and father-in-law, married brothers-in-law with their spouses and kids, and four sisters-in-law. I was not sure I could ever live like that after gaining my own independent space. I realized while seeing her situation that if I were to ever get married, I would need to have my own privacy—which is not something you begin to appreciate until you taste it for the first time. One of the things that Kurdish culture lacks the most is an appreciation for personal privacy.

Media and I grew up together and we constantly competed over grades, as I would usually rank first and she second when it came to class ranking. Like mine, Media's mother was Sorani, and she was also one of eleven children. In fact, our mothers were best friends because they had so much in common. We spent countless days studying together as both of us were interested in the sciences. People had a hard time believing that Media and I were first cousins as we looked so different; she had bright blue eyes, long blonde straight hair, a round freckled face, and was much shorter than I was. I never admitted it to her, but I grew up extremely envious of Media, as she was the baby girl of eleven children and got constant loving attention from her siblings as well as everyone else because of her rare blue eyes.

Everyone in Kurdistan favored girls with blue or green eyes because typically most women were brunettes with brown eyes. Too young to understand the psychological vestiges of European colonialism on beauty standards, I often wondered with resentment why I did not have blue eyes like Media. I felt that if I had blue eyes, I would have also gotten the attention of others like her, especially the boy classmates who were always interested in Media and took good care of her. Media was also my partner in crime as we would often dress up and go to wedding parties together, where we would squeeze ourselves in-between crowds of women to see how the bride looked. Media was much bolder than I was at these parties. She was not afraid to join the older ladies in dances and everyone liked to have the blue-eyed girl join in their celebrations.

Previously, Media and I always agreed on things, but now it was clear how much we had both changed over the years. She found sharing the same house with so many extended in-laws to be a huge help because of her working hours. She could leave her baby boy with someone she trusted.

"Heleen, you remember the tough year where my mother immigrated to England and soon thereafter, my father passed away," she explained. "Having a family is all that I wanted. I was tired of living in between places from one sibling's house to the next." Media insisted that I stay a few nights and I agreed. I was treated like a princess by her in-laws. Every time I sat on the floor (as Kurds normally do, instead of on couches) they placed a pillow behind my back against the wall to ensure I was comfortable. After serving iftar, they always insisted I try several desserts they had prepared for us. I then heard the mother-in-law say how blessed she was to have Media who granted her a blue-eyed grandson. So, it seemed that blue eyes were still favored in Kurdistan after all these years.

After a few days of living in Duhok, the Director of the Office of International Relations came to pick me up and show me the housing options. The first option was in the heart of the old Bazaar of Duhok. With all its noise and activity, it seemed too much for me. The director and I agreed that I should consider alternative housing options. We realized the best choice was an apartment in Zari Land—new apartment complexes built in the city where many American expatriates lived.

I was promised a furnished apartment; however, as soon as I moved to Zari Land, I found that the apartment was missing most amenities. Any housing supplies I asked for needed to go through the president's office for approval and I was reminded that I needed to lower my expectations because "Duhok was not Boston." I understood that Kurdistan was still developing, but I was not asking for anything extravagant. All I needed were basic living items that I was promised in my job contract. The one staff member who was sympathetic to my concerns was a man named Wassfi, who was in his early thirties and had young female cousins living in the United States. He told me how his female cousins had the same frustrations as I when they visited. Wassfi was a Yazidi Kurd, a religious minority group in the Kurdish region. I told Wassfi about our Yazidi neighbors in Guam and how we kept in touch after we settled in different states. After further conversation, we discovered that our Guam neighbors were Wassfi's cousins! *What a small world*, I thought to myself. Wassfi invited me to his house for dinner to meet his wife and two little girls. His wife was also Yazidi from Bashiqa, where many Yazidis resided.

In addition to Wassfi, I met Parween, a humorous, red-haired lady in her mid-forties. Parween, a mother of five, was originally from Sulaymaniyah. She moved to Duhok after marrying Hasan, a distant relative of mine from Zakho. Parween and Hasan met at the University of Baghdad when Parween was finishing her master's studies and Hasan was an undergraduate. Hasan, the only son of two highly educated parents, faced opposition from his family for wanting to marry a woman who did not conform to the family's standards and was four years older than him. Not heeding any of those cultural restrictions, Hasan married Parween. When we met, they had been happily married for seventeen years and had four red-haired little girls and a boy with a sweet round freckled face. I remember going with Parween to pick up the children from school on Thursdays and sharing the same bedroom with them on weekends. The children would fight over who would sleep next to me.

One day, Parween and I were waiting outside the school for the children. Once they spotted me, they ran towards me and held onto me for as long as possible. We then drove around the city with Parween announcing to the kids that it was time to show Heleen around Duhok. We drove by Duhok Dam, which Parween said was a site where couples would meet. Dating was not allowed in Duhok, but it did not stop couples from seeing each other inconspicuously. As we drove out of the dam, we spotted a couple kissing in their car. Parween honked the car horn at them for fun and the man pressed on the gas pedal and drove away as fast as he could. The little ones giggled at Parween from the back of the car. On our way home, Parween stopped to pick up two grilled chickens for lunch. Parween honked twice when we got to the shop as a signal to the owner who somehow knew that meant she needed to pick up two grilled chickens. Five minutes later, the shop owner walked out and presented Parween with two chickens.

Parween had recently been promoted to Associate Dean of Student Affairs of the Medical Campus that housed the schools of medicine, dentistry, pharmacy, and nursing. There were times I waited for her outside her office and heard her talking with faculty members and student groups about various academic issues. However, there did not seem to be anything academic about the encounters. She would never take notes and it seemed as though she was holding business dealings involving real estate. When I told her this, she agreed! She said that all she did was negotiate, making sure both parties heard each other and resolved their disputes.

The academic year finally started. As I walked through the bazaars and along the streets of Duhok, I saw parents and children busy buying school supplies, tailoring school uniforms, and getting prepared for a new academic year. College students were also busy buying clothes and getting ready for their new courses. As a new faculty member, I was worried about how the first day would go. Would they understand my American English? Would I be able to have a collegial professor-student relationship? Would the students respect my class rules and regulations? So many questions were running through my head that I had to finally shut down my brain and head out with an expatriate friend I recently met named Dilband.

Dilband was born and raised in San Diego and was back to marry one of her first cousins. It was a bit surprising that an American would be open to the idea of having an intimate relationship with a first cousin. But I kept an open mind since I was still adjusting to the culture. Dilband was living in an apartment across the street from me with her father. After a long day of work, we would cook and vent the stress from work and cultural dilemmas, helping keep each other sane. Dilband told me her father opposed her marriage to her cousin, Haval. She said that everyone in the family knew she loved Haval, but her father and his did not get along and they had put the marriage on hold. I remembered what Brwa had told me about how his uncles could dictate marriage partners. As a friend, I tried to support Dilband, but I also had my own drama to deal with at the university.

The social culture in Duhok was not friendly to platonic relationships. Also, simple kindness or friendliness to the opposite sex was typically interpreted as flirtation and romantic interest. If you were seen in a park or outside hanging out with someone, it meant you were either his spouse, fianceé, or lover. It was abnormal for two people to meet at a cafe in Duhok for a first date, and if they did meet up at a cafe, their relationship would be assumed to be "official" at that point. Other than hiding in the mountains, or around the Duhok Dam, there was nowhere for aspiring couples to get to know each other without being noticed. Many of the Duhoki guys in our circle who had been in an arranged marriage since a young age, would leave their wives at home to come hang out with our group of ex-pats at cafes until late in the night.

The culture in Duhok was male-dominated, and very much in line with the Islamic teachings found in the four states bordering the Kurdish region. Practicing Muslims were expected to lower their gaze when they encountered a person of the opposite sex. Per Sharia law, you were only allowed to gaze once, because chances were the first gaze was not intentional. But if you gazed a second time, then you would be in the haram category. I joked with Parween that if I were a guy, I would look as long as I could when first meeting a woman, as that was the only halal chance I would get. Then again, the longer you spent in the Middle East, the more you realized that like many things, people were often hypocritically "halal in the streets, but haram in the sheets."

The strict cultural practices and close-mindedness about sex, dating, and relationships had promoted dishonesty, with people having to please their urges behind the scenes. However, my opinions about such things were often rejected, simply because I was the American who grew up in the U.S. that held a U.S. passport. My "outside" opinions were considered completely irrelevant to the current status quo in Duhok.

When I first arrived in Kurdistan, I never doubted my Kurdish identity and was expecting to blend in and assimilate in a matter of weeks. However, with time, I discovered I was developing a distinctive character due to the daily challenges of living as a single woman in Duhok. I was not doing what locals found to be the norm. I was not sneaking off to make out with a guy at the Duhok Dam, but instead preferred to meet men over coffee and talk openly. "Heleen, you will be reprimanded for meeting guys in public," a male friend explained. Over time, I found myself objecting to so many practices and realized that my "Americanized" lens was affecting the way I saw things. I tried hard to assimilate to the cultural norm, but every time I did, I found myself struggling to be who I really was.

My friend, Roza, whom I first met when I was in Boston, was now back in Duhok. When we reunited, I learned that she was Urfi married (an uncommon occurrence amongst Kurds), meaning the bride and groom agreed to marry unofficially through a verbal agreement and signed paper, with neither giving nor receiving any legal rights. Such marriages were usually a way for people to cover up hidden sexual relationships with a veneer of Islamic legitimacy and social protection in case they were discovered. She had kept her love affair with her so-called "husband," Haidar, a secret, while he supposedly decided on their future together. However, it was clear she did not prefer this option.

I was put off by her choice. I felt she deserved so much better, and that her lover was using her as a mistress, since he was already married to two other women. I could not understand why a woman who was a highly educated scholar would lower herself to having a hidden "marriage" with a man who wanted to hide their relationship from the public.

Roza was from a decent practicing family in Sulaymaniyah, who, to their credit, allowed her to be independent and follow her dreams. Roza was the first in her family to have a solid career. She directed a journalism office with twelve reporters under her. She was an exceptional journalist and writer with lots of appearances on TV, which only showed what she was capable of. Yet despite all of this, Roza unrealistically fantasized about a public future with Haidar, a rich politician who happened to be twenty years older than her and clearly (to me) only interested in secretly having her on the side.

Roza had often criticized me for covering my hair when we both lived in Boston. I got to know Roza over the years and she impressed me as a feminist and women's rights advocate. When I learned of her Urfi predicament, I tried to hold her hands and refrain from any judgment. In moments like this, judgment was the last thing a woman wanted to hear. I refused to cast blame on Roza, as I realized that people could do all kinds of foolish things under the spell of love. While some of our mutual female friends questioned Roza's feminist credentials for her relationship choice, she explained her reasons for allowing herself to be the secret third wife, telling us: "Haidar was forced into an arranged marriage with the first wife, and he has told me that his second wife is mentally disabled."

I was not buying any of it and explained to her that she was free to do as she wished, but that in my opinion she was being taken advantage of, since she really desired a monogamous husband.

Shortly after my warning to her, what I feared took place. Roza had asked Haidar to go public about their marriage, but he refused. She finally gave him an ultimatum to either go public about their marriage or she was going to end things between them. Immediately upon this threat, Haidar gave her the marriage paper back and apologized. Roza was upset and heartbroken. Making matters worse, she had confided in several friends about their love affair and news of it leaked out publicly. Consequently, many successful married men in the city began contacting her to supposedly discuss business, but all of them then propositioned her for a secret relationship as they believed she was "that kind of girl."

For someone like Roza, being in a relationship with a man like Haidar meant that she was assumed to owe her status to him, even though it was her own hard work that had made her as successful she was. She grew up in a household that promoted her independence, yet she was still made to believe she was inferior and undeserving of fair treatment. Despite being a respected professional in her late thirties, Roza was still vulnerable to the strict male-dominated culture. When things went sour between Roza and Haidar, it was Roza who suffered all the social consequences. The culture left many women like Roza confused and ashamed of their normal sexual needs and desires. She was made to see desire as a weakness or personal defect, even though her urges were completely normal and common throughout the world. Adding insult to injury, someone like Roza would likely not be taken seriously by her next Kurdish husband if she was honest about her past. Because of this, I had many female friends in Duhok who simply lied to any potential husband, as they felt none of them could handle the thought of their ever dating or even sleeping with another man. Everyone had to wear a mask of supposed innocence, which left women who wanted to have a realistic discussion about their hidden relationships confused and thinking they were in the minority. This fundamental mindset, where men refused to admit that women were sexual beings with similar needs to theirs, ended up causing a lot of stress to women who did not deserve it.

During my stay in Duhok, sex would often come up in my daily conversations with local girls. I was surprised to learn how little these girls knew about sex. Then I began to wonder if they were being genuine, or merely pretending to be so uninformed in an attempt to appear innocent and "pure." Since I realized their society provided almost no sex education, I felt the latter was possible, but I also realized their current world was much different from the one I grew up in, and most women now had cell phones with access to almost anything. Sex was only a word search away.

It had not been until I took my psychology of sexuality course as an undergrad that I understood sexual urges were a normal thing. It also came as a shock to my American friends that at this point I was twenty-eight years old but still a virgin. They simply could not fathom it. Looking back, it is clear to me that the biggest factor in my celibacy was that I had been taught by my religion and culture to suppress my physical needs and see them as deviant.

One morning, I took a cab to the campus to meet with Dr. Hashim, Dean of the College of Pharmacy, to go over my course load and teaching responsibilities. Once I arrived, Dr. Hashim welcomed me in, and I saw that there were six other faculty members seated in his office. I waited for him to take me elsewhere to discuss my course plans; however, we sat with the other faculty and talked about my course plans in front of everyone. During our discussion, two men entered the office and interrupted our conversation for issues that could have waited until we were finished. One of those was the Dean of the Faculty of Medicine and Parween's boss, who was known on campus as the "brutal Dr. Zerak." When he heard my name and that I was from America, he asked, in front of everyone, if I was the one who had "stolen" the university's money. I was not sure what to say, thinking maybe he was confusing me with someone else.

Dr. Hashim, who knew where Dr. Zerak was going with the interruption, attempted to change the subject. However, Dr. Zerak insisted that Helen Sairany was the one that had stolen money from the university. He went on to tell everyone about the book drive I had held when I was at Northeastern and how I cost the university $600 to bring the medical supplies and books from Mosul only to discover the items were used.

I was angry and asked how that made me a thief.

Dr. Hashim tried to calm things down, but it was too late. The room went completely silent, surprised to witness a young female faculty member confront Dr. Zerak. I told him that I did not know who he was, but that he was extremely rude and disrespectful. He had interrupted my meeting with the dean and questioned my integrity without knowing who I was. Finally, I told him I was sorry to learn that he was a professional. I got up and left the room in tears and walked to the president's office.

I submitted my resignation immediately to Dr. Esmat and told him I thought it was inappropriate to treat a new faculty with disrespect in front of others.

Dr. Esmat apologized on behalf of Dr. Zerak and said that he was notorious for being aggressive with new faculty members. He told me he was proud that I stood up for myself. He added that Dr. Zerak's behavior was not acceptable and that he would make sure that he apologized to me.

"Did you just say an old school egocentric doctor will apologize to a young female faculty member?" I asked. I was not sure that was even possible in Kurdish medical culture. And to apologize meant you admitted your mistake and that was not something men of stature were trained to do in Kurdistan.

The whole campus soon learned of—and was impressed by—the position I took with Dr. Zerak. It was also becoming evident that I was the first to confront him. Word went around campus about how this new faculty member from America made a fool of Dr. Zerak. I was fairly sure no one else had ever told him he was disrespectful. Just because he was a high-ranking doctor did not mean he could treat others with disrespect. I could only imagine how he treated his patients in the clinic. He needed a reminder of what the medical profession was all about, and I happened to be his reminder that day!

I found that many doctors in Kurdistan failed to practice what they preached to their patients. Many of them smoked cigarettes. Being part of the faculty at the medical campus in Duhok, it bothered me to see medical residents and students being allowed to smoke indoors. I once took it upon myself to approach a group of residents who were smoking inside the college cafeteria and kindly told them I had allergies to smoking and asked if they would smoke outside. The residents treated me with disrespect, regarding me as a young female wanting to boss them around. The disagreement escalated and news of it made it to the office of the Health Director. The director agreed with me and asked the residents to apologize. From that day on, "No Smoking" signs were posted on every door—a small victory.

I was asked to teach Medicinal Chemistry and Pharmaceutical Formulation for the academic year. The university did not have any faculty who knew how to teach Medicinal Chemistry. If I could not teach it, they would have to hire an adjunct faculty member from Baghdad, who could only teach once each week. I agreed to teach both courses as best I could. My students were second-year pharmacy students from all over Iraq with limited English-speaking skills. There were Bahdini students from Duhok and Zakho, Sorani students from Erbil and Sulaymaniyah, and Arab students from other parts of Iraq. When I attempted to teach a few concepts in Kurdish, an Arab student would fail to understand, and at the same when I tried to teach in Arabic, Kurdish students objected. I told the students I understood Arabic and both dialects of Kurdish perfectly, so they could communicate with me in Arabic, Kurdish, or English, and I would respond to all in English.

For the first day of class, I insisted on wearing a female business suit. Dilband teased me that it was not a job interview, but I said it was my first day, and I wanted to be at my best. I arrived in class thirty minutes early and found only fifteen copies of the course syllabus, although I had requested thirty. Dr. Hashim reminded me that the college could not afford to make thirty copies and the students would have to share (which was a little disconcerting).

Students usually did not take the first week of classes seriously, so I was told not to expect a high turnout on the first day. When class started, I passed around the enrollment sheet, and to my surprise, I had twenty-four students in attendance. We went over the syllabus and, of course, students were curious to know what the exams were going to be like. I told them that nothing was going to be memory-based. Exam questions would all be application-based and warrant critical thinking. I explained to them in class how I had handled previous patient cases that I encountered as a pharmacist. This approach was concerning to many students, considering everything in the region from first grade through college was simple lecture-based memory work. As a start, I introduced the concept of pharmaceutical formulations and the significance of the pharmacist's role.

I ended the class with some key points the students would need to succeed in the pharmacy profession. One of the vital factors was keeping up to date. I asked my students if they understood what that meant. They did, but I knew this was a challenge in Kurdistan, since the college did not subscribe to any pharmaceutical journals, nor did they have access to any pharmacy-related databases. I asked students for their email addresses so I could send them links to some websites that I found relevant to pharmacy. Of all the students, only seven even had email access. I made opening an email account a homework assignment that was due the next class and I took a few students to the campus library after class to help them open their email accounts. While at the library, I saw the books and journals that I had shipped to Duhok when I was a student at Northeastern.

Two months into the semester, students still did not have textbooks for my class. In the middle of one class, we had a power outage and waited for forty minutes for the lights to return. The students told me that power outage was the norm in the region, which for me was frustrating considering Iraqi Kurdistan sat on so much oil. The students were brilliant, but at a disadvantage due to their geographical location. They were all eager to learn but lacked the facilities and resources that enhance learning. That was why I had come back, to serve as their gateway to an American-type education.

Three months into the semester, I had faced countless administrative challenges at the university. They had not paid me the salary we had agreed to and that I desperately needed. Every concern I brought to the attention of Dr. Esmat was met with a bigger concern.

One morning as I was preparing my course lessons, I received a call from Dr. Esmat who asked to see me immediately in his office. Once I got there, he told me he was concerned about my qualifications. I was not sure what concerned him considering I had a bachelor's degree and a doctorate. He questioned my honesty and integrity and said he was frustrated that I had failed him. I tried to remain calm and continue a conversation with him.

Dr. Esmat then said, "Well, you do not have a Ph.D."

Me, "That is correct, but I never claimed to. However, I have a professional doctorate, a PharmD, from an accredited and respected university in the U.S., which makes me qualified to teach pharmacy students."

Dr. Esmat, "In America, one can teach with a PharmD, but in Kurdistan, a PharmD is viewed as equivalent to a bachelor's degree, which disqualifies you from teaching. However, I am willing to wait for the final decision from the Ministry of Higher Education and I hope I am proven wrong."

Me, "I respectfully disagree with your opinion. In fact, I would argue that only those faculty members with professional degrees are qualified to teach professional students. This is important to realize considering the college is going through somewhat of a transition to an American-based education system."

Dr. Hashim had told Dr. Esmat that if I left, the school of pharmacy would likely fail because the school did not have a single qualified faculty member to teach the formulation course.

Dr. Esmat asked me to submit my qualifications to the Ministry of Higher Education for evaluation and the decision to extend my employment would be made after their evaluation. First things first, however, I needed a government ID to prove I was born in the region, and I only had my U.S. passport.

I obtained an official request letter for my government ID on university stationery. Luckily, I had a university driver to accompany me to all the places we needed to go to apply for the ID. We first drove to what was referred to as the "citizenship office." I stood in a long line where I was pushed and shoved so others could get ahead of me. The officer at the front door rushed to help as soon as he spotted the letter from the university in my hand. I told him that I needed my government ID. He said I was in the wrong office and I needed to go to the Gribasi branch in Duhok.

Once at Gribasi, the personnel there told me that I needed an official police agreement to get a personal Iraqi ID. I was directed to the police station, where I was told to go to the court, so the judge could open a new case. I met the judge and explained what I needed. After he opened the case, I was told to collect signatures from all five police stations in the city. It took hours for the driver and me to drive to all the police stations in the city and collect the signatures I needed. I then needed to identify a detective to analyze the case, and from there I had to go back to the court so the judge could sign off on the detective's analysis of my case. After two days of being shuffled between offices, I was finally able to get my ID. This two-day struggle could have been completed in five minutes had I utilized Wasta.

Wasta or Vitamin W is the core of all happenings in Kurdistan.

Vitamin W is an Arabic term that loosely translates to nepotism or "who you know." Vitamin W is so embedded in the Kurdish culture that people living in Kurdistan do not seem to take issue with it, especially when they are the beneficiaries. In fact, it is even seen by many as the glue that holds the entire dysfunctional system together. I was told that Vitamin W could be so powerful, it could grant you your dream job, a college degree, electricity, or anything else you desired. After all, it was about who you knew, not what you knew. In my opinion, Vitamin W provided little hope of making it on your own, little self-exploration, little appreciation, and little opportunity for the drastic changes and reform that Kurdistan needed. I knew I was only scraping the surface of Vitamin W, and my perspective was from someone who was helped more than harmed by it.

A lot of people blame Vitamin W for the bureaucratic culture in the region. Perhaps to Kurdish locals who had lived in the area their whole lives, my reaction seemed unwarranted. But to a Kurdish-American girl who had idealized Kurdistan, seeing the extent to which power and politics insidiously harmed the progress Kurdistan needed to make was something that concerned me. I was a college professor with an official request letter from the university who had to shuffle between countless offices for two full days. I could only imagine what my experience would have been had I been an ordinary citizen with no official documents—long waits in lines only to be told I was at the wrong office or sitting outside in the brutal heat of early September waiting to be called for my turn.

Once I had my government ID, I submitted my degrees to the Ministry of Higher Education to validate my qualifications. Four weeks after the submission, I met with three Ph.D.-degreed pharmacists who were faculty at the College of Medicine in Erbil. I explained the process of getting my degrees. They repeated that my degree was equivalent to a bachelor's degree in pharmacy. I was informed that I had to take an exam to validate my skill set as a pharmacist. I reminded them that my degrees had already been authenticated by the Iraqi Embassy in Washington, DC, but the committee did not seem to care.

With my time at the university becoming more stressful, I decided to focus on other aspects of Kurdish culture in Iraqi Kurdistan that I had been ignorant of as a child. One of those that came to mind first was Yazidism, based on my new local friend, Wassfi. Their religion Yazidism, their holy place called Lalish, their main angel named Melek Taus, and several other fascinating things about them had been on my mind recently. Moreover, I wanted to examine some of the likely unfair things I had heard growing up about Yazidis. I vowed to visit Lalish and learn more about this faith. Of course, who better to guide me through Lalish than Wassfi? He spoke extensively about the faith as we walked around Lalish barefoot, a requirement to visit the holy complex.

Although they speak Kurdish, Yazidis are a distinct group within Kurds. They are notable because they have been ignorantly stigmatized as "devil-worshippers," which has tragically led to constant persecution by the dominant Islamic culture of the region and many attempted genocides.

As a child growing up in Erbil, a common misconception was that Yazidis worshipped Shaitan (Satan), and I am ashamed to admit that as a young kid I foolishly would yell "Satan!" at my Yazidi neighbors and run back to my house. I would also spit on the floor or pour hot water on the ground in front of the Yazidi children to frustrate them, as I foolishly did not know any better. The Yazidis discouraged spitting or pouring hot water on the floor because they believed that spirits or souls might be present and would be harmed or offended by such actions. This ignorance caused them to be angry with me and never want to interact with me again. Looking back, I understood I was taught intolerance and not properly educated about their rich culture and religion.

As an adult, however, I was fascinated by the Yazidi faith. The Yazidis are regarded as having descended from Adam alone, while other humans are descendants of both Adam and Eve. As such, Yazidis do not believe in inter-religious marriage, even with other Kurds, and they accept no converts. Anyone who attempts to marry a non-Yazidi is excommunicated from the faith, and some have even been killed, showing that like all religions in the world they also suffer from fundamentalist elements. They believe that God gave life to Adam through his own breath and asked all the angels to bow to Adam. All angels obeyed except for Melek Taus. When questioned by God why he refused to bow to Adam, Melek Taus replied, "How can I submit to another being? I am from your illumination, while Adam is from dust." Yazidis argue that the order to bow to Adam was a test for Melek Taus, for if God said something, it dibe (happened). God could have made Melek Taus bow to Adam but gave him the choice as a test. Yazidis believe that their respect and praise for Melek Taus (often portrayed symbolically as a colorful peacock bird) is a way to acknowledge his majestic and sublime nature.

Confused, I asked Wassfi how the Yazidi faith was different from the Zoroastrian faith. He explained that Zoroastrians strictly believe in the teachings of Ahura Mazda, the lord of wisdom and light that holds both men and women equally responsible for defeating the evil forces on earth. To defeat these forces, human beings should be righteous in word, thought, and deed. Just like the Yazidi faith, Ahura Mazda only created a good spirit. And now mankind has a free will to do good and bad, but there is punishment in place for those who do harm, either in this world or in the one to come.

As we continued our tour around Lalish, we spotted trees around the sanctuary with pieces of colorful cloth tied to the branches. Wassfi said that the sick in Lalish tie the ribbons to the trees surrounding the sanctuary to ask for recovery. I was honored that they let me inside their "Mecca," the birthplace of the universe, only because I showed up and showed interest. Watching the sunset after being welcomed at the birthplace of the Yazidi universe, I felt there was nowhere else in the world I would rather have been at that moment. I loved their birthplace and the Yazidis. I then began to feel shame at the lies I had believed about them as a child. It taught me the importance of doing proper research before passing judgment. As a Kurd, I gained a new appreciation for Yazidis and found it wrong how some Muslim Kurds insulted them. The Yazidi holy texts were written in Kurdish, while us Muslims read the Holy Quran in Arabic, so perhaps the Yazidis were the "most Kurdish," not the least.

On our way out of Lalish, we were greeted by Ferash, a young man dressed in white, a sacred color to Yazidis. Ferash was responsible for the daily preparation and lighting of the torches in Lalish. Ferash started lighting the holy lights and Wassfi explained that fire represented the sun in his faith, a sacred belief. I admit that during my stay in Kurdistan, I was intrigued by the religious diversity in the region and coexistence among all the religious groups, something that I failed to experience elsewhere in the Middle East.

Another thing I wanted to focus on during my time in Iraqi Kurdistan was charitable ways to give back. When I returned to Kurdistan, I encountered countless refugee patients who were suffering unnecessarily from preventable and treatable diseases due to public health policy failures. Ideally, proper patient education and awareness on simple preventable and treatable diseases could do wonders, but it was not easily available. The medical supplies and number of providers simply did not meet the patient volume and demand. In Kurdistan, years of war, oppression, and imposed sanctions played a role in patients' illnesses. This unfortunate pattern is seen around the world.

In Kurdistan, physicians usually contracted or even owned pharmacies and some would only prescribe medications that came in their pharmacy formularies. As a result, a pharmacist degree was transforming into a license to conduct business transactions where pharmacists would sell their licensure to providers as soon as they were done with their training. Therefore, patients who saw these physicians were now limited to the medications that were available in their pharmacy. I could not imagine a worse way to conduct health policy and found this an unethical insult to my profession.

I was approached a few times by physician faculty colleagues of mine in Duhok to see if I was willing to sell my American pharmacy licensure for $2,000 a month. To convince me even further, they informed me I did not need to practice or even physically be present at the pharmacy. I was shocked and affronted. To me, being a licensed pharmacist meant being a healthcare provider where I would apply my expertise in medication to my patients, not make money from the licensure number I got from a state board of pharmacy in America. "There is no way the state board would know that we are using your licensure here," they added. Clearly, I was not being firm enough about what it took to be a public health servant or a healthcare provider.

Pharmacies in Kurdistan routinely sold medications without proper prescriptions from a medical doctor. Many pharmacies failed to employ certified pharmacists to properly counsel patients about the correct use of medications and often handled and stored medications under unsafe conditions. It was shocking for me to learn how much prescriptive autonomy pharmacists had in Kurdistan with scarcely any knowledge of disease management. Therapeutics was not commonly taught in pharmacy curricula in the region. In the U.S., we graduated with a wealth of clinical knowledge about disease management, yet had no authority to prescribe medications to patients. When I had to demonstrate my therapeutic knowledge, almost everyone wondered how I had so much clinical knowledge when I was only a pharmacist.

I soon approached the Medical Director of Duhok City to see if he would permit me to practice on days when I did not have office hours or classes. Word reached the director about my knowledge of therapeutic topics. The director, recognizing who I was, approved my practice at the diabetes clinic in the city. The director's approval letter was sent to Dr. Hashim's office, who told me that I had the green light to practice at the Duhok diabetes center.

Once I started my practice treating refugees in Duhok, I had to keep myself up-to-date and remember the ethics of how to interact with patients. I reviewed information about the tools that enhanced patient compliance, which included the use of a pillbox, alarm, chart, calendar, and a logbook to remind patients to take their medication at a specific time. I had to remind myself that sometimes health management meant involving all family members. I was always a strong believer in empowering my patients. Once I laid out the problem, I would ask patients for their input on how to address the problem, using motivational interviewing skills when I needed to intervene. I needed to empower my patients for they had far more power over their bodies than any healthcare provider.

Having a practice site in Duhok was one of the jobs I had dreamed of doing after graduation. However, having so many patients kept me from giving each one the personal attention and care that they deserved as human beings. I would see between 150 and 200 patients a day. There were often twenty patients in my office at once wanting their prescriptions with no regard for patient privacy. I had to hide the stethoscope I kept in my office because we simply did not have time for blood pressure measurements, and I was not able to counsel my patients the way I had hoped. Strangest of all, some patients refused to come to the clinic, and instead, sent a family member with their medication book for the next month's supply of medication. Some patients complained about the long commute to Duhok from the surrounding villages and thus asked if I could write their prescription for a three-month supply.

I knew from the first month of practicing at the clinic that I could not accept this broken system passing for healthcare. If I did, there was no point in my return to the

Kurdish region. I had to do something to provide better care to the hundreds of patients I saw at the clinic. I soon learned that comprehensive healthcare was not what some patients needed when they came to the clinic. My experiences had taught me that making a small difference in someone's well-being can be as simple as a smile, a gesture, or a touch. There were little girls in the refugee camp who were victims of sexual assault and forced to follow strict cultural guidelines, who wanted to be like that American healthcare provider giving care in Arabic and Kurdish. They would stand outside my clinic door and look at me until I looked back and walked toward them for a quick chat. I found that giving my attention to these girls and doing simple things like teaching them how to blog or play sports was even more rewarding to me than it was to them.

Most patients I saw lacked awareness about the seriousness and progression of their diseases. They did not understand the long-term consequences of their diabetes remaining uncontrolled. I had to be careful recommending any changes in lifestyle, such as regular exercise, knowing the cultural restrictions about women being out in public. Plus, the city lacked suitable parks and trails that could be used for walking and jogging.

In this clinic, diabetes management was based on a single finger-stick blood glucose reading that patients would receive from a nurse as soon as they arrived. I reminded the nurse that a single reading was not enough to diagnose a patient with diabetes, nor was it enough for providing a therapeutic recommendation. She told me that with the limited resources available, a single reading was the best they could do. I asked if patients utilized a glucose meter at home or logged their glucose levels. She said that due to the high illiteracy level in the population we saw, glucose meters or logs were hardly used. I once even had a female patient present with a serious diabetic foot infection. Her breath smelled fruity, and my heart started racing as I understood the gravity of the situation even though the patient did not. I called the senior attending physician over, and we finally convinced her to go to the emergency room to seek immediate care.

Three weeks into my practice at the Duhok Diabetes Center, I managed to put a sample logbook together for my patients. I was waiting for approval by the Department of Health in Duhok so we could hand them out. I also started teaching patients how to prick their fingers twice daily to check their glucose levels. I taught patients about the appropriate timing for administering their insulin or taking their oral medications and I continued with my group counseling. I got approval from the director of the center to run seminars for patients on how to take care of their feet, modify their diet, perform a finger stick, and log their daily glucose readings to bring with them to the clinic.

I hoped that I could continue teaching at the University of Duhok so I could start bringing my students to the clinic to help manage patients under my supervision. But the archaic system of higher education and bureaucracy took precedence over the needs of patients and my students; so, when my contract was terminated by the university, all the initiatives I started ended upon my departure.

Despite my hard work at the University of Duhok, I was only making $1,500 a month, half of which went to my student loans, with the rest barely covering my expenses. Luckily, my rent and transportation were provided by the university. Dilband told me that one of her student's mothers, Shayan, wanted to learn English and was willing to pay me $500 a month to teach her. Knowing I could use the extra money, I agreed.

Married to a wealthy man of status in Duhok who was very jealous, Shayan had to stay within her fancy villa. Her husband would send the family driver to pick me up twice a week for Shayan's lessons. She and I would speak in English for an hour or two. At times, Shayan was paranoid about her husband's jealousy, so I would let her share her frustrations with me under the theory that it was a way to practice her English.

Fridays were my favorite day in Duhok. The streets were usually empty, and families would gather around a sofreh (a food spread) to share traditional dishes and good laughs. Knowing that I lived on my own, Shayan invited me for lunch on a Friday to meet her family and I took a cab to her house that day. In Duhok, there was no navigation system to get you where you needed to be. Once I got in the cab, I told Shayan that I was going to hand the phone to the driver so she could give him directions. She replied that there was no need because their house was right behind Khayal's house, and if I just told the driver about Khayal, he would know the way. I asked Shayan who Khayal was. She replied that Khayal was famous for eyeball licking (removing particles and small disturbances from people's eyes with her tongue). This whole eyeball licking technique was fascinating to me. I remembered when I was a kid in Zakho, I had a piece of sunflower shell stuck in my left eye. My parents took me to see three ophthalmologists to see why I had a red eye and was in excruciating pain. It was not until they took me to this old lady in the neighborhood, who licked my left eyeball and got the piece of shell out, that my eye started to heal. A fascinating example of indigenous techniques surpassing modern technology.

And Shayan was right! As soon as I mentioned Khayal's name to the driver, he knew exactly where I needed to be dropped off. For lunch, Shayan fixed the most traditional meal in Kurdistan, called sar u pe (stuffed animal gut and body parts cooked together). Having learned more about the grease content of this dish since I was younger, I concluded that my life was going to end with a heart attack right then! I shared my opinion about sar u pe, explaining that such food should not be eaten because it could potentially cause fatal conditions to humans and even lead to an early death from heart disease. Shayan's husband told me that he knew it was bad for his health, but he was young, and his body could resist the dish's negative effects. People who enjoyed this meal failed to understand the long-term consequences of eating it. It contained thousands of calories and a ton of cholesterol.

After the meal, Shayan served chai that was brewed on charcoal with a tray full of sunflower seeds. Interestingly, the seeds were named after Obama, because they were "dark and long" like the U.S. President at the time. Shayan got permission from her husband to accompany me to Seka Duhoki (the oldest historic bazaar in Duhok) to look for a nice set of Kurdish clothes for me. As we made our way to Seka Duhoki, Shayan and I looked at the beautiful colors of Kurdish fabrics in the shops. As I was busy looking at the various fabrics, I heard a woman ask the shopkeeper if he carried "Obama."

Had I just heard *Obama* again? I continued listening to the conversation. In this case, "Obama" was used to refer to the finest quality fabric for Kurdish clothes in the region. I asked how they come up with these names for fabric. The shopkeeper explained that the names were usually chosen by the female customers. In Kurdistan, "Obama" was used to refer to sunflower seeds, a Chrysler car model, or the finest quality of Kurdish fabric for ladies. So, I guess we did have an Obama in Kurdistan, but in our own little way.

As we continued through the market, I saw a line of shops selling peneri pesti, a brand of cheese prepared in animal skin. Shayan bought a few kilograms of this cheese, at $25 per kilogram. Peneri pesti got its name from its method of production. Pest means sheep's skin or simply skin in Kurdish. The cheese was made with sheep, cow, or goat's milk. The curd is then let rest in animal skin during its preparation. Peneri pesti is served at every breakfast in Duhok and Zakho with fresh naan. I had been obsessed with peneri pesti ever since I had my first bite of it and I always asked my family members to bring me some of this cheese every time they went back to Kurdistan for a visit.

Shayan, like the average confined housewife in Duhok, was expected to abide by the rules put in place by her husband and had very little say in the matter. The final word always belonged to her husband. Her only way of expressing herself and projecting some degree of self-agency was through her physical appearance. Kurdish women often paid little to no attention to their body fitness (since it would be covered to the public), and instead focused on their faces. Every outing with Shayan meant she took at least an hour or two to apply makeup in front of the mirror and put an Arab jilbaya (full body covering) on, which was the new trend in Duhok. However, this bothered me, as it seemed foreign to Kurdish culture and tradition to cover our beautiful colorful dresses with long black fabric. Such jilbaya were often expensive and came in a variety of styles. So, when we would go to the Duhok Bazaar, the place would be filled with masses of black jilbayas, which to me resembled a swarm of black ghosts or ninjas. Being a Kurdish woman who took so much pride in our rich colorful clothing, this was sad for me to see.

Since their fashion focus shifted to their faces, Kurdish women's makeup was what some might describe as excessive. Cosmetic plastic surgery was also starting to grow in popularity. The beautiful Kurdish facial features that most exhibited were now seen as a burden among the upper class in Duhok (since the procedures were expensive for most). The thick eyebrows that I grew up to cherish and take pride in among my American friends, had slowly morphed into thin tattooed lines among the city's wealthy women. Botox was also the new thing and natural lips were viewed as too thin. If families had money and the ability to travel, they would go even further and announce they had traveled to Iran (the hot spot for plastic surgery) or Lebanon to get various procedures done.

For her part, Shayan began pressuring me to consider plastic surgery. I liked my face and how I looked, so I was reluctant. I also felt that a natural Kurdish-looking face was more beautiful, and I was more concerned with staying physically fit than making tweaks on my facial features. Shayan and my cousins insisted that as a young college professor, I should not be so humble and maximize my appearance to be more successful in a world where women were judged by their appearance. Eventually, after peer pressure, I agreed to at least attend one of the sales pitches to see what procedures were on offer.

I met Shayan's plastic surgeon of choice, Dr. Sabri, a charming smooth talker who was skilled in exploiting the many insecurities Duhoki women had about their looks. In his office, there was a big screen of before and after images of the miracles he had performed "fixing" women. Right next to the flat TV screen hung all of his medical degrees. He was foreign-trained, something that was a huge bonus when it came to practicing in Kurdistan and to attracting customers of Shayan's type, since she valued foreign qualifications over local ones, believing the latter to be inferior.

Dr. Sabri immediately began trying to convince me that my nose was too big for my face, and he promised he could fix it for a fraction of the cost I would pay back in America. He then looked me in the eye and asked me to take my glasses off, which I did. "You have two big beautiful eyes, but the glasses are hiding them because your nose is too long," he diagnosed.

All of a sudden, I began to doubt the pride I had in my features. He then held up a mirror and left me for ten minutes to stare at my face and examine my nose from every angle. As I kept looking closely at my nose, I actually began to see myself differently and feel that perhaps my nose was, indeed, too big. When he returned he was not finished. He then told me I also needed botox. "You have a beautiful smile, but your lips are not thick enough and so we cannot see it well enough." He assured me that one little injection would do the magic and fix my face. With all these procedures I was told I needed, I started to feel overwhelmed.

Luckily, my confidence returned. I was only nearing thirty and did not need chemicals injected into my face to "nab a man" as Shayan put it.

I tried to visit Jowan during the holidays. While in Erbil, I did my best to connect with my expatriate friends, most of whom lived in Erbil. At times, male friends would offer to pick me up from Jowan's house. This made Hatam uncomfortable because the neighbors would see a different guy friend picking me up from their house every time I was there. Jowan finally asked that when I visited, I stop having men pick me up or, if necessary, walk to the main street in the dark and have them pick me up from there. Only then did I understand why Hatam had been giving me the silent treatment. I was putting my sister and her husband in a difficult spot with their neighbors. It never occurred to me that I was doing anything wrong. I also needed my ex-pat friends because they could relate to what I was going through in coping with all the bureaucracy and cultural misjudgment in the region.

One of the things that was difficult about living in Kurdistan as a single woman in my late twenties was the fact that almost everyone emphasized the need for me to be married. It was as if I was a walking, breathing threat to the entire social fabric and they did not want my "bad" example rubbing off on any of the others. The locals would bombard me with inappropriate personal questions like how old I was, why was I still single, why was I living alone in Kurdistan, where was my family, and why was I so skinny? So many times, Dr. Esmat said that he could get me married off in Duhok, which made me extremely uncomfortable. It was as if my primary value to society was my availability as a potential wife, not as a person with her own aspirations.

Since I was single, I was introduced to many men while in Duhok. One was a physician and a professor at the College of Medicine. He was also a Fulbright scholar who obtained his master's degree in the U.S. It was determined that we would be a good match because he was just back from the U.S. and highly educated. When we met in the college cafeteria, he would not even look up so I could see his face. Thirty minutes into our conversation, I felt I had done 90% of the talking and he agreed with everything I said. After a few days, I started getting bored because he simply did not bring any excitement to the table. I was sure he was skilled at his job, but to me, a husband had to be more than what he did for a living. Three weeks into talking with him, I told him that we were too different and recommended that we go our separate ways, to which he agreed.

After these essentially platonic dates and several others in the Kurdish region, I realized the local men were intimidated by my independence and strong personality. I was reminded that I would not make a good wife because I was too opinionated and Americanized. Plus, I knew that I could not fill the role of the wife they were envisioning, since my career and world travel were of greater importance to me than household duties. My family recommended that I suppress some of my assertiveness when I met new suitors. My family also reassured me that a husband would put up with my personality better once we were married than when he first met me in person. I felt there was nothing about my personality I needed to suppress! I believed in honesty in dating, as it was through dating that couples got to learn each other's habits and see for themselves if they could put up with each other. After all, it was easier to break up a relationship than break up a marriage.

March had finally come to Kurdistan, a month full of events that were significant to how the region had been shaped. Every event in March was like a holiday. What did all these holidays and time off mean to me as a college lecturer? Frustration! As an ambitious faculty member who wanted to cover as much information as I could and stay committed to the course syllabus, these days off were difficult. However, there was only so much I could do with all the last minute, unannounced holidays. I had to change the course syllabus and course plan many times. I thought to myself, "*Was it even worth having a syllabus in this country*?" Every time I finalized the syllabus and intended to email it to my students, I was informed of another day off. Exam schedules continued to change, and quizzes and appointments were postponed because of holidays.

The Kurdish region is one of the few places in the world that celebrates three New Year's days: Newroz (which marks the first day of spring), January 1st, and the first day of the Islamic Calendar also known as Muharam. During the holy month of Ramadan, office hours were cut short by three hours daily because most office personnel would be fasting. Following Ramadan, a whole week was granted as a holiday to celebrate Eid ul-Fitr. Two months later, another week-long holiday was granted for Eid ul-Adha, followed by the first day of the Islamic calendar and the 10th day of the holy month of Muharam. All these days were sacred holidays.

Then came the non-sacred holiday, winter break, which was celebrated in two weeks. Next came the month of March, one full of celebration since it contained the Kurdish New Year on March 21st and the anniversaries of many past Kurdish uprisings. Often, when New Year's Day (Newroz) fell in the middle of the week, students would lobby the dean to give them the days between the holiday and weekend off. Obviously, this was not the workaholic American culture I had become accustomed to.

I loved everything about spring in Kurdistan: the greenery, wildflowers, beautiful weather, vegetables and fruits, and beautiful colors of women's Kurdish clothes. Most locals would picnic in the mountains and valleys on Fridays. During one of my visits, Jowan and Hatam decided to take a family picnic to Masif, which was about an hour's drive from where they lived in Erbil. On our way to Masif, we were stuck in traffic. As we were waiting, a group of children stopped by the car, carrying bunches of nargis flowers for sale. We bought several bunches, which excited the children immensely.

Nargis only grows during the spring season in the outskirts of cities in Kurdistan. When you smell nargis, you almost feel hypnotized. The smell is one of a kind and I am told that cologne industries cannot even make perfumes that smell as heavenly as the nargis flower. When classes were back in session, my students brought me bunches of nargis so I could fill my office with the smell. Nargis dates all the way back to Greek mythology, to King Nargis or Narcissus, who was so proud of his beauty that he refused to leave the pool where he saw his reflection in the water and fell in love with it. Due to the flower's beauty and fragrance, which lasts for days, it is no surprise that many Kurdish families name their daughters Nargis.

For Kurdish New Year's Eve, it was tradition to have a bonfire on mountains in Kurdistan and even jump over the fire to mark the new year. I told Jowan and Hatam that I wanted to go to Akre. Akre was the town in Kurdistan that, in my opinion, portrayed the rituals of Newroz best. I was happy that they agreed to accompany me to see the Newroz bonfire in Akre, considering how challenging it would have been for me to go to Akre alone.

Every year, thousands of Kurds go to Akre to watch the flames beautifully illuminate the evening sky. Hundreds of the town's young men carry fire touches and climb the 354 steps to the top of the highest mountain in Akre, known as Kale. What I really wanted was to join these young men. As always, I wanted to be among the locals and part of their cultural rituals. To my mother, my determination was blasphemous, considering I would be the only woman among all the men in town.

Two of my students, who were from Akre, met us there. I told them I wanted to carry a torch and climb the mountains. They discouraged me, considering the risk associated with carrying a torch and the speed at which I needed to climb to keep up with the others. There were also many gunshots as part of the celebration which made things riskier. However, at that point, I had my mind made up and nothing could have stopped me from climbing up the mountain. They wrapped my shoulder with a jamadaniya, a Kurdish scarf. Instead of a torch, they asked if I was willing to carry a Kurdistan flag for them. I was happy to get their agreement, so a Kurdish flag it was. They asked me to stand at the beginning of the line. The march to the top of the mountain was going to start at sunset.

I was told to wait for the gunshots to begin the hike, and was warned about making any stops, because if I did, I would disrupt the marching for all the men behind me. As I waited for the sunset, I could see all eyes staring at me, thinking that I was out of my mind for wanting to attempt the climb. Then I heard my students whisper, uncomfortable that everyone in the neighborhood was talking about my wanting to climb Kale. They had never seen a girl wanting to climb Kale for Newroz.

At the sound of the gunshot, I raced up the steps. As I climbed, my breathing became difficult. By step number 200, I was struggling, considering that I was climbing and there was less oxygen, but I was determined to continue my quest. At that very second, I remembered our struggles back in the 1990s and how we had to leave everything behind and climb many mountains in the extreme conditions of winter while running for our lives from Saddam's bombs. I reminded myself that today my struggle was different. It came with joy.

I made it to the top of Kale and started waving the flag

of Kurdistan. Only then did I realize that as a Kurdish-American, I have come a long way and my people have surely endured every oppression possible. We adapted to new homes in the west and have thrived, but our hearts still belong to the motherland, Kurdistan. Words could not describe the feelings I experienced. As I turned around, I saw cameras recording me to show the first Kurdish female who had climbed Kale on Newroz; I could only imagine my mother's reaction to seeing me on TV, waving the Kurdish flag in Akre.

Lighting a bonfire on the mountains is significant to every Kurd on Newroz. This dates to the mythical story of the Kurdish hero, Kawa the Blacksmith, and the evil King Zuhak. King Zuhak had an unfortunate birth defect involving two giant snakes growing from each shoulder. The snakes were from a curse placed on Zuhak by God for his evil doings. These snakes had to be fed with the brains of two children every day of the year. Zuhak's doctor could not bring himself to kill children every day so he would smuggle one of the children to a land beyond the mountains and feed the snakes a mix of human and sheep's brains. One of Zuhak's victims was Kawa, a poor blacksmith who already had many of his children sacrificed in this way. When he was told that his last remaining child, his beloved daughter, was next to be sacrificed, Kawa marched to the land of the smuggled children where he raised an army and marched on the palace of Zuhak. Kawa killed Zuhak with a single blow of his mighty hammer.

The sacrificial children who had survived Zuhak set out for the mountains and lit fires to tell the people of the world that the evil Zuhak was gone and freedom and peace would now reign in the world. Kurds, the descendants of those mountain children, light bonfires and celebrate the downfall of Zuhak every year on the eve of March 21st, which marks the Kurdish New Year or Newroz. In the western world, March 21st marks the end of winter, where the days begin to stretch and nights shrink. To the Kurds, March 21st is a rebirth. It is a reminder of victory over the murderous tyrant, Zuhak. It has also become a significant day for many Kurds from Bakur (Northern Kurdistan) or southeastern Turkey, because Kurdish prisoners from the PKK symbolically would light themselves on fire on Newroz to protest their torture and mistreatment in Turkish prisons. Their self-immolation was mimicking Kawa's fiery signal to others. But to all Kurds, regardless of which region they are from, Newroz is a promise, a release from the burden of winter, which will one day be accompanied by freedom from political oppression in all four parts of Kurdistan.

After finishing my formulation course, I wanted to take my students to Awamedica, the only pharmaceutical company in Erbil. I wanted the students to see how the various drugs were being formulated in the region. I proposed the idea to Dr. Hashim, who asked that I draft a proposal outlining the relevance of this trip to my course so he could present it to Drs. Zerak and Parween.

Once I received approval to take my students to Awamedica, I called the company to ask if we could have a tour of the facility and a question-and-answer session with my students. Everything went according to plan until the day before the trip when I was called to Dr. Hashim's office. He told me that he had asked a male colleague to lead the trip. He added that I could just enjoy the trip with the students and not worry about the logistics involved when we needed to stop at the checkpoints between Duhok and Erbil. When I asked how this last-minute decision came about, he explained that the checkpoint guards might not take me seriously, and it made better sense to have a man meet with the Awamedica leadership. I did not buy any of this nonsense and went straight to Parween to have her explain it to me.

"Welcome to Kurdistan, my dear," she said. "This is how they treat women here."

My frustration continued. The day before the trip, I met with the students and asked them to meet me at 7:30 a.m. the following day outside the campus. As I was taking attendance, I noticed that three students, who were the children of political leaders in the city, were missing. I asked their classmates if they knew the missing students' whereabouts. They told me that Dr. Hashim had permitted them to go to Erbil in their private vehicle.

I called Parween to ask how this was even possible when I was responsible for the course and students. Why was Dr. Hashim allowing students to bypass me and making exceptions for these supposed VIP students?

Parween promised that she would not let this one pass. She asked that I be patient, and things would be revisited when I returned.

We finally made it to Awamedica, and the first thing I saw as we entered the building were the three VIP students seated in the office of the director. They tried to avoid eye contact with me, knowing I was not happy with the stunt they had pulled. We broke the class into four groups for the facility tour. After the facility tour, we had our question-and-answer session. The male professor with the three VIP students stood at the front of the room with the director of Awamedica. Vitamin W was now having my students run the show for me.

When we were back from Erbil, Dr. Hashim and I met to discuss matters related to the students' performance. Indirectly, he wanted to make sure I was not planning on failing any of the three VIP students. One of those students had twenty-seven days of absenteeism, so I had to push back. I believed it was not fair to pass a student who did not even bother to show up to class and handed in blank exam papers. However, the message was that we needed to pass him because of who his father was.

I told Dr. Hashim I did not leave my career and life in the U.S. to be part of a corrupt system. The student, just like any underperforming student, needed to retake the class next year. Plus, how was I going to trust them as pharmacists to treat patients.

After an hour-long meeting, we were clearly not on the same page. I reminded him about the field trip to Awamedica and how disappointing it was for him to allow my students to go around me. I explained that this would enable students to continue going behind my back if I did anything that was not in line with their desires. He started to stutter when I told him about the likely outcome of his decisions. He realized that if I stayed on board the following academic year, I was going to cause him trouble with the politicians in Duhok. He did not have time for political trouble considering he had a privately-owned clinic.

When we failed to reach an agreement, Dr. Hashim stated that there were no classes for me to teach the next academic year, and I would have to seek a job elsewhere. With my qualifications under scrutiny by the Ministry of Higher Education, almost no one stood up for the good work I had done for the patients and students in Duhok. I then had no choice but to pack my belongings and leave for Erbil. As I was packing, I said to myself, "All this trouble because of Vitamin W?"

CHAPTER VIII:
CITIZEN OF THE WORLD

Jumping was my dream as a child. I wanted to jump as high as I could so I could see my house and the city where I grew up. It was a jump of joy. Now that I can fly, I can see not only the city, but the entire world, I fail to find the joy that I used to have as a child. The city has changed and so have the people and the childhood dreams that I used to have within me.

Photo courtesy of the Kurdish photographer, Jamal Penjweny.

On August 21, 2011, while I was in Erbil with Jowan, I received a call from my mother that my father had passed away. My father had settled in Detroit and lived in a small Arab community after he had most recently left my mother. Once we knew he had cancer, however, my mother, Omed, and Shayma drove to Michigan to help him sell all his belongings and brought him home to stay with my mother and siblings until he died. The small consolation was that he was at least with our family when the end came.

Yet, even though we knew and were prepared for some time for his death, when that phone call came, I felt something had been taken away from me, something I was never going to get back. My father had heroically battled lung cancer for four long years. I knew it was time for him to be at peace and not suffer any longer, but I could not help but feel the pain that he was no longer with me. Growing up in Kurdistan, my father had been my stern guardian angel, quiet, judgmental, but loving and protective; now who would shield me in a world that often seemed cold and lonely?

I felt like the little girl in Erbil whose father had been her sole audience was now standing in an empty stadium. Who would I brag to about all my accomplishments? Who would listen when I needed to talk about the trouble I was having in Kurdistan? Who would I tell about the countless number of times I had to stand for the values with which he raised me? It aggrieved me to think of all the pain that my father had endured over the years as a prison inmate and how that had detached him from all of us. Part of me was still in denial. This could simply be due to the culture we live in, a culture that prefers to deny and avoid the reality of death. However, when I lost my father, the reality that life was finite and that I, too, would someday die became apparent. I could never think of anything more than a canned answer when people asked how I was doing. What was there to say? Guilt that I had not done my daughterly duty in keeping my parents together nagged me. I also felt selfish for letting my dreams distance me from my parents and for the pain that my father went through alone. Until my father passed away, I had not truly understood the impact of my parent's separation. How lonely my father must have felt to see his body being consumed by disease while living on his own. Cancer ravaged him, and now his absence would eat away at life's little joys in the same slow way. I could not think of anything but how my father was the most important patient I had failed.

My father's last wish of me was to serve the underserved in life, and since his death, I have promised myself to continue to fulfill that wish with whatever gifts and talents I possess.

Even though my father died in Atlanta, my aunts and uncles wanted to observe an official period of formal mourning in this honor in Zakho. I was not too thrilled about this idea. The money we would spend on another period of mourning could have been used to feed the poor instead, continuing my father's legacy. Plus, formal mourning periods in Kurdistan were often opportunities for women to gather and gossip.

Life for women in Zakho was not easy. Seventeen years later, Zakho was still the same Zakho I had left in 1996, as not much had progressed in the town. There were no proper shops, one university, one hospital, and limited female doctors. Many of my cousins had left for Europe to secure a better living standard for their families by transferring Euros which were worth a lot in Iraqi dinars. Those who did not risk going abroad remained in Erbil to do construction work and staff the airport. Women in Zakho were still hiding their faces whenever they left their homes, and they could not speak to men who were not blood related. With the limited social opportunities, it was usually during the formal mourning of our loved ones that women got a chance to catch up and talk about jewelry, new babies in the family, any divorces or breakups in town, and their baking and holiday plans. It was also during mourning events where girls showed up without makeup, a cynical opportunity to see what they actually looked like without excessive accessories. As such, mothers with single sons found mourning events to be the prime environment to find the right girl to marry into their family.

Unfortunately, the decision to have a formal mourning period was made and I had no choice but to make the commute to Zakho. According to Kurdish culture, a formal mourning was held separately for men and women. The men gathered at one of the oldest mosques at the heart of the bazaar in Zakho, where they listened to the Quranic readings for an hour or two. As they left the mosque, immediate family members of the deceased were waiting so the men could convey their condolences. The women gathered at my aunt's house from morning until late at night. Tradition required the immediate family of the deceased to dress in black, which I resisted, considering black stood for grief. My father lived a good life, and I felt a formal period should celebrate and cherish that.

I soon learned that the communal grief from my father's death had taken over our area of Zakho. A wedding for my cousin had been canceled and all TVs were shut off for weeks. At times of mourning a loved one, it was customary to be careful about how we expressed our joy and happiness, so as not to offend the grieving family. Mourning periods themselves in Kurdistan lasted anywhere from five to seven days for women and two to three days for men. My father's mourning period was a painful experience, considering I had to sit in a room full of women dressed in black all day long. On the first day, some of my cousins started slapping their faces with their hands and pulling their hair out, a way to show their sadness over my father's death. Terrified by what I saw, I immediately told them they had to stop, or I was going to leave the house. Hurting themselves over my father's death was unacceptable, and I added that we had gathered to celebrate my father's good life. Ritualized pain would not bring him back and adding suffering to the world (even if personal) was an insult to his memory.

Three days into the mourning period, I was done with the gossip and needed some quiet time to reflect on what I was going through. I asked Jowan to let me leave for Erbil. My aunts overheard and told me it was ayba (shameful) for me to leave the affair. They also reminded me that I was being rude. Not being able to hold back, I said that the mourning was bringing nothing but harm to my father's soul with all the gossip and nonsense. But I had had it with people reminding me how certain things I did were ayba. Refusing to dress in black for my father's mourning was ayba. Leaving my father's mourning, a day early for some solitary time was ayba. Smiling at strangers in public was ayba. Dressing a certain way for work was ayba. Eating during Ramadan while having my monthly cycle was extremely ayba. Being given a ride by a male friend was ayba. Socializing with my students at the campus was ayba. Dating was ayba. Laughing too much in the company of men was ayba. Being too happy was ayba. Focusing too much on myself was ayba. Debating the logic of absurd customs and whether they still had relevance in today's society was ultra ayba. And the list continued. By then, I wanted people to mind their own business and stop interfering in my personal life.

People in Kurdistan had many bad habits that needed to change, but nobody cared because those bad habits were not perceived as ayba. I found myself noticing all the things wrong with Kurdish culture, not because I hated it, but because I loved it, and wanted it to be better. Things like smoking indoors and leaving cigarette butts on a teacup saucer, showing up late to events, insulting your wife or children in public, throwing trash from the car window or leaving it behind in public areas, harassing females you did not know by sending them countless text messages—to me these were the sorts of behavior that should have been perceived as ayba.

By August of 2011, I had been living in Kurdistan for a year: a year full of challenges, adventures, and positive experiences. In that one year, I met some incredible people who played a vital role in my life. I accepted the challenges I faced in Duhok as a life experience. I never thought of an experience as bad, since all my experiences had shaped my outlook on the world, something that was underappreciated by many in Kurdistan.

In one year, I had shadowed offices in the region, networked, and learned that institutions often fail to place the right person in the right position. By the right position, I mean the best fit, the most competent, and the one who had years of experience and specialization. Having a respected degree of some sort did not by any means make the candidates fit for positions that differed from their specialties. So many people in Kurdistan were interested in growing but refused to go through the natural processes that ensured a healthy growth. I also noticed a tremendous amount of insecurity by those who were in high-ranking positions, almost as if their guilt told them they did not deserve their status. Years later in business school, I would learn that once an individual earns a sense of position, he has increased confidence and ownership of that position, and tends to share very naturally. However, in Kurdistan, most individuals did not earn their positions and therefore were often reluctant to share and felt a sense of vulnerability that prevented them from collaborating and sharing information with others. If you know you are not the best person for your job, you will constantly remain scared they will find someone who is and replace you. Opportunity was something to give out to one's friends in the hopes they would repay the favor, instead of those who deserved it.

Individuals in Kurdistan were fascinated by foreign technology, ideas, and systems in a way that showed they lacked self-confidence in their own people. They admired foreign intellect and practices. For example, foreign workers were granted a higher wage, better accommodations, and better treatment. Institutions would go as far as they could to implement a foreign concept, believing it to be superior by the mere fact of not having been from there. For a short time, these skills and techniques appeared to work. However, with no follow-up or maintenance, the foreign technique would fail to sustain itself. They often failed to ask or wonder if the foreign idea was suitable to the Kurdish institution. They failed to have a search committee in place that analyzed and studied the foreign practice. Instead, the institution would rush in and apply something with no prior exposure—like planting an orange tree in Antarctica and expecting it to grow.

After my last unpleasant encounter with Dr. Hashim at the university, I moved to Erbil and stayed with Jowan for a couple of weeks. I had more opportunities for finding a job there, and it was where all my American expatriate friends lived. Erbil was more metropolitan than Duhok. It was where old met new—a blend of history, mosaic mosques, bazaars, and roller coasters, that appealed to both the young and old.

Erbil's famous Qalat, resting on top of a hill at the heart of the city, is one of the oldest continuously inhabited settlements in the world. The Qalat was first created by many generations of people living and rebuilding on the same spot, including the Assyrians, Mongols, and Kurds all dating back to Erbil's late Ottoman phase when it was most active. During the Ottoman Empire, when fully occupied, the Qalat was divided into three mahals (neighborhoods): the Serai, Takya, and Topkhana. The Serai was occupied by notable families. The Topkhana was where the craftsmen and farmers lived. And the Takya was named after the homes of respected Sufi Darwishes. The fortress stretched over 100,000 square meters and rose between 82 to 105 feet (25 to 32 meters) from the surrounding plain. In 2012, in coordination with UNESCO, the Kurdish Regional Government started relocating most of the inhabitants in the Qalat for renovation work. In June of 2014, the Qalat was listed as a UNESCO World Heritage Site. Currently, there was still one family living in the Qalat, so it remained the longest inhabited city in the world.

I was fascinated by how the city was engineered. The historic Qalat was at the heart of the city and all the main city intersections circled around it. The streets were numerically named—30, 40, 60, 120, and 150—with each numeral representing the width of the street in meters from sidewalk to sidewalk. Hawleris often said that getting lost in Erbil was impossible. If you missed your intersection while driving, you could continue driving and the street you were on would bring you back to your starting point.

I loved the nightlife in Erbil. My favorite neighborhood was Isktan, where we would stroll in the market that served as a gathering center for people from different backgrounds in Iraq. The market housed many popular restaurants and cafes and was always crowded with young people, especially when there was a soccer match between Barcelona and Real Madrid. The majority of Hawleris were Real Madrid fans and you could always tell when the main player, Cristiano Ronaldo, would score a goal by the roar of the crowd. And you could equally tell when Messi from Barcelona scored a goal through the anger and the swearing by the locals; that felt like music to my ear. It was my way of learning some street slang and bad words in Sorani that I had missed after all these years living abroad.

I would go to Iskan with Jowan and Hatam to grab my favorite shawarma or falafel sandwich. We would then sit at a teahouse to enjoy some Kurdish chai freshly brewed on charcoal with a cone full of roasted sunflower seeds. Conversely, it was a heart-wrenching experience to see so many street children walking around selling chewing gum, who were told to never take no for an answer. They followed me everywhere and insisted I buy a pack of gum from them. The same kids cleaned Hatam's front car window at a traffic light, hoping they could make some spare change.

A physician friend named Riza volunteered to accompany me to the Cardiac Care Unit in Rizgari Hospital, where I was monitoring patients to research the long-term use of heparin (anticoagulant) therapy. Once I arrived and started looking through patient charts, I overheard some residents say that my research topic was not going to work because cardiology specialists do not follow standard practice guidelines. At Rizgari, Heparin was given as needed, and not every patient for whom Heparin was indicated got the therapy. After surgery, most patients were rushed out of the unit to make space for incoming patients, even though they were medically indicated to stay longer.

The residents at Rizgari were wonderful. I went on rounds with them and they told me how the system worked in the cardiac unit. As we were making rounds, I noticed that the families of the Peshmergas, who were often undereducated, had preventable cardiac conditions that had long been neglected. We ran into an urgent case that the residents needed to see. The first thing I noticed was the patient's gangrenous feet. They were so purple I thought it was purple toe syndrome until I heard the resident say that this patient's feet needed to be amputated as soon as possible or the gangrene would continue to progress. I looked at him with tearful eyes and asked what brought the patient to the cardiac unit. The patient's chief complaint was heart failure with shortness of breath. When we looked at the patient's medical chart, I recommended a few changes to the patient's medications. They agreed. However, they were not allowed to change any therapies without input from the specialist. The resident told me that the cardiologist would probably discharge the patient despite his condition to make space for more urgent cases. *Can anything be more urgent than this case in front of us*? I thought.

I left Rizgari Hospital somewhat shocked at the cases I had to witness each day. On one occasion, we were stopped at a traffic light while leaving when suddenly, my physician friend jumped out and ran toward a young man who had been hit by a car. The man was convulsing and bleeding. With no ambulance service in the region, my friend and I, along with a few other volunteers, picked up the man, placed him on the back seat of our car, and rushed him back to the emergency room. Once we got hold of the young man's family and made sure he was stable and in good hands, I told my friend that I needed to get home. I was starting to develop a terrible migraine from all the stress I had been through that day.

On our way back, we took a shortcut and drove on Gulan Street. It was impressive how much investment the KRG had put into Gulan Street, from five-star hotels, high-rise buildings, apartment complexes, shopping malls, cafes, and restaurants. It felt as though there was Erbil and then there was Gulan Street. The disparity between parts of the city was stunning and shocking. Gulan Street looked like a typical street in the United States. All the expatriate and foreign investors I knew lived in those fancy apartment buildings lining the road.

"Gulan is used to show that Erbil is becoming the next Dubai in the Middle East," said Riza.

"Is turning into the next Dubai even possible without proper healthcare for the locals who have been through years of war and economic sanctions?" I asked.

"I am not sure the leaders care about your point of view, considering they all seek healthcare in Europe or the United States when needed," Riza said.

"And the locals and the families of Peshmergas deserve the kind of healthcare we just witnessed?" I asked angrily.

"Looks like you are starting to get a taste of reality here in Kurdistan," Riza quipped with a smile.

When in Boston, I use to run during stressful times. However, I had to stop running for a year after I had a bad experience in Duhok at sunset. On that occasion, men driving by started whistling at me and thought they could catcall me for running alone. At one point twelve cars in a row honked and flashed their lights at me, while several shouted they wanted a kiss or a date. One driver even rubbed his fingers together signaling he would pay for my services if I got in the car with him. I then realized that women were essentially given two unfair options in Duhok: refuse simple pleasures like jogging at sunset or be labeled a whore for being out alone and thus face harassment.

Instead of running, I would call some of my ex-pat friends to hang out at a local Lebanese-owned family restaurant in Ainkawa. We liked Ainkawa because it was a predominantly Christian neighborhood and more accepting of women smoking and drinking, something my friends did. The restaurant soon became our favorite spot where we met up to vent about the stress we all experienced from our daily struggles living in Kurdistan. One of those friends, Shereen, had been a clinical pharmacy specialist at Vanderbilt who left her career and life in the U.S. for a man she met through her family. Shereen was thirty-five when we met. She shared that her family was worried about her age and not being able to find a husband if she got any older. She smoked half a pack of cigarettes every time we met in Ainkawa. At least I had some appreciation of the culture, considering I was born and raised in Kurdistan. For Shereen, who was born and raised in America, the culture and living standards were overwhelming. She told me that her husband expected her to "shine and dine" with his business partners throughout the day and she was simply not cut out for this lifestyle. She was also disappointed in not being able to practice pharmacy in Erbil.

Then there was Nadine, who was going through a second divorce. In this culture, a woman going through a divorce was blasphemy, let alone for a second time. She kept her divorce secret from the whole world except our close ex-pat circle and continued to wear her wedding ring even after she was no longer married. She later shared with me that her husband would hit her every time they argued.

Not long after my father passed away, I learned about my dear Mati (aunt) Soad being admitted to Nanakaly Cancer Center for non-Hodgkin's lymphoma. I called my physician friends at Nanakaly and they confirmed that my aunt was indeed there getting chemotherapy. I dropped everything I was doing and rushed to see her.

On my way to her room at the hospital, I saw lines of immunocompromised patients on hospital beds in the hallway getting therapy. I found my aunt in a decent-sized room, but she had to share it with three other families who had a loved one getting cancer care. My aunt looked so frail and pale. I rushed to hold her, and we both sobbed from the joy of reuniting after all the years.

This was the same mati who had defended me when my grandmother, Miriam, who played favorites, would pick on me to get me in trouble. Whenever I craved a plain jam sandwich, my aunt would make it with one hand because her other hand had been severely burned and did not function well. She would brag about how yummy the sandwich was and talk about the health benefits of the jam.

Mati Soad did not marry until my grandmother Miriam passed away. She realized that while living in a patriarchal society, it would be difficult to live alone as a single woman. When my father was around, he had invited her to live with us, but she refused to be a burden to any of her siblings. Her only way of surviving in Kurdistan was to marry. However, being forty-five years old then, her options were limited. She ended up marrying an uneducated man who was already married and had a dozen adult children. The man she married was abusive to her and would often insult her for being unable to bear any children for him. We asked what made her put up with the abuse and she reminded us of a woman named Kurdi who went missing from Zakho after she was raped. Kurdi was a mentally unstable woman who lived on her own. She eventually got pregnant and that was when she went missing. Rumors circulated that her father had committed an honor killing to stop the shame she brought upon her family. Mati Soad felt that living with an abusive man was far better than being harassed by society for being a single woman. Marriage should not be the only solution for a woman living in Kurdistan. With a lack of mental health facilities and resources to support women like Kurdi and my aunt, women would continue to be the victims of a system that was designed to fail them.

I loved visiting my mati and enjoyed her company and the stories she shared about my childhood. She used to call me Tineen (little dinosaur) for being so loud. When she was in Nanakaly, I held her burnt hand and could see the bruises from the needle insertions for the chemotherapy infusion all over her arms. I looked her in the eye and told her I was committed to taking care of her and would stay by her side. I placed a call to Dr. Anwar Sheikha, who was known to be the father of cancer therapy in Kurdistan. Dr. Sheikha was the reason I returned to Kurdistan to serve. I admired how he gave up the perks of practicing in the U.S. to serve his people in Sulaymaniyah.

Upon further review of my aunt's medical chart, I learned that my aunt had kept secret the fact that she had been living with breast cancer for years. I was discussing my aunt's case with Dr. Sheikha when he stopped me and said, "Helen, you are a pharmacist so I will be straightforward. Your aunt is sixty-seven years old with non-Hodgkin's lymphoma. The prognosis is not promising."

"But you brought cancer therapy to Kurdistan and you have cured thousands like my aunt. Why not her?"

He asked me to leave my emotions aside and reviewed all my aunt's risk factors with me.

Some other doctors I knew overheard my tense conversation with Dr. Sheikha and agreed with his assessment. Three days after she was admitted to Nanakaly, my mati developed a pulmonary embolism and shortness of breath. We knew she was approaching the end of her life, so we rushed to get her transferred to the intensive care unit at Rizgari. However, as soon as that occurred she passed away. The medical team and I performed CPR, but my dear mati did not respond. I kept pressing on her chest, refusing to give up until the team stopped me.

"Doktora, please stop! Her soul has rested."

I refused to accept the death of another loved one. The staff walked me away from my aunt's body and I sat in the hallway speechless with dried tears on my face. It occurred to me then how blessed I had been to be with my aunt in the last few seconds of her life. Losing my father and my aunt eight months apart made me realize how short life was and that I simply could not take a back seat and wait for life to pass me by.

Not long after I moved to Erbil, I was offered a position teaching pharmacology to third-year dental students at Ishik University, a private institution inspired by the Turkish Sunni clergyman, Fethullah Gulen. Known to locals in Erbil as the Turkish school, the faculty and staff at Ishik were all followers of the Gulen movement. While at Ishik, I did not want to get involved in any movement. My goal was to focus on my students, do research on the side, and enjoy living in Kurdistan. However, working at Ishik came with its own religious prerequisites. Almost all the female Turkish faculty members I worked with wore a hijab as I did. However, I was constantly criticized for wearing makeup, tights, and jeans. I worked hard to limit my interaction with the overly judgmental Turkish faculty, but there was only so much I could do when I had to share office space and meals with everyone.

During lunch, one Turkish faculty member asked to sit with me. Her name was Ayeshan and she went by Abla Ayshan. One day Abla Ayshan noticed I was using my left hand to eat (since I am left-handed) and she started schooling me on the importance of using my right hand.

"Are you not aware that Muslims should eat and greet with their right hand?" she asked.

"No, not really. I have always been left-handed and never been asked why I was eating or writing with my left hand until I started working here at Ishik," I replied.

"Well, now you have! Muslims use their left hand to wash their backside after visits to the toilet. And it is sort of filthy that you are using the same hand to eat with," she informed me.

I did not know what to make of the awkward conversation. "It is pitiful to learn that men have made it to the moon and here you are worried about me eating with my left hand," I told Abla Ayshan and excused myself from the lunch table.

During the academic year at Ishik, I was tasked with the additional role of faculty advisor to the first-year dental students who started class in November 2011. I already had a full course load teaching the third-year dental students. Plus, the freshman class needed a lot of handholding since they had no prior college experience. On the first day, I asked the freshmen to line up for course registration outside my office. As soon I started registering them, two live ducks with pink bowties were thrown into my office. I shrieked, jumped onto my office desk, and waited for the ducks to waddle out of my office.

At the end of the academic year at Ishik University, I decided to finalize the student grades and publish them on my office wall to give students an idea of their class standing. Little did I know, a group of students who were displeased with their grades approached the dean to have him make me change their grades. The dean asked them to talk to me and see if I was willing to adjust them myself.

As I was wrapping up office hours with a group of first-year dental students, a group of third-year dental students barged into my office. I asked them to wait until I was done with the first-year students, but the students started to threaten ominously that I had until 3 p.m. to change their grades or I would only have myself to blame for what would happen to me next.

I called the dean, but he refused to address the

situation. When I looked through my office window, I saw the dean talking with the students. I notified the president's office, and he called the dean to inquire what had happened. With the reputation of the university in jeopardy, other faculty and university officials joined the president in the office.

The next thing I knew, I was the only female in a room full of men speaking in a language (Turkish) foreign to me. They called the dean and had him on the speakerphone to explain what had happened. The dean explained his view of the situation in Turkish. Once they hung up the phone, and after further conversation, a decision was made.

I was told that they were afraid I was causing too much trouble with the wrong kids on campus. The president and a few other faculty members continued to try and talk me into changing the student's grades. "We do not want to escalate matters, and these students need to pass for the university to maintain relationships in the region," they explained.

I stood by my principles, but with my safety in jeopardy, I thought it best to submit my resignation. As I was packing my belongings in my office, several of the first-year freshmen students came to me in tears and asked me to please rescind my resignation. As their faculty adviser, I had become attached to them and it pained me to leave, but I knew I had no future at Ishik.

After my resignation from Ishik, I was recruited to teach at the American University of Iraq in Sulaymaniyah

(AUIS). After two tough years in Kurdistan, I wondered if Sulaymaniyah could be any different. Because the university was ostensibly American, I hoped I could cope better with the institutional culture. At the very least, perhaps they would be willing to stand up to Vitamin W because that was not the way things were in the U.S. I agreed to an interview and AUIS offered me free housing for two days and a driver to pick me up in Erbil and take me home after the interview. I thought to myself if nothing went right with the interview, I would at least get a two-day trip to Sulaymaniyah.

When I arrived at the campus, I was fascinated by the marble buildings with a beautiful view of Sulaymaniyah, also known as the city of life. The people of Suli (how the American expatriates referred to the city) were known to be the most liberal in the region. They used to tell me that the liberal mindset was from the Persian influence due to the proximity of Sulaymaniyah to Iran. On the first day, the staff at AUIS offered to show me around the city. Unlike Erbil and Duhok, Suli was the cultural capital of Southern Kurdistan, where you could feel the real Kurdish culture and not a Dubai-like consumer culture. The authenticity was evident in the way people presented themselves, the Kurdish artwork on the streets, the shops, and the architecture.

I loved everything about Suli. Unlike Duhok and Erbil, in Suli I could live a judgment-free life more easily. I could date and socialize with my male friends without anyone judging me. Plus, I was guaranteed to make a decent salary so I could enjoy some world traveling and spend time with friends in restaurants and cafés. AUIS had all the American faculty housed in one building in Pak City, a fancy apartment complex. In hindsight, I am not sure how wise that was if Americans were ever seen as a terrorist target. During the interview, I was allowed two nights in Pak City to experience the faculty housing for myself.

On the second day, I had interviews scheduled with the department chair, the dean, and the president of the University. My interviewers had no shortage of questions, but it was nothing that I was not prepared for.

After a long day of interviews, I left feeling extremely confident about my performance. It was not until late that Friday evening, when I was attending a friend's wedding in Erbil, that I received a call from the dean extending me a job offer.

The music at the wedding was uplifting and I could not help but notice how my whole body was moving to the beats of the electric tambur (musical instrument). I was impressed by how long the singer went on singing the Bahdini lyrics without taking a deep breath—which was itself a skillset. The singer was the famous Saed Gabari, who is blind yet plays on his tambur while singing at the same time. I soon learned that the same Saed Gabari was married to three women.

The wedding night was incredibly special because I was seated with some of my close friends. One of them was the well-known and talented Kurdish designer, Della Murad, who had designed the bride's wedding dress. She was famous for adding a modern or a practical touch to the traditional Kurdish fashions. Many girls, including me, loved her taste, while others criticized her way of modernizing the traditional. After the wedding, I treated all my friends to some famous kanafeh (a Middle Eastern pastry made from semolina dough and soaked in sugar syrup and layered with cheese) at a neighboring Turkish pastry shop where I broke the news about my job offer from AUIS.

I took the summer off to spend time with my mother back in Atlanta, Georgia. When I arrived, I went to my bedroom and to my surprise, everything was the same. I saw the novels and books from my days in high school and college. Everything was left untouched from the day I left my room in 2010. I took a shower and came downstairs to the aroma of my mother's delicious cooking, her fresh homemade bread waiting for me.

My favorite thing about Atlanta was my mother's garden and my favorite thing in her garden was the dirty tomatoes. One time, I joked on Facebook that if for any reason a Kurdish parent upsets you, go outside and pull out all their tomato plants by their roots. The next thing I knew the phone was ringing with a call from Kurdistan. It was my oldest sister calling from Erbil to check on our mother's tomatoes!

During my stay in Atlanta, I would run for six miles in Stone Mountain Park, join my mother for a fresh breakfast, sit by the window of the living room, waiting for the first rays of the sun to shine, and find myself trembling with loneliness. I was not a stranger to that city. How could I be? I grew up there. But after two years in Kurdistan, I was used to my days being filled with personal interactions and more human intimacy than I found back in Georgia.

Like so many Americans, my friends from Agnes Scott had misconceptions about Kurdistan and the Middle East as a whole. "Does every Kurdish woman have to cover her hair with a hijab (which they mispronounce 'heejab')?" ... "Women can drive in Kurdistan?" ... "Wait, you can actually date in the Middle East?" ... "Hold on, women can go out without men?" ... "Wait, that means you do not need a man to accompany you everywhere?" As for fasting during Ramadan, "Wow you do not eat anything for thirty days? I would never be able to do that!"... "Are you trying to lose weight?" ... "You can eat something; we will not tell anyone."

I did not blame my friends for not knowing much about my faith, culture, and Kurdistan, but I also did not have the patience for these types of conversations anymore.

I was now approaching thirty, still searching for a home and a sense of belonging. To me, the idea of home was always where my heart was and my heart had always nostalgically belonged to my childhood memories, to Kurdistan. Yet, I suspected that time had made those days rosier than perhaps they really had been. While growing up in Kurdistan, I felt out of place because how can you call a place home when your safety is in constant danger, when your cultural identity is denied, and when you are not even allowed to listen to music in your mother tongue?

When I came to the U.S., I suddenly could comprehend all the possibilities of what a home–in the larger philosophical sense–could be. Yet, even in America I felt a different kind of cultural exclusion. My language was allowed, but it would never be something in the public sphere. I would be the sole person displaying my Kurdishness, not surrounded by it. I gradually realized that what made a place home was being able to soak in your culture in the presence of others. It was not a solo performance, but a communal play.

To solve this dilemma, I filled the void by living a nomadic life where I would not be forced to choose. And whether it was genuine or me merely convincing myself, I enjoyed the constant packing and unpacking while moving from one city to the next, with my two suitcases full of clothes and books. By deriving belonging from my books, I felt I was never alone, even when I clearly was.

For years, the definition of home was very transient, and it was about leaving and not staying. After moving to Kurdistan, I realized I was part of two different worlds: The West and the Middle East. I also realized that I would always be treated as the American girl in Kurdistan and the Kurdish refugee in America. Every time I got ready to leave one part of the world I belonged to, I failed to give it a proper goodbye. So, I stopped saying goodbye! Every time I got ready to leave Kurdistan for America or America for Kurdistan, I felt the pull of the other. The yearning, which I learned to embrace, was a simple reminder that I was one whole soul but composed of two different cultures.

By the end of August 2012, back in Erbil after a two-month vacation in Atlanta, my heart had yet to heal from seeing my mother's tears at the airport as she saw me take off once again for Kurdistan. I was still asleep when I heard my phone ring. "Dr. Helen, where are you? I am on my way to get you." It was my driver from AUIS. I immediately jumped up and tried to comprehend the driver's words.

He was in my neighborhood, and I was not even ready.

I rushed to take a shower. The transition from life in the U.S. to life in Kurdistan had once again begun. This time the jet lag was brutal. I had been up all night and had the hardest time waking in the morning. The drive from Erbil to Sulaymaniyah was close to three hours, and the driver named Kaka Faiq (brother Faiq) had a litany of questions for me.

As he flipped his rosary while driving with one hand, Kaka Faig asked, "Dr. Helen, are you Kurdish?"

"Yes, I am, Kaka," I said.

"I figured, since you look and dress like a Kurdish girl. Where in Kurdistan are you from?"

"I am mixed, my mother is Hawrami and father is from Zakho."

"How come your Sorani dialect is Hawleri?"

"I know it is strange. I have formed a Kurdish dialect of my own because my father spoke Bahdini with us and my mother spoke Sorani. However, my primary schooling was in Arabic, and we left for America when I was little. Thus, my Kurdish has been morphed with an American accent, like all the diaspora's children."

"Um, I understand. So how did your parents meet?"

"Well, it is a long story, but nothing can explain qismat u nasib (destiny)."

"Why do you have a western name?"

I was starting to get a bit irritated with all those personal questions. "Kaka, my name is Heleen, but when I went to America, they misspelled it and gave me Helen for a name."

"Americans are so smart; how can they make such a careless mistake?"

"Americans are human just like we are."

"Heleen has such a beautiful meaning. Can I just call you Heleen Xan instead of Dr. Helen?"

"Yes, of course!"

"Are you married?"

Now it was starting to feel awkward. I rolled my eyes and thought about how many more times people were going to ask me this question. "No, Kaka, I am not married. I am single."

I got tired of answering his questions, so I started yawning hoping he would get the hint.

"You look exhausted. You can just take a nap in the back seat."

"Yes! I am jet-lagged and did not have any sleep last night. I need to rest my eyes for an hour."

It did not take too long to gather that Kaka Faiq was a proud Kurd who loved Kurdistan.

"Heleen Xan," he began, not too long after he let me take a nap, "do you like to picnic?"

"Yes, Kaka I love to picnic."

"You see that beautiful lake?" he asked, pointing to Lake Dukan, which was turquoise green and nestled in snowcapped mountains. "That is Dukan and it is so beautiful in the spring. For Newroz time, all beautiful young girls like yourself from Sulaymaniyah wear Kurdish dresses and fill the area with colors. Here, take my number. We would be honored to have you join us next time."

"Supas, Kaka Faiq. I will sure to be in touch once I get all situated in Sulaymaniyah."

As we rode, I observed the beautiful mountains with Adnan Karim's voice (a famous Kurdish singer) playing in the background. I closed my eyes and wondered how I had been able to be away from Kurdistan for two months. Would I ever be able to return to America for good?

In Kurdistan, at any given hour of the day, half a dozen people knew where I was and what my plans were for the week. In America, I could get hit by a car, and no one would find me for a week. So, I was not surprised that Kaka Faiq, who just spent a few hours driving me from Erbil to Suli, offered me his number and asked that I call him whenever I needed anything.

As Kaka Faiq and I continued our drive through the mountains approaching Sulaymaniyah, I wished that I could enjoy the natural beauty of Kurdistan with my loved ones, nieces, and nephews, hearing them call me by "Mati Heleen."

We entered the Tasluja checkpoint, which was colored in green (the PUK party color) and I spotted a big picture of Mam Jalal (the PUK's leader) hanging on top of the checkpoint. Kaka Faiq rolled down his window. The officer at the checkpoint asked who I was and where I was coming from. Kaka Faiq told him I was an American there to teach at AUIS. The officer then knocked on my window to welcome me in person to Sulaymaniyah. He slapped the front of the SUV twice indicating that we could continue the drive.

As soon as we were clear, I received a call from the AUIS housing staff asking where I was. I looked at Kaka Faiq who was focused on getting me to the campus and asked if we were close. He replied that we were almost there. Then I asked myself, could it be possible that I was jealous of Kaka Faiq? Why not! He belonged to one world while I was torn between two.

While at AUIS, I was able to participate in enjoyable activities with the girls in Sulaymaniyah. One of those was being a faculty adviser for the Blogger's Club, where I taught the students how to express what they felt about certain events happening in the region and publish their opinions on a blog. This activity was desperately needed since females were not encouraged to voice their opinions, nor were they encouraged to express how they felt about issues that involved politics. I also volunteered to be a coach for the female basketball team. The sport was not something that many girls played in the Kurdish region. Seeing a faculty member with a hijab run around the campus in the afternoons and coach female basketball players motivated more women to join and exercise. These two initiatives were in line with a new course I developed while at AUIS on Health and Wellness. In this course, we discussed the power of giving and the role of living in a healthy community. Students were not only encouraged to practice healthy hygiene, exercise, and eat a healthy diet, but were also encouraged to promote healthy practices in the communities where they lived.

One thing I learned about the other faculty members during my stay in Kurdistan, whether they were Kurds or Arabs, was that they were very well trained in their fields, but as a rule, had no interest in going outside of them. It seemed that broad learning was neither encouraged nor rewarded by the system. As for me, besides my passion for healing patients and empowering my students, I loved learning about new cultures and different religious beliefs.

I believed health was connected to everything. Soon, I found I was regarded by those around me as virtually omniscient because of how much I had picked up about fields other than my own specialties! It was kind of odd, since I am aware of my limitations.

I once approached a world religion scholar after a talk to show my interest in learning about the Zoroastrian faith. I asked if he was willing to grant me thirty minutes of his time for a possible interview about the religious minority groups in Kurdistan for a blog piece. He asked for my specialty. "I am a pharmacist, "I answered.

"Pharmacy?" he asked. "Why would a pharmacist be interested in learning about religions?

Heaven forbid someone might enjoy reading outside of her career discipline, I thought to myself.

AUIS was the first-ever liberal arts school in the country and Kurdistan needed more of them. I was confident that AUIS would allow me to teach students how to think outside of the box, have the confidence to ask difficult questions, connect the dots, and master the synthesis of a big picture from differing perspectives. With the patriarchal mindset that was plaguing the region, this was exactly what the new generation of Kurds needed. After all, the world was dominated by critical thinkers, so the ability to communicate effectively and work well on a team was imperative for Kurdish students and for the region to transform.

High school graduates in Kurdistan were expected to identify a long-term career as soon as they got their twelfth-grade final exam scores. Based on their exam grades, they struggled to fit themselves into one of the few narrowly defined career paths with medicine, engineering, and law being the most popular. The admission requirements for the major government-based universities were becoming extremely competitive due to the influx of refugees into the region from other parts of Iraq, who competed with Kurdish students for college admission. In this stressful setting, students had no choice but to accept what would get them a job, making their college experience analogous to "technical training" rather than intellectual exploration.

The one year I taught at AUIS turned out to be the best year of the three I spent in Kurdistan. The students were rowdy and would intentionally do mischievous things in class as I was teaching, so I would playfully pick on them. Nevertheless, they were thoughtful and respectful of my class boundaries. My students introduced me to the culture in Sulaymaniyah and their families and we celebrated most Kurdish holidays together. I was amazed by the amount of gold the female students would put on for the holidays, which ranged anywhere from one to two kilograms of pure gold in the form of bangles, earrings, and belts. Gold usually represented a female's social status, so the more gold she put on, the higher her socioeconomic standing.

They say a Kurdish woman's best friend is gold. Most women in Kurdistan have no reliable source of income and though their role is slowly evolving, gold remains a woman's most valuable asset. Kurds usually used the phrase "yellow gold" for a dark day. The gold that a woman gets when she gets married is hers to keep. She can sell the gold for income if faced with divorce or can use it to help her husband and his family if finances become tight. While the idea of being given gold at marriage can seem like she is being purchased, it also gives her a degree of power and mobility that she would not have without it.

Among all the gold pieces my students wore, I also saw blue-eyed jewelry that came in various shapes. The blue eye, in our culture and many others in the region, was used as a mechanism to deter the evil eye. I also saw blue eyes in the form of the Hamsa hand. The word Hamsa, also spelled as khamsa, meaning five in the Arabic language, referred to the five fingers of the hand. In Jewish culture, the Hamsa was called the hand of Miriam, and in Islam, it was called the Hand of Fatima. Although this practice of wearing the blue eye and hand of Hamsa was condemned as superstitious by some Muslim scholars, many people still liked them.

This was understandable, as most Kurds I encountered in the region believed envious looks could themselves contain destructive power. However, they did not genuinely believe a blue eye or a hand served as a protective mechanism to deter the power of the evil eye. To adhere to Islamic teachings, most locals merely used blue eyes and hands for decorative purposes. To protect against the evil eye, Kurds refused to talk about their accomplishments, relationships, and health. Some families even went so far as to say they had to borrow money to build the house they owned (even if it was not true). When a compliment was given about one's looks, it was mandatory to say Mashallah (God has willed it) in Arabic. If you forgot to end your compliment with Mashallah, the locals would remind you to say it because of the evil eye and to guard against the pitfalls of too much pride.

It was Friday, my day off. I grabbed my phone and saw that it was only 6:30 a.m. Was it time to get up? I tried to go back to sleep, but at that point, I was wide awake. I jumped out of bed and started my weekend. I turned on the angelic voice of Fairuz, opened my windows, and found myself meditating to the beautiful view of Sulaymaniyah while inhaling the biggest dose of fresh air possible. I looked down from my balcony and saw a few old men with their cute traditional Kurdish shalwal and qamis on with bags of fresh bread in their hands. Drooling for some myself, I changed quickly and ran downstairs to get some from the neighborhood bakery. As I walked by the teahouse, I heard the stirring noise of the teaspoons in the chai istikan (little teacups), the closest noise to my heart. I thought to myself, what a beautiful start to my day.

The phone soon rang. It was one of my best friends whom I had met when she was finishing her master's degree in the States. "Helene gean, chaki? (you okay?) What are you up to today? Mom wants to have you over for lunch. She is making dolma."

Did I just hear dolma? Of course, I had no choice but to accept the invitation. She offered to pick me up. She did not want me to take a cab even though Suli was very safe.

Knowing how traditional her family was, I dressed properly for a Kurdish house: a long dress, light makeup, and some jewelry. They picked me up, and as we arrived, to my surprise I found the house full of ladies dressed in Kurdish garb. They all got up and each one gave me three or four kisses. By the time I kissed this fourth random lady

I did not know, I figured three was the right number of kisses. I also realized that some men were not okay with shaking hands with a female. They offered me a seat. By that point, I had attention overload with everyone looking at me. I kept my arms tightly folded on my lap. I kept smiling and wondering how many eyes could be looking at me, what could they be thinking?

Then, it was time to eat. They called me to have a seat at the sofreh (they had the food laid on the floor). The sofreh was packed with a variety of Kurdish dishes. They stuffed my plate with red meat. It almost broke my heart to state that I was vegetarian and could not eat any. I then heard a cute grandma say, "Vegetarian chia (What is a vegetarian)? She must eat meat!" Kurds never accepted no for an answer. I realized that no matter how much you ate in Kurdish culture, they always complained about your not eating enough. After a delicious meal, they served chai with desserts. My mother's voice started buzzing in my head, "Heleen, when you are around Kurdish locals, you need to smile less, talk less, and suppress all the cockiness you inherited from Americans."

The next day, I was invited to a meet and greet party by one of the American faculty members at work. This party was to meet all the new and old faculty, hear their stories, and learn their reasons for wanting to work in Kurdistan. For this party, I found myself putting on a pair of plain leggings with a T-shirt. I realized there was no need for any makeup or proper dress code. The environment was very different. Everyone had a story to share about their experiences in Kurdistan. I found myself giggling, expressing myself, and filling my dish with whatever satisfied my appetite. The servings of food were nothing like what I'd had the previous day.

After a while, I became distracted at the party. I began thinking about what my life had been like since I moved back to Kurdistan. I thought about everything: the friendships I had formed, the families that had given me a warm welcome to their houses, my job, my students, societal expectations, the compromises I had made, and the changes I had noticed in myself. What got me thinking the most, however, were the two lifestyles I had been living since the move to Kurdistan: one with the American expatriates and the other with locals. I realized how differently I had been behaving in each setting. Then I remembered a one-liner from a friend about living a different lifestyle every hour like a "crazy person" in Kurdistan. Yes, I maintained two completely different cultural standards in my brain at the same time, with different voices constantly telling me what to do to meet each cultural expectation.

Every semester, AUIS would plan a field trip to Erbil for all the American faculty. The university would rent a big bus to drive us to the Erbil Family Mall for shopping. From groceries to clothes, the Family Mall had it all. As soon as we arrived, I took a taxi to Erbil Qaysari to visit Mam Khalil. Mam Khalil, or Uncle Khalil, was in his seventies. He took pride in serving tea at his little tea house. I was not sure why I was so attached to his tea house, but I was guaranteed to leave in better spirits. I loved Mam Khalil and the joy he would find in the simple things in life. His smile, kind heart, and hospitality were contagious. Every time I visited him at his tea house, he would grant me his unconditional love and attention.

The traditional Kurdish music and atmosphere at the tea house, which held traditions in place and decades of memories, would take me back to my childhood when I would accompany my father when he was still employed in Erbil. The tea house had been in operation since 1963, making it the oldest café in the city. It was a living museum of photos from all those famous Kurds who visited Mam Khalil. Many local chai drinkers had been coming to the teahouse since childhood. After drinking two to three payala (cups) of strong chai with lots of sugar, I would have to beg Mam Khalil to allow me to pay for the tea, and he would not let me. The man barely made a living from serving tea in his old age yet refused to accept payment from me. He looked at me as a guest and not a customer, and in Kurdish culture money from a guest is an insult.

I continued my stroll through Qaysari and found myself chatting with a group of retired elderly men outside the bazaar at the Qardaran Teashop. Qardaran was a name given to the teahouse back during sanctions because poor locals would need a qard (loan) to purchase their tea. After further conversation, the same retired uncles requested I play backgammon with them. I admitted that I was not skilled in the game, but they offered to walk me through it. They pulled up another chair, ordered me a cup of chai, and clarified the cost was on them (ironically not on loan based on our location). They handed me the dice and one uncle guided me through the game against his opponent. The uncles I met took pride in playing the game. During many years of war, backgammon had been one of the only sources of entertainment in Iraq. After I deployed a fierce play, the uncle guiding me theorized that I was a risk-taker in life, based on my backgammon strategy. I raised my eyebrows and I asked how he knew.

"You left many spaces open and were constantly taking risks," he explained.

I smiled back because I knew he was right.

As bad luck would have it, during that summer of 2013, the Islamic State of Iraq and Syria (ISIS) and their barbaric ideology began starting to spread like cancer in the region. Although Kurdish guerrillas of the PKK, Kurdish fighters of the YPG and YPJ, and Kurdish Peshmerga from the KRG would soon be battling ISIS all across Rojava (Syrian Kurdistan) and Bashur (Iraqi Kurdistan) respectively, Kurdish citizens from other nations were encouraged to leave for their own safety.

The State Department soon issued a warning for all expatriates to return to the U.S. as soon as possible. At the age of thirty-one, my journey in the motherland had come to an abrupt end. Sadly, it was time to head back to Atlanta and put an end to the dilemma of which world I belonged to. For three years, I gave the region my best until my safety was in jeopardy. "I tried, I really did," I kept reminding myself. I tried my best to blend into the culture and be a part of the change the region needed. However, the region was simply not ready to make the changes it claimed it needed, nor was it safe for me to stay. I had lived in all three major cities in Kurdistan and worked with a government, private, and liberal arts college. As a young professional, I felt I had not accomplished as much I needed to. I did, however, fulfill my duties as a public health servant. With the successful completion of an academic year at AUIS, the engineering students threw me a beautiful goodbye party. At the party, they asked if I had plans to return to the region.

"Of course, I do," I reminded them. "Kurdistan will always be my original homeland that I will miss and return to." You can take the Kurd out of Kurdistan, but you can never take Kurdistan out of the Kurd.

After three years of living in Kurdistan, I was back in America. For the first few months, I felt I was again a refugee in the country where I'd grown up. Everything felt strange and foreign to me. I had no job, hardly any cash in my bank account, two degrees that had not landed me the positions I'd wanted in Kurdistan, and I owned only two suitcases full of clothes. Friends and family were also telling me how I had changed over those three years. I was proud of how I had grown and become more independent and resourceful. However, the one disappointing thing I noticed about myself was a lack of self-esteem. I felt I was not good enough to serve the underserved.

Sometimes, I could almost read my mother's thoughts through her stares. She feared that no man would ever want to marry me. Her looks also carried her fears of what bad things could have happened to me while I was in Kurdistan, a place she had not wanted me to return to alone, as I had. But I knew that venturing to Kurdistan was a journey of the heart. I had done what I could for my homeland, and I would not live with any regrets. I did not fail in Kurdistan, rather the archaic system in the region failed me. I had planned so many projects that would have benefitted my patients and students, but most had not come to fruition because I failed to comply with "Vitamin W."

Maybe it was also because I was a woman with Kurdish blood who had my head covered (i.e. perceived as too timid)? Or maybe I was too honest about how I felt about certain subjects and failed to sugarcoat things for those high-ranking officials (i.e. perceived as too bold)? Such a dichotomy was something I wrestled with every day.

What was undeniable, was that American expatriates with lesser qualifications and fewer connections to the region were far more respected, better paid, and more pampered than I had been in my own home country. In my last few weeks at AUIS, I told the chairman they needed to give equal attention to foreign staffers and Kurds. He responded that I had returned to my country, but the Americans had left their families and friends for Kurdistan (as if this made their commitment or sacrifice to be there more laudatory). I had also left my career and family in America to help Kurdistan, but the fact that I was a Kurd meant that I did not get the same treatment.

While in Kurdistan, I had seen many disappointing deeds done under the umbrella of Islam, things which were completely contrary to its teachings. Many of my students in Erbil and Duhok wore a hijab. Yet, I found that those wearing a hijab were more likely to engage in disappointing deeds like cheating on my exams and quizzes, complaining about how difficult the homework was, and lying about the reasons they were tardy to class. I found this confusing because I was taught that the hijab was a signal that you were an ambassador for the righteous deeds of Islam.

In America, we had to be extra careful with how we talked and treated others because our hijab flagged us publicly as Muslims, and any bad deed on our part was automatically associated with the faith. My students did not know the meaning of the hijab that I was taught, as they had started wearing the headscarf as young children and no one explained the significance of modesty associated with it. Many girls were simply obligated to cover their hair more on a cultural level and because of family pressure, so they failed to understand that the hijab was a symbolic veil tied to one's behavior and speech over hair visibility. They failed to understand that lying and cheating were far more serious than whether you covered your hair with a scarf. However, to many of my female Muslim students, the hijab was a cultural tradition they needed to uphold regardless of their actions, and it acted as an easy way to "virtue signal" that one was pious—regardless of the reality.

At the local bazaars, there was a good deal of swearing and casual use of the name of God in vain. The local grocery shop owners, butchers, and farmers would swear by God (Allah) and the Prophet Muhammad to convince you of the quality of their inferior merchandise and cover their lies. Lying was against the teachings of Islam, and those same merchants would then rush to the mosque to pray as soon as the call to the prayer went up.

After 9/11, I had to fight my family to keep wearing my hijab because they feared for my safety. After close to two long decades of wearing the hijab, however, I was exhausted from the never-ending public service announcement I had to make because of it. I would often choose the most colorful and fun patterns for my hijab to show that covering my hair did not mean I was oppressed, and I found myself speaking and laughing louder at gatherings to overcompensate and show that girls wearing a hijab could also have fun. But I had become frustrated at how every conversation turned into a discussion about my faith. I decided the hijab was a visual barrier that made it difficult for people to see the real me, the interesting and complex person underneath.

After living in the Middle East for three years, my outlook on religion and its application to life started to change. The Quran does talk about how women must cover their bodies to maintain modesty, but the Quran leaves room for interpretation, depending on which Hadiths (various attributed sayings of the Prophet Muhammad) one relies on to supplement their guidance. While in Kurdistan, I learned that men were the ones who set the parameters for the different religious interpretations. With all the permissible interpretations of the Quran, religious scholars—mostly men in the Middle East—were doing Islam and the hundreds of millions of Muslim women around the world a disservice by interpreting the Quran as one-size-fits-all. As a result, I started to focus instead on the parts of my faith that were compatible with my lifestyle in America, an approach that many religious fundamentalists from Kurdistan would object to.

After my return to Kurdistan, I learned the Islam that I practiced in America was far different from the Islam practiced back there. The Islam I grew up with was based on doing good deeds. The rituals associated with the faith such as praying in the mosque and fasting came second. Muslims in the Middle East are more prone to follow religion by the book (theory), while many Muslims in America turn Islam into a way of life (practice). Essentially, it is the difference between focusing on rules versus behavior. In Kurdistan, people were more focused on mandatory rituals and less on actions—which lacked clear instructions.

So, when I left Sulaymaniyah, I left my hijab back in Kurdistan and came back to the U.S. as a new me, with a new philosophy about how my faith should be practiced. I knew in my heart that my religion was more than the veil I wore to cover my hair. I maintained my commitment to be a good human and would remain private about the Islamic rituals I practiced. It was nobody's business that I was praying five times a day or fasting during the month of Ramadan. Wearing a hijab simply exposed the rituals I now wanted to keep as a personal matter between me and God.

After working in Kurdistan, I felt I had also lost the bond I had with a higher power. I used to sit on my prayer rug and ask God for guidance on things that bothered me; however, after my return from Kurdistan, I did not feel as though I had access to Him. I tried to pray, but my thoughts were never on the prayer, and I would finish praying without feeling any resolution or sense of peace.

Once back in the U.S., I found myself struggling with severe depression. The years of internal conflict had led to an identity crisis I could no longer ignore. I could not fight this personal war alone. I needed help and to be surrounded by loved ones. For the very first time, I saw the need to open up to a therapist about my emotions around struggling to find myself while simultaneously feeling like I belonged nowhere. In every therapy session, I repeated the same story about my grief over yearning for home.

My therapist asked how I was coping with the pain. "I have been avoiding the whole world," I responded. Being from an ethnic minority group herself, my therapist could relate to my pain and understood where I was coming from. She and I discussed my culture, childhood, and strict upbringing. At that point, I became comfortable enough with her that I started sharing everything from my childhood. I told the therapist I was from a culture that valued group terms, meaning if one family member was in trouble, it simply meant that the whole family was. Moreover, to my detriment, at age fourteen I was put in the "American wilderness" amidst a society where culture, language, and people were so different from what I was used to. I was forced to grow up in a society that stressed individual responsibility. I was ill prepared to face life in the U.S., as I was taught to believe that I could live in the West and make the transition without paying the heavy cost of choosing between mutually exclusive clashing values.

I had been brought up in a culture that refused to take no for an answer, a culture where you were supposed to do whatever it took to please others. This had negatively impacted me in my relationships with those who refused to respect my boundaries. I had difficulties confronting people and telling them to stop doing things that made me uncomfortable. Instead, I normalized their behavior and internalized the pain they caused. I ended up facing the consequence of my decision for not being able to set boundaries. Often in department stores, I wound up buying merchandise that the salesperson pushed on me because I had difficulty saying no to the sale. When it came to conflict, I found myself changing my attitude about things that I felt strongly about to please the other party or to get me out of the conflict. This was partly because I was not taught to address conflict or say no to things that made me uncomfortable.

Over the sessions, my therapist reminded me that deep inside me, just like any American girl with Kurdish roots, I carried every ingredient needed to turn my experiences into joy. All I needed was guidance in how to mix those ingredients and accept assistance. She warned me that therapy was a slow, growing process that would require patience and work. She reminded me how impressed she was with my hard work and intellectual level, but we both agreed that due to my upbringing, I was still extremely naïve about certain aspects of life.

During one session, my therapist asked about some of the things that I enjoyed doing. I told her that I used to love the adventures I had seeing the world and returning with stories to share and blog about. I missed those excursions so much and my encounters with locals overseas. She asked, "What is stopping you from getting back to traveling?"

Nothing was. I was now ready to get back to doing something about which I was so passionate.

"You only are free when you realize you belong no place—you belong every place—no place at all. The price is high. The reward is great."
— Author Maya Angelou

I realized I needed and wanted to get away and travel to as many countries as I could. I knew traveling to destinations full of unknowns was the only way to rejuvenate and rediscover myself. I started to keep a travel diary to document the things I experienced while traveling. Every destination I went to added something special to how I perceived the world. After each trip, I would reflect on my experiences by looking back at my journal and reminding myself about the therapeutic value of each experience.

My journey to recovery and self-discovery started in India with a visit to the Taj Mahal, which took me back in time to the magical Mughal era, giving my mind a break from the present. The stones used to build the mausoleum embodied the Mughal culture and the love Shah Jahan had for his second wife, Mumtaz Mahal. As I stood facing the mausoleum at sunset, I could only imagine the amount of labor that had gone into constructing this building, the attention to detail, and the emotions that Shah Jahan had felt for Mumtaz. Love is what gives life a fullness and completeness, and that is what I had been missing.

My journey continued to a place where I had a chance to restore my faith in humanity—the Golden Temple, the most sacred place to the world's Sikhs. With thousands of pilgrims, I celebrated as we shared food prepared and donated by volunteers. It was the need for community that pushed me to serve along with thousands whom I had never met before. From the Golden Temple, I celebrated the end of life and rebirth with thousands of Hindu pilgrims in Varanasi, the oldest city in the world. It was believed that whoever died on the land of Varanasi, was freed from the cycle of birth and rebirth. At sunrise, I washed my face and body in the sacred Ganges River, which Hindus believe has the holy power to wash away the sins of mortals. Through that intimate bond with pilgrims at the Ganges, I learned to surrender to God, let go of my worries and painful past, and have faith in what God would bring my way.

From India, I continued my search for happiness in the small Himalayan kingdom of Bhutan, a country that measures progress through Gross National Happiness (GNH) rather than Gross National Product (GDP). From the Bhutanese, I learned that happiness is only possible when your body, mind, and action are all in agreement. I also learned about Buddhism, which says that human existence involves suffering and that suffering has causes, cessations, and paths to cessation. Bhutan is famous for its beautiful fortresses built on ridges overlooking scenic valleys and for its Tibetan Buddhist pilgrims traveling throughout the country while preaching. I embarked on my journey to learn about those truths by trekking for five hours to the famous Buddhist Monastery, the Tiger's Nest, which is perched on a cliff about 3,000 feet (900 or so meters) above the ground.

My search for the truth continued through China and the forbidden country of Tibet, the birthplace of the Dalai Lama. In the former, standing atop the Great Wall and looking out at it snaking over the mountains showed me that regardless of what kind of barrier you construct, it will be breached or eventually become obsolete in our ever-changing world. So, we should not think that we can isolate ourselves from all threats or plan for every danger coming our way. In Tibet, my soul was moved by the teachings of the Dalai Lama and the pure heart of local Buddhists who displayed a dedication and devotion both to their land and faith.

Next, I made it to Nepal, where I challenged myself both physically and mentally to summit Mount Everest's base camp. As I was climbing, I learned that the body can do everything in the world, but it is the brain you must convince. Once I conquered Everest's base camp, I spent a few days in a nunnery at the outskirts of Kathmandu watching the little girls and the joy they found in the small things in life, like jumping rope for hours, cleaning the neighborhood, and feeding the poor in their communities.

From Nepal, I continued my journey through Southeast Asia to experience Thailand and Vietnam, where I enriched my soul with the kindhearted smiles, hospitality, and cuisine of the people there. After months with no appetite, I finally found myself craving delicate Vietnamese cuisine in Halong Bay. I learned to maintain the balance between my mind and body through meditation and yoga in front of Angkor Wat, Bagan, the Bay of Bengal, and the Mekong riverside in Cambodia, Laos, and Myanmar. I found myself integrating yoga with my five obligatory daily prayers, one of them at sunrise and one at sunset. I realized the religions of the world have so much in common and that it is the imperfect human interpretation that drives our faiths apart.

From Southeast Asia, my journey continued to the Middle East where I came to terms with the land that left me heartbroken countless times. I started in Dubai, known as the "Vegas of the Middle East," where locals took pride in having the tallest, largest, and most extreme of everything. But by then I knew that a country's legacy is not about having the tallest buildings but in its treatment of humanity. I soon learned that pretty much everything in Dubai was built by thousands of exploited laborers from Far East countries who were not allowed citizenship in the Emirates. They slaved to build glittering skyscrapers that they would never be able to enter once they were completed. I learned that racism by all ethnicities was possible, and humans can be cruel simply because of someone's skin color or country of origin.

From the Emirates, I continued to Palestine, Israel, Jordan, and Lebanon. My visit to the Holy Land allowed me a glimpse into the complex interwoven conflict around areas held sacred by all three of the world's Abrahamic religions and how regardless of your opinion, you are guaranteed to offend someone. In the West Bank, I visited displaced Palestinian refugees in the Jenin refugee camp and listened to their tragic stories of being displaced by religiously zealous Jewish settlers. The old Palestinian Amoos (uncles) looked like they had the weight of the world on their shoulders from years of Israeli military occupation. I was even repeatedly interrogated by Israeli soldiers at the Temple Mount/Dome of the Rock in Jerusalem, where it is said Jesus Christ expelled the greedy money changers, and that later the Prophet Muhammad led prayers with all the world's prophets before he ascended into the sky.

I saw the other side of the coin in Tel Aviv, where I was shown kindness by a Jewish man and learned of his family who had perished in the Holocaust which caused his parents to emigrate, and other family members of his that had all their possessions seized before having to flee to Israel from Iraq. For one afternoon, we exhibited our own small version of a "peace process" between Judaism and Islam.

From Jerusalem, I crossed the border to Jordan, making a stop at the Um Qais valley, where I gazed over one of the most controversial pieces of land on earth, the Golan Heights. I considered the number of lives lost and the bloodshed at that very place in the name of religion, but really because of greed and the desire for power. I continued through Petra, where I had an episode of low blood sugar and almost fainted. Luckily, the local Bedouins brought me sugar, cheese, and bread. In that gesture, I was reminded how there is nothing more powerful than the human bond, regardless of our differences. Next, I was on to Lebanon, where no one is ever looked at as a stranger. Lebanese people invited me into their homes and insisted that I share their morning coffee with them. Living in conflict from years of civil war had turned the Lebanese people into the most easy-going I had met. They knew how to have a good time regardless of the situation because life was just too short.

After the Middle East, I continued to Kenya and Tanzania in Eastern Africa where the hunger and poverty I witnessed crushed my spirit. Yet, regardless of how bad the living conditions were, people exhibited the brightest smiles of any place I visited and constantly spoke of how things would be better tomorrow than they were today. The tribe of Maasai Mara in Kenya taught me that living a simple life was indeed all life needed to be. They lived in small huts made from mud with no running water or electricity, yet they seemed more genuinely content than I was.

Soon after, I was climbing Mount Kilimanjaro while in Tanzania, which was the hardest thing I have ever done, mentally, physically, and emotionally. For seven long days I lived in severe conditions without showering, fighting altitude sickness with a migraine all along the way. As I summitted at sunrise, I took a few seconds to reflect on what it had taken to get me there. I learned I was more resilient and tougher than I had ever thought. I learned there was nothing wrong with allowing myself to be vulnerable and letting others help me when needed. I learned about the power of teamwork and the spirit of how we were in it together to make it to the top of the mountain. As we descended, I reminded myself that life is full of stressors, social pressures, and doubt, and it is only through trust, resilience, and a supportive team that you can overcome the challenges you face.

Later, while in Morocco, I met a sweet old lady who was a fortune teller in the old Medina (city) of Fez. When she read my fortune, she told me that I had taken life way too seriously. She reminded me that when God closes one door, he opens a million others. I needed to believe in a higher power and in myself. She said that in instances where I am unable to control my destiny, to let the invisible force guide me.

I continued my journey to Marrakech, a beautiful and complex city, with many incomplete projects and infrastructure, and learned that to the locals, the joy in the journey was more rewarding than the actual destination. Consequently, I was slowly coming to the epiphany that instead of focusing so much on reaching my goals, I should embrace the work that I have done to reach each step along the way.

I then went to Europe where I used the time during train rides between Holland, Germany, France, Switzerland, Belgium, Portugal, and Spain to log my travel experiences. From great cities, monuments, museums, and learning about important people in history, I saw it all. Perhaps there was one common denominator in all the greatness I saw in Europe, and that was how excellence requires time and patience. For example, Van Gogh only sold one piece of his artwork while he was alive.

My next stop was a weeklong stay in Rio de Janeiro, Brazil, where I learned not to judge people by the way they dress. Brazilians are known for wearing the skimpiest bikinis, but they are strict Catholics. A foul mouth and bad manners got a few people on my tour group in trouble for being disrespectful. Afterward, I learned how to adapt my habits in Argentina, a country known for its lax attitude towards time. Locals do not start their day until 10 a.m. and do not dine until 10 p.m. or later because to the average Argentinian, there is no reason to rush.

In Peru and Bolivia, I learned the best thing about traveling the world was interacting with locals, and I did not need proficiency in Spanish to develop a bond with Peruvians, Bolivians, and trekkers from all around the world. As I was hiking on the Inca Trail to Machu Picchu and Valle De las Animas, I learned to stop doubting myself. The treks were not easy and there were times I wondered why I even started. However, as I continued the journey, I was awestruck by one of the most scenic landscapes in the world. And only in Patagonia, Chile, can one experience all four seasons in five days while hiking the amazingly scenic

W Circuit. Rain, snow, sunshine, and humidity happen all in a matter of hours. This taught me the importance of flexibility when making plans, because things in life can change rapidly and be unannounced.

Later, while in Cuba, I was least connected to the internet, which meant a break from some of my millennial habits. I was forced to develop new routines and network with locals, discovering things I never thought I would enjoy. I realized how important it is to appreciate those around me and that I could make someone's day by simply listening to their stories. Walking through the streets of Havana, my soul was filled with exciting sounds of salsa, reggaeton, and the daily greetings of "buenos dias" (good morning)! Through Cubans, I learned about resilience. Despite over five decades of embargo, poverty, and limited resources, Cubans impressed me as the most intellectual people I had ever met. What they lacked in material goods, they made up for in moral virtues.

In Mexico, I found that people with the most basic life needs are also the friendliest and most helpful. It truly is the case that those with the least are the most willing to give the most. Mexico City was big, and I have always been challenged by what large cities have to offer. Meeting locals in Mexico City was an easy way to explore the hidden jewels of a big city. The locals helped me find places with decent food and the little secrets that only locals know. This showed me the value in relying on local wisdom over outside supposed "expertise."

And finally, Canada! Although a young nation in America's shadow, there is much leadership to be learned from the Canadians, as they are not afraid to take full responsibility when things do not go right or when they notice a level of dissatisfaction from those they are dealing with. In fact, Canadians apologize for almost everything, which I found to be their way of ensuring a smooth conversation. This taught me the value of admitting failure or your mistakes, as nobody is perfect.

After visiting countless countries, I knew traveling the world was the best investment I could have made to feed my soul and fill the void I felt in my life. The kaleidoscope of different people and beliefs I met taught me how to belong to myself; I realized that I did not have to accept the false dichotomy that had been haunting me all these years growing up Kurdish in America. Limiting myself to one individual variable—Kurd, Muslim, woman, American—would be doing my sense of self a disservice.

The Kurdish writer Yasar Kamal once said, "The world is a garden of culture where a thousand flowers grow." Indeed, our universal human experience, like any healthy ecosystem, benefits from a rich diversity. This richness comes from deep within the human heart and cannot be contained by any man-made border or artificial boundary (as hard as some may try). I did not need permission to behave a certain way to brave the wilderness. From expert assimilator to finding value in being different, I discovered the courage to be bold and contrarian when life often feels like a combat zone. No matter how the world may try to package my identity, I know who I am.

Not bad for a young girl who once was so desperate that she traded a grenade for a bag of candy.

ABOUT ATMOSPHERE PRESS

Atmosphere Press is an independent, full-service publisher for excellent books in all genres and for all audiences. Learn more about what we do at atmospherepress.com.

We encourage you to check out some of Atmosphere's latest releases, which are available at Amazon.com and via order from your local bookstore:

The Swing: A Muse's Memoir About Keeping the Artist Alive, by Susan Dennis

Possibilities with Parkinson's: A Fresh Look, by Dr. C

Gaining Altitude - Retirement and Beyond, by Rebecca Milliken

Out and Back: Essays on a Family in Motion, by Elizabeth Templeman

Just Be Honest, by Cindy Yates

You Crazy Vegan: Coming Out as a Vegan Intuitive, by Jessica Ang

Detour: Lose Your Way, Find Your Path, by S. Mariah Rose

To B&B or Not to B&B: Deromanticizing the Dream, by Sue Marko

Convergence: The Interconnection of Extraordinary Experiences, by Barbara Mango and Lynn Miller

Sacred Fool, by Nathan Dean Talamantez

My Place in the Spiral, by Rebecca Beardsall

My Eight Dads, by Mark Kirby

ABOUT THE AUTHOR

Helen Sairany is a Kurdish-American born in the Kurdistan region of Iraq. She lives in Columbia, SC, with her two French bulldogs, SeVay and Jango—the Kurdish names for apple and hero—where she serves as the Chief Executive Officer for SC Pharmacy Association. Helen holds a Bachelor of Art from Agnes Scott College, a Master of Business Administration from the University of Maryland, and a Doctor of Pharmacy from Northeastern University. She was recognized by the *Washington Business Journal* "40 Under 40" for her work on combating opioid abuse nationwide through pharmacist patient care services.

Helen's greatest passion is traveling the world. Throughout her years of travel, she has embarked on many adventures including trekking in Southeast Asia, summiting Everest Base Camp in Nepal, W circuit in Patagonia-Chile, Machu Picchu and Rainbow Mountain in Peru, and Mount Kilimanjaro in Tanzania. After visiting 70+ destinations in the world, she has developed an appreciation for a diverse mix of cultures, people, and traditions.

Helen's work frequently takes her outside of the U.S, beyond the bounds of the pharmacy profession into the fields of education, discrimination, immigration, and workers' rights. She has worked overseas at the frontline to provide urgent care to displaced children in conflict zones.

Helen's love for writing started when she blogged about her experiences living as a single woman in a male-dominated field in the Middle East. In her free time, she served as a faculty adviser for the All-Women Blogger's Club, where she taught young women how to voice their opinions through writing. She also served as a basketball coach for the women's basketball team in Sulaymaniyah, Iraq.